FLORIDA STATE
UNIVERSITY LIBRARIES

MAR 2 2001

TALLAHASSEE, FLORIDA

From Birth to Death

From Birth to Death
A Consumer's Guide to Population Studies

William Petersen

Transaction Publishers
New Brunswick (U.S.A.) and London (U.K.)

HB
3505
.P48
2000

Copyright © 2000 by Transaction Publishers, New Brunswick, New Jersey.

All rights reserved under International and Pan-American Copyright Conventions. No part of this book may be reproduced or transmitted in any form or by any means, electronic or mechanical, including photocopy, recording, or any information storage and retrieval system, without prior permission in writing from the publisher. All inquiries should be addressed to Transaction Publishers, Rutgers—The State University, 35 Berrue Circle, Piscataway, New Jersey 08854-8042.

This book is printed on acid-free paper that meets the American National Standard for Permanence of Paper for Printed Library Materials.

Library of Congress Catalog Number: 99-056520
ISBN: 0-7658-0006-3
Printed in the United States of America

        Library of Congress Cataloging-in-Publication Data

Petersen, William.
   From birth to death: a consumer's guide to population studies / William Petersen. p. cm.
   Includes bibliographical references and index.
   ISBN 0-7658-0006-3 (alk. paper)
     1. Untied States—Population—Statistics. I. Title.

HB3505 .P48 1999
304.6'0973—dc21
                                                                       99-056520

For Renee

Contents

1. Population: The Fundamentals — 1
2. Age and Sex — 23
3. Population Composition — 37
4. From Fecundity to Fertility — 49
5. Mortality — 73
6. Health — 97
7. Prehistoric and Primitive Populations — 109
8. Population Theories — 123
9. Forecasts and Projections — 133
10. State Control of Population — 145
11. Conclusions — 165
    Notes — 169
    Index — 191

1

Population: The Fundamentals

The word *population* derives from the Latin *populus*, people. Like most verbal nouns, a "population" once designated either a process or a state. One of the charges made against George III in the Declaration of Independence was that he "endeavored to prevent the population of these states," but in this sense of "growth in numbers" the word has become archaic. The English language never developed a full equivalent of the French *peuplement*: "peopling" is not standard professional usage, and the usual term in geography, "settlement," has special connotations.

There is also an obsolete word, *population*, derived from a different Latin root, which means devastation or laying waste. With the word in that sense, the last reference in the *Oxford English Dictionary* is from 1747, but it is surprising that one of the more zealous proponents of controlling the increase in the world's human beings has not revived it.

What is a "Population"?

As demographers understand the term, the population of a designated area is the number of persons who, by specified criteria, are there on a particular date. This is similar to the understanding of the word in biology, but biologists are likely to concentrate only on the number of individuals per unit area and the rate of their increase under varying conditions.[1] In counting the members of a nation or of another areal unit, the census can enumerate either all who in some sense belong there (whether or not they are currently present) or all who are physically in residence (whether or not that is their legal domicile). The first is called the population *de jure*, the second, the population *de facto*. Some nations count one, some the other, and some both. Since neither system has been generally accepted, any comparison of human populations—to be as precise as possible—ought to be made with an awareness of how each country arrives at the number of its inhabitants.

What is the population of the United States? To this seemingly simple query, there is no single correct answer.

There are three official totals: the civilian population, the total resident population, and the total population including Americans living abroad. Military and diplomatic personnel are not the only ones who may reside outside their country, but also—among others—tourists, professionals of various types, businessmen, Gastarbeiter, missionaries, employees of voluntary services, and students. The practice of the United States in distributing census forms abroad is to use whatever facilities seem to be useful, such as Army and Navy units for their personnel and airlines and passenger ships for others. American consulates have the forms available, but persons not on the public payroll who live abroad are recorded only if they themselves take the trouble to register.

The accuracy of the count may be affected by the complicated definition of nationality. In works on politics authors often use "nationality" rather loosely, meaning more or less a community that defines itself by some process of self-determination, and population statistics sometimes reflect this usage. In typical practice, however, the meaning of the word is based on legal definitions of citizen or subject, which differ considerably from one country to another.

In the United States, the 1940 census was the first in which the census count of aliens was supplemented with a registration by the Immigration and Naturalization Service. There was a disconcertingly large difference in the number of aliens between the enumeration (based on each person's self-identification) of about 3.5 million and the registration (a summation of persons so defined in a legal context) of about 5 million. One can assume that in every census many aliens report themselves as citizens.

The concept of citizenship has undergone fundamental changes. Under laws enacted in the United States during the first decades of the twentieth century, a naturalized American relinquished his citizenship if he indicated a dual loyalty—as, for instance, by becoming a citizen of another state, or serving in its armed forces, or voting or being a candidate in a foreign election. In a series of subsequent decisions the Supreme Court abandoned all these restrictions on how one defines an "American." Under today's law, a person may commit himself to another state without losing his American citizenship unless it is proved that he intended to forgo it. Rabbi Meir Kahane, a rabble-rouser repeatedly arrested in both the United States and Israel, was a striking example. Elected to the Knesset, he pledged to be "faithful to the state of Israel," but he challenged the revocation of his American passport by claiming that he did not "intend" to forgo his United States citizenship—for he wanted to continue visits to the States in order to raise money for his cause. The subsequent legal battle in American courts became moot when the Israeli parliament passed a law, aimed directly at Kahane, requiring its members to relinquish legal ties to any other country.

As another interesting example, ethnic Japanese living abroad used to be obliged to register with a Japanese consulate, noting both the place of their *honseki*, or an ostensibly permanent legal residence in Japan, and where they were currently living. The dual record, however, was not very well maintained. Children were sometimes omitted from the prescribed listing, while names of deceased persons remained on it for years; and in countries where the assimilation of Japanese was in process, some did not register their *honseki* because to do so was considered a symbol of continuing political adherence to Japan.[2]

From random beginnings, dual citizenship has spread widely. A native-born American with one Irish grandparent, for instance, can obtain an Irish passport and thus the right to work in any country of the European Union without fussing about restrictive regulations. In 1998 Valdas Adamkus, a naturalized American citizen and a former federal employee, was elected president of his native Lithuania. On March 21, 1998 a Mexican law went into effect permitting the citizens of that country to hold an American passport, and the already porous border thus became still more permeable. Scholars in several social disciplines are analyzing the effect of such changes on the actual meaning of nationality, and there is a new periodical, *Diaspora*, dealing with such issues. Millions of Americans are eligible under the laws of their own or their forebears' native countries to apply for dual citizenship, but no statistics exist on how many have done so.[3]

Demography

The word demography is derived from two Greek words meaning "people" and "description of." It was coined by the French political economist Achille Guillard in his *Eléments de statistique humaine, ou démographie comparée* (1855). Earlier writings about births and deaths, the growth in numbers, and the relation of population to other social processes went by different names: "political arithmetic" (used to denote the pioneer efforts of such mercantilist writers as the English professor of anatomy William Petty, who coined the phrase); "political economy" (the term current at the time of Thomas Robert Malthus to designate the study of population, among other topics); and "human statistics" or simply "statistics" (used particularly by German analysts of the early modern period).

In some ways demography is a fully developed discipline, with its own national and international professional societies, a wide range of journals, and many persons who identify themselves as demographers. Yet it has also been and to a certain degree remains a rather amorphous congeries, made up of bits and pieces of other disciplines that everyone in the field assembles for himself. As the late American demographer Frank Notestein wrote in his last published paper, "Since the major part of our scientific equipment lies in our background professions, all of us tend to come to the subject with modes of thought, orientation, and prejudices of our background disciplines."[4]

This kind of haphazard training, more or less inevitable for a pioneer of Notestein's generation, has largely continued at least in the United States. Demography is usually taught in departments that offer advanced degrees not in that discipline but in sociology, economics, geography, statistics, or public health; and most aspiring demographers are thus required to become adept also in another set of skills. The consequence is that their training in mathematics and economics may often be less than optimal for population studies, and that in biology and history typically close to nil. It means also that members of the same discipline with diverse points of view may find it difficult to cooperate or even to communicate intelligibly.

There is a more or less fixed interrelation among fertility, mortality, and the structure of the population by age and sex. What is called formal demography, which often is based on technical and mathematical intricacies that laymen may not follow, is essentially the analysis of that interrelation and its reflections in population structure and growth. So-called social demography or population studies, on the other hand, comprises analyses of how population interacts with social, economic, political, geographic, and biological factors, all part of what an early compendium by the United Nations called "the determinants and consequences of population trends."[5] As the nineteenth-century Belgian statistician Adolphe Quetelet pointed out, there is a polarization between practitioners who believe that demography is a natural science with the same kinds of discoverable laws as physics and chemistry and, on the other hand, those who hold that the immutabilities of life and death can be truly understood only in relation to their enormously varied cultural and social settings. The regularity to be found in what he termed "moral statistics" (including data on marriage, divorce, crime, etc., as well as population per se) he saw as a social law comparable to a law of physics. As he conceived them, the characteristics of "*l'homme moyen*," the average man, is based on "constant," "perturbative," or "accidental" causes that together set a central point and the dispersion around it.[6]

The French economist and demographer Paul Vincent, who helped compile the first multilingual demographic dictionary, wrote a cogent article describing how difficult he found it to ferret out an acceptable definition of demography and thus an appropriate range of its terms and concepts. He found that participating in the compilation of such a work forced him to rethink matters that he assumed he already knew.[7] After he finished his own comparable work, Roland Pressat, another French demographer, wrote a similar appraisal of his experience.[8] For four years Renee Petersen and I worked to write another *Dictionary of Demography*, with again the same series of perplexities about the nature of the beast we were trying to describe.[9]

In each case the basic dilemma, as Vincent put it, was whether to define demography in a "restrictive" or an "extensive" manner. In arguing for the second alternative, he asked the reader to imagine the reaction of someone who, "in order to translate a work *on demography*, had to resort to a whole series of technical dictionaries—sociological, juridical, medical, economic, etc.—after having vainly searched his 'demographic' dictionary for terms currently used in demography." To satisfy fully the supposed user of a dictionary, in short, would require at least brief excursions into all the fields associated with population: biology in relation to birth and death; medicine and epidemiology; law in its regulation of such matters as euthanasia, abortion, international migration, and so on; mathematics, statistics (in particular, vital statistics), and computer science; such social disciplines as sociology, political science, economics, anthropology, geography, and psychology; as well as some notice given to national and international organizations and research institutes. From the 1950s on, moreover, there was a marked shift from earlier description or analysis to a frequent emphasis on recommended policies, with important consequences on how demographic data and techniques were regarded.[10] About the same time a new approach emerged called demographics, meaning the analysis of population data as these relate, for example, to markets for particular commodities. Since obviously no single discipline can be all-inclusive over so vast a range, to some degree the limits of demography remain indeterminate and mutable.

Several recent comments on the diversity of demographic works are indicative of new emphases. It is not surprising that Gunther Ipsen, a German demographer in favor during the Hitler period, tried to create a specifically German population theory compatible with National Socialist ideology.[11] One article makes the point that there are three quite distinct histories of demography.[12] In an interesting paper the American demographer Nathan Keyfitz attempted to resolve differences in analyses of population matters by persons in various disciplines. For example, he argued that physiologists and demographers come to divergent conclusions concerning how nutrition affects population growth because of their predisposition to pose different questions to the data.[13]

Real or Fabricated Data

International statistics encompass a basic contradiction. For scholars, the cold quantitative record of nations' achievements and failures is the neutral subject matter of their discipline. Those more concerned with what they deem to be the national interest, however, have often objected to the public display of such facts, and many have used their countries' publications to broadcast misleading or false data. In 1853, at a statistical congress meeting in Brussels, representatives of 26 countries tried to establish the definitions and procedures that would make the data collected by all governments fully comparable. The permanent commission that evolved out of that congress, however, could get no more than partial and reluctant cooperation from the nations involved. Over the years Germany objected even to the convention that the proceedings were published in French, at the time the standard language of diplomacy. The commission lasted until the Franco-Prussian War, and its successor, which met at irregular intervals between 1878 and 1912, almost foundered during the First World War. Yet the International Statistical Institute did survive, and its serial *Aperçu de la démographie des divers pays du monde* became for a period the most important source of international population data.[14] Eventually they were superseded by the several series of the United Nations and other international agencies established after the Second World War. Though such works reflect the substantial improvement in professional demographic standards over the past several decades, they also display the spread of statistical recordkeeping—of a sort—to a wide array of countries with neither the ability nor usually the will to maintain reasonable standards of accuracy. The technicians of the bureaus who organize such records into international compilations might, in the best case, endeavor to correct the faults and present the highest quality of data feasible. In fact, of course, the technical agencies have not been insulated from the steady politicization of the United Nations as a whole.

How should a responsible reference work deal with the publications of a country that combines in its intricate bureaucracy some technical work of a high quality with a frequent disregard for scholarly objectivity? The issue is fundamental to a large body of work in various disciplines in which such data are unquestioningly accepted. Specialists express doubt about the statistics of the former Soviet Union or of Communist China, but the usual practice is to cite, for instance, population figures of African countries as given, with no warning to the uninformed reader that these are, at best, estimates and, in many cases, figures that have been falsified in order to present the regimes with the best facade possible.

A more general deficiency of population statistics is analyzed in the various works of the American demographer Eugene M. Kulischer, especially in his principal book, *Europe on the Move: War and Population Changes, 1917-47*.[15] In his view, history is a continuous battleground. As demographic institutions ordinarily define their task, "the role of cataclysms is minimized," but in fact changes take place "not only by 'normal' fertility and mortality but also by wars, epidemics, and other forms of excess mortality, as well as by the uprooting of peoples." When I introduced into an elementary textbook on population a detailed account of politically sponsored mortality in totalitarian states,[16] this new departure was criticized by several more traditional demographers. In my opinion, my implied definition of the discipline represented not only a fuller but also a more realistic view of twentieth-century trends.

Problems in Aggregation

The issue of whether, when, or how much to accept the authority implicit in official data is far broader than that posed by the statistics of less developed countries or totalitarian states. In all versions of data assembling, whether the census, vital statistics, or surveys, information is gathered from individuals and then presented as concerning categories. Take as an example—one lacking any ideological content—the way the United States is divided into regions. How persons living in "the Middle West" or "the South" differ statistically from other Americans depends in large part on how these places are delineated. The regions of the United States were drawn following the 1870 census by one Henry Gannet, and with minor revisions his schema has been maintained ever since.[17] However useful the partition into four regions (and, within them, nine divisions) may have been at the time, it is relatively meaningless today. The principal fault is that, as defined, the regions are composed of whole states, which are generally too heterogeneous to make useful building blocks.

Far better units, for example, are the so-called BEA (from Bureau of Economic Analysis) economic areas, each of which consists of a Standard Metropolitan Statistical Area (SMSA) or similar core and the surrounding counties. A total of 183 economic areas so drawn covers the entire country, and by combining them one can fashion larger units that are relatively homogeneous in specific cultural or economic attributes. This was done by one marketing firm, with interesting results. Down the Atlantic Coast the regions it proposed are the Yankee Belt, Boston-Washington, Dixie, and South Florida. In western New York State is the Eastern Foundry, and next to it the Western Foundry. Below them are Southern Appalachia and the Mid-South. Across the top of the country from the Great Lakes to the Pacific are the Great Plains, the Western Energy Belt, the Empty Corridor, and the Pacific Northwest. Central Texas is identified as the region of South Plains Energy, and the expanse from western Texas to southern California as Hispanic America. The two noncontiguous states, finally, are grouped into Alaska/Hawaii.[18] The fact that businesses are willing to pay for such information in order to pinpoint their prospective customers suggests that such alternatives to the official partitioning could be useful also for the analysis of how social and economic attributes are distributed.

How to define a region is only one instance of a general problem in population statistics. No matter how meticulous demographers try to be, when they combine data about individuals into statistics about categories of the population, they introduce a false note that often even they may not be aware of. An example from a completely different context is the widely used index of contraceptive efficacy proposed by the early biologist and demographer Raymond Pearl:

$$R = \frac{\text{Number of pregnancies} \times 1,200}{\text{Total months of use}}$$

Among any sample of women that start to control births, however, those that discontinue over the following months are not representative of the whole. Any who find the method objectionable shift to another; any who have an accidental pregnancy are presumably less conscientious or more fecund. Month by month, the original heterogeneous population is reduced to a more and more homogeneous residue of satisfied, highly motivated users, including all the sterile and most of the subfecund.

In any work about population the frequent statements comparing the attitudes of the middle class with those of the working class, discussing the incomes of blacks and whites, analyzing the relative success of Asians and other Americans in school work, and so on and on--all such assertions are based in part on how the aggregates were compiled, and that is seldom a procedure that can be called independent of how the person or institution involved viewed the data.

Population Counts

In a strict sense the census is a product of modern times. The counts made by various ancient peoples were only of the portion that, for example, paid taxes or could be conscripted for military service. In order to estimate Rome's population, including females, children, slaves, and other categories generally omitted, scholars have had to resort to such other sources of data as shipments of grain from the provinces to the center or tombstones in ancient cemeteries.

The most general supplement to periodic counts of all the people in a designated area is one or another form of vital statistics. These are made up of a continuing registration of births and deaths (or of the religious ceremonies accompanying them), as well as changes in civil status marked by a marriage; a divorce, annulment, or separation; an adoption or legitimation; as well as sometimes fetal deaths, the state of health, moves from one residence to another, and so on. In the Western world such data were compiled first by churches, only later by secular institutions, and there are serious deficiencies concerning the accuracy and completeness of especially the earliest records. In the United States the so-called "registration area" comprised all states in which registration was judged to be at least 90 percent complete. It was not until 1933 that both all the births and all the deaths in the whole country were included in this rather casual definition of completeness.

International migration, formally defined as a movement across the border between nations, has been recorded in modern times, but with much ambiguity and sloppiness. Many analysts have omitted those who cross borders without permission, but illegal migrants have constituted a very high proportion, perhaps even a majority, of those who have moved across international borders since the Second World War.

The fact that data on international movements are an adjunct of state control means that national concerns largely determine the statistics. Thus, the countries' far lower interest in those departing than in those arriving has meant that there is a wide disparity between the number who leave one country and that who arrive at another. In 1977, the U.N. Economic Commission for Europe (ECE) published a study of how migrants were counted at both ends of the 342 paths between any two ECE countries. The number of recorded immigrants was 57 percent greater than that of emigrants.[19] With that much inaccuracy in the documentation of even legal migration within a region with the world's best population statistics, one must be very wary of conclusions about other categories or about recorded movements anywhere else.

Errors

Errors occur in every type of demographic data, and a good deal of professional demographers' expertise is concentrated on pinpointing deviations from accuracy, estimating their probable size, and making suitable adjustments. An undercount is generally more frequent and larger than an overcount. As long ago as in a volume supplementing the 1900 U.S. census, the outstanding demographer of that period, Walter F. Willcox, defined the class most likely to be passed over, and the reason:

> Census returns are obtained by enumerators who inquire from dwelling house to dwelling house, [but] a small minority have no dwelling house even in the loose sense in which that term is defined by the Census Office, namely, the place where a person regularly sleeps.[20]

More generally, sectors at a society's periphery—not only the homeless but casual laborers, criminals, and near-criminals—are always the most difficult to count and therefore the most likely to be overlooked. Throughout the world, census bureaus often exclude (or, at best, enumerate with less precision) such marginal sectors of the population as illegal immigrants, residents of the shantytowns that ring the cities of less developed countries, the "Indian jungle population" in parts of South America, or the nomads in some countries of northern Africa.

One common source of error is that some respondents misunderstand the instructions concerning census questions. The U.S. Bureau of the Census tests each query in several locations before it is included in the schedule, but even so the wording sometimes generates bizarre replies. Haley Barbour, formerly the chairman of the Republican National Committee, likes to recall an incident when he was director of the Mississippi census:

> One day a bunch of us were sitting around the office in Jackson looking at some business census forms. I'll never forget, we got one response from a little mom-and-pop operation up in Iuka, Mississippi. As they went down the questionnaire they came to the question, "Number of employees broken down by sex." And they answered that question, "None broken down by sex, but we have two with a drinking problem."[21]

In 1970 the United States census schedule asked persons to identify themselves as of Mexican, Puerto Rican, Cuban, South or Central American, or other Spanish origin. The total count of all these Hispanics (or Latinos) was 1,508,886, contrasted with fewer than 600,000 in both the 1969 and the 1971 Current Population Surveys. As the Bureau later noted, "Some respondents apparently...interpreted the category 'Central or South American' to mean central or southern United States."[22]

When the 1920 census reported that there were only 81,338 foreign-born Japanese in the United States, some racist newspapers questioned the accuracy of the datum. Ten years earlier the census count had been 67,655, and during the decade the net immigration amounted to 67,108. Seemingly, if one took into account the probable death rate of a population with many old people, the 1920 figure represented an undercount of some 55 percent. In fact, the apparent error was due to the different ways that two federal agencies defined "the United States." By the usage of the Bureau of the Census, the territory of Hawaii, with its sizable number of Japanese Americans, was excluded, but the Commissioner of Immigration included territories. When the figures were assigned to the proper populations with estimates of the probable changes during the decade, the count in 1920 proved to be not lower but slightly higher than an extrapolation from 1910.[23]

The residence, the place where one customarily or legally lives, can be interpreted in various ways, which affect not only the stated size of a population but also its recorded characteristics. Occasionally persons establish a pseudoresidence in order, for instance, to gain a tax advantage or to run for electoral office. When unmarried college students, previously counted as residents of their parents' homes, were redefined as residing where they were temporarily living, this increased by sometimes significant proportions the official populations of small towns that included a college. For example, the population of Chapel Hill, the site of the University of North Carolina, jumped from 3,654 in 1940 to 9,177 in 1950. Not only the number of people but also their median age, income, occupations, sex ratio, and other characteristics changed radically when a redefinition of a technical term recorded a large influx of teenagers.

Errors occur not only in the count of persons but also, more generally, in the designation of their characteristics, and thus in the relative size of various categories. One might suppose that the age of a person is so unambiguous an attribute that it could be recorded with a full assurance of its accuracy. In fact, the concept is defined differently in various cultures. In China a child, assigned the age of 1 year at birth, becomes a year older at the beginning of each successive lunar year, so that by the Chinese reckoning everyone is between 1 and 3 years older than by the Western convention. In Bangladesh there is a confusion among the Western, Bengali, and Muslim calendars, all of which are in current use. Many persons in less developed countries do not know how old they are; and in literate populations age is often misstated, because the respondents do not know it, report it only approximately, or refuse to respond altogether. As estimated by Giorgio Mortara, the last generation's top expert on Latin American populations, in 1950 half a million Brazilian women aged 30 to 69 declared their ages to be 15 to 29; and are the women of Brazil vainer than those of other countries, or the men? In the censuses of most countries, the schedule asks for the age at either the last or the nearest birthday. The practice in France, to ask for the date of birth, is both unambiguous and possibly less likely to elicit false responses. Why other countries have not adopted this usage is puzzling, for it is important in many types of demographic analysis to get as accurate a measure of age distribution as possible.

Whenever it is possible, statisticians try to find a quantitative measure of a qualitative attribute.[24] In United States censuses, for example, education is measured by the reported number of years of schooling completed. Over the decades this index has risen appreciably, though by more meaningful measures the population's learning has not improved nearly so much and during some periods may even have declined.

Editing and Imputation

The returns of an American census are subject to various types of editing. The 1990 census schedules, sent in by mail, were then reviewed in the field against lists of local residences in order to pick out those lacking any information about the people supposedly living in them. In that year I took a temporary job as such a field editor to pursue these no-shows in two towns in California. In Pebble Beach many houses are the second homes of well-to-do families who actually live in, say, San Francisco; the dwellings were often empty, and neighbors knew little or nothing about the owners. In Carmel, which prides itself on maintaining a village-like ambiance, such routine urban conveniences as house numbers are verboten. On the list I was given, homes of presumably missing residents were identified as, for instance, "a green house catty-corner from the two-story brick building." Though sometimes I could not find such places, I was able to fill in many gaps and correct some errors. I was also made aware as never before in my professional career as a demographer why it is impossible to compile a fully accurate record of a population of several hundred million.

Once this field editing has been completed, the data are processed at one of the offices of the Bureau of the Census. When data are fed into a computer, it is programmed to perform a so-called validation check, detecting such errors as coding "3" for sex when only "1" or "2" is permissible. The program also fills in some information omitted on the form but unambiguously implied in other responses. If the space specified for sex is left blank, for example, it can be indicated by a given name or a self-identification as a wife. The computer can also correct such impossible combinations as a male "housewife," a "widow" aged 10 years, a native-born "alien," and the like—though it may not always be obvious which half of the contradiction is in error.

The computer is also programmed to use bits of evidence from the rest of the questionnaire or from other sources to make a plausible, but not necessarily correct, emendation in or addition to the reported responses. Even more dubiously, not only the characteristics but even the existence of a person or a household are assumed from data on supposedly similar components of the neighborhood. In the 1960 census of the United States, for instance, some "occupied" housing units had no one reported as living in them; and a total of 776,665 persons, or 0.4 percent of the official count, were "imputed" merely by replicating nearby households on which there were data. In 1970, the census form asked a sample of households to give the 1969 income from wages or salaries for each person in the household who had worked, but for 11 percent of the households some part of the total income was imputed. In some critics' view, such a difference between 0.4 percent and 11 percent is one between editing to which they do not object and so great a revision that the user of the resultant tables can hardly be sure what they mean.[25] This is particularly so since the person using the statistics is given no warning of how they were fabricated.

These issues were given a thorough public airing when lawsuits were brought to challenge some of the results in both the 1980 and the 1990 censuses, especially statistics that had been based on such imputations. The fact that in both cases the Bureau of the Census won the court cases is important; but in the second round of suits the matter was closed only when, in March 1996, the Supreme Court declined to review appeals by several large cities, which claimed to have lost millions of dollars in federal funding because of inaccurate counts of the poorer sectors of their populations.

An alternative to imputation—and one that is, in my opinion, much to be preferred—is to revert to the practice used before computer techniques were fully developed. That was to list at the foot of each table a residual proportion labeled "Not stated" or "Unknown." This procedure would give users of the data a more honest representation of what we really know about the population, as well as indicate whether respondents find particular questions excessively intrusive.

The Future of the American Census

In 1990 the Census Bureau recorded a total population of 248,709,873, and it estimated that more than 8 million were not counted and more than 4 million were either counted twice or incorrectly included. This degree of inaccuracy, though less than in prior counts, made a more significant difference in a number of ways. During the 1990s the Bureau conducted a series of tests in search of an improved procedure, and in 1996 the Bureau announced a plan that, in its words, had the "twin goals of reducing costs and increasing accuracy." The new emphasis would be on collecting better data on fewer people rather than duplicating the futile effort to get unsatisfactory statistics on everyone.

The tentative plan for the 2000 count was to enumerate only about 90 percent of the population—that portion that presents fewest problems—and then to complete the census using sample surveys. Subsequently, the Bureau proposed to begin sampling as soon as the mail-in deadline passes, adjusting the sampling rate accordingly. In a Census Bureau press release dated March 11, 1997, the proposed procedure was described as follows:

> For example, a census tract with a small response rate of 60 percent will have the balance of its households sampled at a rate of 3-in-4 to achieve a 90 percent response rate. Census tracts with initial mail response rates of

better than 90 percent will have the balance sampled at 1-in-10....The Census Bureau changed its methodology...to assure responses from at least 90 percent of all addresses.

This revised plan, it was maintained, would give a more reliable result concerning the households not counted directly. This second procedure was suggested, one should recall, in response to criticism of the original plan, which was also defended as fully adequate to serve as the basis of apportionment. Indeed, in the months leading up to the date of the census opposing forces were engaged in a continual conflict, with new arguments advocating changing procedures.

Whether either of the procedures proposed by the Census Bureau would conform with the provision in the Constitution prescribing the decennial count was tested in federal courts. A special three-judge panel, with two members who had been appointed by President Reagan and one by President Clinton, decided unanimously that using sampling would not conform with the law setting census procedures. The issue was appealed to the Supreme Court, whose decision is discussed later. At a preliminary session of the Court on November 30, 1998, several justices indicated their lack of enthusiasm about being asked to resolve a dispute between the executive and legislative branches. Justice Antonin Scalia suggested that the Court's stature would be diminished if it got involved in an essentially political dispute. Chief Justice William Rehnquist reminded the litigants that preparations for the count had to begin the following spring, and if the case were to be brought before the court again, "we'll do well to get [a ruling] by June."[26]

During 1998 the Bureau responded to several hundred congressional inquiries, had three full-scale audits by the General Accounting Office (representing in effect the House Republicans), participated in twenty-two formal hearings before congressional committees, was carefully supervised by overseers from the Commerce Department and the Office of Management and Budget (representing in effect the White House Democrats). A new Census Monitoring Board was installed within the Bureau itself. Its budget of $4 million a year was used initially to pay lawyers to clarify rather vague sections of the legislation under which it operates.[27]

After months of wrangling between the Democratic administration and the Republican Congress, a temporary compromise was announced. The Bureau could experiment with statistical sampling, but it agreed to test also the traditional method of head counts. Its rehearsal focused on three areas: Sacramento, Calif.; Columbia, S.C. with eleven surrounding counties; and the Menominee Reservation in Wisconsin. An AP dispatch of January 16, 1999 gave the results of a test count in Sacramento:

Traditional count	349,197
Sampling	403,313
California State estimate	392,834

From this much variation in the reported population of a single city, it became obvious that the choice of procedure would be of indisputable significance. But it did not solve the dispute over which method to adopt.

On December 13, 1997, *Science News OnLine* printed a number of letters responding to its earlier programs on the controversy over the 2000 census. One viewer suggested that mail delivery should be discontinued to persons who fail to return the census schedule. Another proposed that the Bureau restrict its mission to an enumeration; "the arrogance and intrusiveness of the census taker alienates people who would otherwise cooperate in answering a simple head count." The Bureau was not likely to follow such suggestions, which are nevertheless interesting in that they reflect the fairly widespread concern that the ostensibly technical issues generated.

The matters to be decided are both important and complex, and it is helpful to divide them into the three categories: (1) constitutional, (2) statistical, and (3) political.

1. When the framers of the Constitution tried to lay a foundation for a new national unity, one of the major issues they faced was the potential discord between large and small states. They fashioned a bicameral Congress: in the Senate, with two members from each state, the smaller ones would have relatively more power; in the House of Representatives, with members apportioned according to the number of each state's inhabitants, the larger states would have more power proportionate to their population. This required that there be a regular count of the nation's population in order to record a district's population that each House member would represent. The Constitution therefore stipulated that there would be a census every ten years, conducted "in such manner as they [the members of Congress] shall by law di-

rect," and in 1976 the Census Act was amended to explicitly prohibit the Census Bureau from using statistical sampling as part of the decennial census. No census bureau existed in 1790, when the first count was made, and during the first years federal officials from presidents down supervised the details of enumeration and apportionment. Field operations were undertaken by United States marshals, who appointed assistants to travel about and put the queries to everyone in the assigned area. Since no census form was sent out, each enumerator acted on his own. The unit was not the individual but the household, and in 1790 the data were limited to the answers to only six questions.

Carrying out the directives was more complex than the framers had anticipated, and an excellent analysis of how each challenge was met is given in Margo Anderson's *The American Census*.[28] The first problem was that the district's population, when divided by the number of seats in the House, did not generally result in a whole number. This meant that an entirely fair representation was not possible, for the several alternatives proposed affected the various states' representation differently. If the size of the first House was set at 112 Representatives, with each representing 30,000 constituents, members from the South held that that region would be cheated. It took two years to set the size of the House, following Thomas Jefferson's proposal: 105 members with each representing 33,000.

The 1976 Census Act was the principal basis of the suits that were brought to the Supreme Court. The manner of counting the population would probably affect, or in large part determine, how the 435 seats in the House would be allocated among the electoral districts, how districts at state and local levels would be redrawn, and how about $180 billion in federal funding of various programs would be distributed.

On January 4, 1999 the entire Court voted 5 to 4, according to the usual press reports, that the Census Bureau may not carry out its plan to use sampling in the 2000 count. In fact, the split might better be called 4½ to 4½. Justice Sandra Day O'Connor, who cast the swing vote, wrote a decision that reflected the Court's preference for avoiding taking any position. In the words of the majority opinion, using sampling is unconstitutional "in calculating the population for purposes of apportionment," but sampling was allowed to set the population base for funding decisions and possibly also for state and local redistricting.

Matthew Glavin of the Southeastern Legal Foundation, who had brought one of the original suits that the Court decided, announced that he would sue again to prevent the use of sampling to guide redistricting at any level. Since the Court's decision resolved the "substantive issues presented," it dismissed the parallel case brought by the Republican-led House, but that suit would probably also be brought again to bar the use of sampling for any allocation of political power.

In April 1999 the Republican Congress threatened to cut off funding on June 15 if the dispute over sampling was not resolved to its satisfaction. Presumably not only the Commerce Department, which includes the Bureau of the Census, would be affected but also the Justice and State Departments, which have been grouped together with Commerce in the federal budgets over the past three-quarters of a century. Chief Justice William Rehnquist sent a letter to the congressional leaders expressing his fear that the dispute might close federal courts. "I urge in the strongest possible terms," he wrote, "that funding for the judiciary quickly be made available for the remainder of the fiscal year."

2. One legal objection to the proposed procedure for the 2000 count is that the Bureau of the Census supposedly has never before used such a combination of enumeration and sampling. Even though a head count has been recognized as less than perfect, it was continued in part because it was seen as relatively impervious to manipulation. In fact, of course, all recent censuses have been based in part on sampling. The Bureau distributes two schedules, called a short form which is supposed to be filled in by everyone, and a long form with additional queries, put to one in every so-and-so many respondents. No one has ever objected to this procedure, for it ensures that the expanded questionnaire will be distributed to a random sample of the whole population, with a known range of probable error in the reported figures.

Whether a sample is a suitable substitute for a full count depends on whether there is a random, or at least a representative, selection among the people to be enumerated. How can the Bureau of the Census draw an appropriate sample from a segment of the population that is being approximated in this manner because it is deemed to be otherwise unreachable? The Bureau's record does not give one confidence that it will find a procedure that will satisfy critics. To repeat: not only the characteristics but even the existence of thousands of Americans have been imputed in past counts. Strangely, the extensive dispute about the proposed procedure has, so far as I have seen, passed over this earlier record of an arguably dubious procedure.

Many social analysts propound a rather simplistic environmentalism with respect to slum residents, holding in effect that anyone living in a poor neighborhood is likely to have the characteristics of "problem minorities." Each of a number of interrelated factors—low income, ill health, poor education, high crime rate, unstable family pattern—reinforces all the others; and the sum of all of them, in turn, reinforces the majority's negative appraisal, which then reinforces the alienation of the minority. Yet this widespread assumption is not in accord with the facts. Many poor blacks, for instance, strongly resist the baneful influence of the destructive environment in which they live, and a surprisingly large proportion succeed, against all odds, in retaining a law-abiding and responsible life style. It is not at all appropriate to extend the characteristics of a (necessarily) poorly drawn sample to any portion of the American population.

3. The minorities that are undercounted with the usual enumeration are especially blacks and Hispanics. These sectors of the population are two of the principal supporters of the Democratic Party, and it is not surprising that the Democratic administration would like to have a larger number of such voters included in the count that will be the basis of electoral districts for the following decade. Similarly, the Republicans that control both houses of Congress are hardly enthusiastic about a project that is likely to reduce their party's representation. But this difference is only the beginning of the political dispute. Sampling under the jurisdiction of a Democratic official can involve various types of fraud, and the record of the Clinton White House suggests that it is not unreasonable of citizens to be wary of that possibility. Moreover, Republican members of the House have argued, the Bureau of the Census has not exhausted all the other means of getting a fuller count while still relying on the standard procedure of enumeration.

On March 2, 1999, Kenneth Prewitt, director of the Census Bureau, testified before the supervisory subcommittee of the House. He did not mention, except indirectly, the debate about sampling, and he stressed the technical expertise of "the dedicated, hard-working professionals at the Census Bureau." But the principal import of his testimony was to list a number of ways the Bureau would use to improve enumeration in 2000, and to point out that almost all of them would require additional funding. A more intensive preparation for the census would involve cooperation with state and local officials as well as schools and private organizations, the greater use of paid advertising, and other innovations or extensions of past practices. Some 3,500 welfare recipients had been hired to check lists of addresses, and he recommended that welfare recipients, veterans, and American Indians be allowed to take temporary jobs with the Bureau and continue to receive federal benefits. A letter will be mailed before the questionnaire to inform respondents of its imminent arrival, and a reminder card will be mailed to those not returning the questionnaire promptly. The schedule will be simpler and "user-friendly," printed in Chinese, Korean, Spanish, Tagalog, and Vietnamese as well as English. The Bureau anticipated that the number of follow-up visits will be of the order of 45 million housing units, rather than the 30 million in 1990.

One of the main means of improving the accuracy of prior counts used to be what was called a post-enumeration survey, which Prewitt labeled a Post Census Local Review. A sample count was taken in areas with low returns in order to estimate the number and characteristics of those omitted in the enumeration—essentially on a smaller scale what has been proposed as a new procedure for 2000. This was, Prewitt stated, an expensive and inefficient means of improving the figures; in 1990 only about 125,000 persons were added to the reported population, or "only one-twentieth of one percent of the overall population count."

The dispute over the American census is not unique. The world over, disputes over counts have become common.

In 1976 the Slovenes in Carinthia, Austria's southernmost province, tried to sabotage a census called to determine how many citizens spoke languages other than German. Great Britain omitted the unsettling question on race from the 1981 schedule. More general protests against a census took place in Switzerland. In West Germany more than a thousand suits against the government charged that the questions invaded respondents' privacy, and the count scheduled for April 1983 had to be postponed. In the Netherlands the 1970 count was postponed a year, and in 1971 many respondents were "not at home." Pilot surveys to prepare for the 1980-81 count had so high a nonresponse rate that the responsible minister decided to postpone it until 1983, when again it was not held. A Dutch demographer raised the question whether "census taking may not now be a viable form of data collection in the Netherlands." Indeed, up to the mid-1990s there has been no Dutch census for two decades, in spite of the law requiring an enumeration every ten years.[29]

The reasons for the hostile reaction derive in part from local conditions, very often from interethnic disputes. More generally, the greater role of the state bureaucracy in managing an expansive social welfare has often resulted in more extensive questionnaires, with a greater likelihood that some portion of the population will resent what they see as either an invasion of their privacy or, worse, a means of corruptly depriving them of their fair share of control over governmental affairs.

International Comparisons

If each American demographer, as Notestein remarked in his paper, evolves along a partly unique path, the same must be said a fortiori of each national school of demography. Since the last quarter of the nineteenth century, the dominant social issue related to population studies has differed from one country to another: in the United States, for many years, immigration and race relations; in Britain, historical demography and the statistics of less developed countries; in France, the low birth rate and how to raise it; in Italy, what is termed "constitutional demography," whose practitioners have stressed biological factors far more than in population studies elsewhere; in Central Europe, multinational populations; in Russia and the Soviet Union, economic productivity; and, more recently, in many less developed countries, excess fertility and measures that might reduce it.

In each context such emphases, while setting priorities for the most significant work, have also impeded the exchange of findings between one locale and another. In the enormous American corpus on ethnicity, for example, remarkably little attention has been given to the large body of writings in Austria-Hungary and the neighboring countries; for in the American context the problem was long seen as identifying and mitigating impediments to full assimilation, while in Central Europe it was, on the contrary, how minorities could maintain their own languages, religions, and ways of life. From such differences in nuances of the discipline, dissimilarities arose not only in the main topics that demographers study, but also the major problems they face in their task.

2

Age and Sex

For a demographic analysis the most important classification of any population is one by age and sex, for which the term is population structure. The reason, of course, is that almost all behavior patterns diverge along those two dimensions, partly because of physiology, partly because everywhere cultural norms differ between males and females and between children, adults, and the old.

It may be enlightening to exemplify from several actual cases how tricky it can be to interpret statistics that have been offered without taking population structure into account:

- In a 1905 Massachusetts state census, married women were asked how many children they had borne (an average of 2.77) and how many their mothers had borne (an average of 6.47). There had been, in other words, a disastrous decline in family size over only one generation—the consequence, undoubtedly, of one or another deleterious custom.
  But the fertility-in-process of the respondents, who ranged in age from 18 up, was compared with the completed fertility of the respondents' mothers, all of whom were past the childbearing period.
- During the Spanish-American War, the secretary of war used his annual report to respond to public criticism about the large number of soldiers dying in the Philippines. Their death rate, he pointed out, was almost identical with that of the civilian population of Washington.
  But the soldiers were all in the age group with normally the lowest mortality; the civilians were of all ages.
- Proponents of the restrictive immigration laws that were enacted in the 1920s often contrasted immigrants' birth and crime rates with the much lower

ones of the native population (and a similar restrictive policy is now being supported with the same argument).
But immigrants are mainly in the age group from which both parents and criminals come, and in the first decades of this century well over half of them were young males, who are everywhere more likely to commit crimes.
- The family income of various ethnic groups in the American population ranges from well over one and a half times the national average (Jews) down to under two-thirds of the average (American Indians). Of the many reasons that could be given for the differences, the one most often cited is discrimination.
But an important factor is the median age—ranging from the mid-30s to the mid-40s (Jews, Poles, Irish, Italians, and Germans), or from 18 to the low 20s (blacks, American Indians, Puerto Ricans, and Mexicans). Men and women of whatever ethnicity who are well along in their careers earn more than those who recently entered the work force.
- The 1979 census of the Soviet Union included the usual question on age, as we knew from the published enumeration schedule. However, except for a few partial citations of minor importance, no age data were published. In spite of the new era of *glasnost* that had been proclaimed, Soviet officials omitted what in most other countries would be a routine element of a census report.
Murray Feshbach, among the most knowledgeable of American sovietologists on such matters, acquired the age and sex data for four republics of the USSR and published them in 1985, six years after the census.[1] The change in children's sex ratio from 1970 to 1979 suggested that during that intercensal period infant mortality had increased by between a third and a half. Statistics for the four republics, which approximated four ethnic components of the USSR, showed that the Russian, Ukrainian, and Latvian sectors were declining relative to the Uzbek, which could be assumed to resemble the other Muslim sectors. Because of shifts in the age structure, growth of the work force would be not only much slower but also concentrated in the non-Slavic populations.

In other words, the mere publication of age and sex statistics could inform demographers of trends with highly significant economic, social, and military implications.

Population Structure in Demography

As exemplified by the false interpretations I have listed, an axiom of population analysis is the need to pay careful attention to how the age and sex structure affects whatever is being discussed. Take, for instance, the difference between "crude" and "refined" rates. Any rate is a device for comparing the actual with the potential. Thus, we take the number of births in a year as the numerator and the population in which they occurred as the denominator to get a figure, called the crude birth rate, that can range from around 10 to 50 or more per thousand persons in the population. It is called "crude" because some portion of the presumably potential mothers in the denominator are in fact children, males, or women beyond the age of childbearing. So in a first adjustment, we change the denominator to females aged 15 to 44, the approximate age range during which a female is able to bear a child. But both the physiological ability to have children and the cultural norms that influence the timing of births vary greatly over that age range; and to be more precise we calculate separate birth rates for females aged 15-19, 20-24, and so on, and then sum up these several rates. Various other refinements are made occasionally (such as, for instance, a differentiation between legitimate and illegitimate births), but the most fundamental ones are those that distinguish the sectors delineated by age and sex.

The sizes of various age groups, male and female, are conventionally represented in what is called a population pyramid. If we arrange the elements of a bar graph to represent successively higher ages from the lowest at the bottom to the highest at the top, each divided between males at the left and females at the right, the shape of the graph will typically approximate a pyramid. For of those born, say, in 1900, some will have died each year since then, gradually reducing the length of the bars representing each higher age. The shape, however, is not a perfect pyramid, for mortality varies by sex and from year to year, and fertility and migration also affect the population structure. A depletion caused by a past famine or epidemic, or by a period of especially low fertility or large emigration, is represented by an indentation from a smooth pyramid; and a period of exceptionally high fertility or of a considerable immigration is represented by a corresponding bulge. These irregularities remain on pyramids of consecutive dates, gradually moving up to the top of the graph and disappearing only when the persons concerned die off.

The population pyramids of three countries at the specified dates are shown in the figure. These examples were chosen because their shape is close to that of the three stylized figures above them. A broad-based pyramid indicates an expansive population, for the proportion either in the fecund age group or about to enter it is large, while the proportion of the aged about to die off is small. A constrictive age structure, such as the one corresponding to Sweden in 1935, has the contrary characteristics: a small proportion currently or soon able to become parents and a relatively large proportion that will soon die of old age. The middle diagram represents a population between the two extremes, neither growing nor contracting.

Figure 2.1

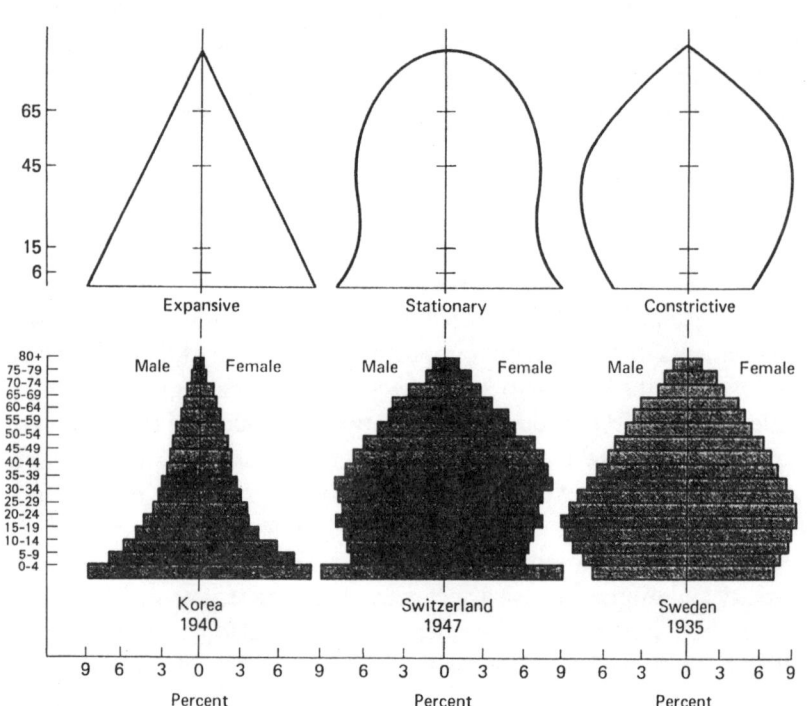

Connections between various parts of the age structure are analyzed by cohorts. Until rather recently dictionaries defined the word *cohort* as one of the ten divisions of a Roman legion or, by extension, any band of warriors, with citations in both senses back to the fourteenth century. Among demographers, "cohort" is used to mean all those who during a single year (or other period) have gone through a particular demographic experience, such as being born (a birth cohort), getting married (a marriage cohort), and so on. We have all become familiar with the use of the concept in commercial or political writings—he Young Marrieds; the Gray Panthers; the baby boomers, who grew up to become the Yuppies and then moved into post-Yuppydom.

Population Structure and Growth in Numbers

Several decades ago, at the height of the movement to usher zero population growth (or ZPG) into the United States, a student asked me to sign a petition endorsing that goal. To realize his objective, I tried to explain to him, was more complex than its sponsors seemed to realize: zero growth would mean that more than half the population would be aged over 30—the sector that the same student was denouncing as untrustworthy. He thought I was pulling his leg. What did growth in numbers have to do with the relative size of age sectors?

The campaign that the student had joined was conducted vociferously by his organization, Zero Population Growth, Inc. It reflected the well-publicized views of its first president, Paul Ehrlich, author of such works as *The Population Bomb* (2nd ed., 1971) and the most persistent of the country's antinatalist zealots. According to two surveys of the organization's membership, it was virtually entirely white and predominantly male, with an average education well above the national norm. The most striking characteristic of the members was their youth, with a median age under 30, and the proportion of full-time students among them rose in the one year between the surveys from 37 to 46 percent.[2] To the extent that this organization can be taken as typical of the movement, the pressure in the United States for ZPG was generated largely by male college students and young men who had recently graduated from college. These were the boom babies on the threshold of maturity, whose recommended policies reflected their experiences with overcrowded schools and, after graduation, shortages of attractive job opportunities.

The term "zero population growth" has been used with several meanings, and the phrase hardly represents the *mots justes* for several of them. The brochures of the ZPG organization, like most popular accounts of efforts to affect the birth rate, ignored a key determinant of population growth—namely, the age structure. If efforts to reduce fertility focuses only on cutting the number of children per family, and if the number of families increases, the population will continue to grow. And, vice versa, if the number of families is small, even a sizable progeny per family will not reverse a trend toward depopulation. The boom babies who reached childbearing age could form so many *new families* that even if each couple had only two offspring the total number of children in the country would have grown by a considerable number. That is why virtually every demographer then believed that the baby boom would have an "echo"; the actual decline in American fertility was the unexpected consequence of a fall in family size so drastic that it more than made up for the larger number of young people entering the prime reproductive ages. Because American women postponed longer than had been anticipated both getting married and, subsequently, starting a family, the echo came later than expected. By the late 1990s, thus, there were some 72 million boys and girls of school age, with again an especially heavy crowding in the country's high schools.

In several interesting publications, the American economist Richard Easterlin has used the details of this cycle to build a theory of family formation. When the national birth rate is high (as during the baby boom and, again, during the delayed echo), the competition within the large cohorts will tend to result in a higher rate of unemployment, lower wages, and slower advancement. Therefore, members of that generation will tend to marry later and put off longer having children, and more of the women will seek jobs outside the home. Economic strains will result in higher rates of divorce and other social pathologies. When, on the contrary, cohorts entering the work force are relatively small, economic opportunities will be abundant and young people will marry earlier and have more children.[3]

A second meaning given to "zero population growth" is also simplistic—that, with no regard to age structure, the total population remains constant from one year to the next. But with no change in size over a short period, the resultant shift in the age structure would generally result in significant changes in the subsequent rate of growth. The slogan calling on Americans to achieve zero growth by the year 2000 was visionary, for it assumed that in each year up to the new century policies would be adopted in order to shift the age-specific rates of births, deaths, and net migration. These rates, however, sum up the behavior of a large number of individuals, which can be forecast (with usually inadequate accuracy) mainly in the sense that the population's age structure indicates the probable ranges in the components of population growth.

If there is no net migration and if age-specific birth and death rates remain constant for as much as a century, the fluctuations in the population's rate of growth will finally end. In the so-called stable population that is thus brought into being, both the age structure and the rate of growth (which can be negative, zero, or positive) remain fixed. A stable population with no growth is called stationary, and this is the meaning that demographers assign to what the antinatalists term "zero population growth."

Males and Females

A person's sex is obviously a major determinant of his or her behavior. Both biology and culture set many differences between males and females, and often a distinction is made between "sex," related to physiological impulses and constraints, and "gender," the comparable effects of the culture. However, some in the social disciplines are so inclined to understate biological factors that they use "gender" to denote the whole range of characteristics: there have been journal papers in which the authors discuss what they term "gender hormones."

The usual measure, or the sex ratio, is defined as the number of males per 100 females. The primary sex ratio, or the number of males conceived per 100 females, is not known, and demographers' usual assumption that it is very high would mean that a far larger percentage of male fetuses than female die in the womb. This premise (not shared by some physicians[4]) could be validated only by checking the sex of an adequate sample of fetuses, including those lost in spontaneous and induced abortions. The secondary sex ratio (or the number of males born per 100 females) has ranged worldwide between 104 and 107. In the United States it fell from 105.3 in 1969 to 104.9 in 1995, and the breakdown of this change is more interesting, because more than a bit puzzling, than the decline itself. When controlled for maternal and paternal ages and the infant's birth order, the sex ratio at birth fell among white mothers but rose among black mothers. The shift is significant: a change of <1 per 100 females represents nearly 4,000 newborns per year. Among the possible reasons cited, perhaps the most likely is that black females typically have higher levels of estrogen than whites.[5]

In most cultures parents generally prefer a boy to a girl, especially as their first child. A gynecologist has devised a method based on the relative acidity/alkalinity of the uterus that may enable a couple to realize that preference by timing the conception at a particular point in the menstrual cycle.[6] If this procedure works and if many parents were to adopt it, the changed sex ratio of children would alter various characteristics of the population. For example, if a population with a typical sex ratio at birth of 105 doubled itself in 118 years, raising the sex ratio to 116 would increase the doubling time to 178 years.[7]

A grossly skewed sex ratio has effects that permeate the entire culture. Of the early Chinese immigrants to the United States, for instance, virtually all were young males; the more than 100,000 Chinese enumerated in the American censuses of 1880 and 1890 included only about 4,000 females. Since in most of the country racial intermarriage was then illegal, usually men could satisfy their sexual urge only with prostitutes: a civil society built on normal family life was manifestly unachievable. Similarly, the culture of the Old West, or of most European colonies during their heyday, or of almost any other frontier area, reflects the effects of a surplus of males and the consequent dearth of family life.

When the sex ratio is close to parity, according to the conventional view, men and women in a Western society pair off and form families. The actual process is likely to be more complex, as suggested by the fact that the word *family* has been ambiguous since it entered the language. It derives from *famulus* (feminine, *famula*), a servant, and the route to its present meaning has been circuitous. The earliest definition given in the *Oxford English Dictionary*, with citations going back to the fifteenth century, is "the servants of a house or establishment; the household." The primary present-day meaning is "the group of persons consisting of parents and their children, whether living together or not; in a wider sense, the unity formed by those who are connected by blood or affinity"; but in this sense the earliest citation is from a 1667 work of John Milton. That is to say, the confusion between a household and a family, a frequent problem in interpreting demographic statistics, is found also in the etymological history of the word.

Since data are often not available to distinguish precisely between a family and a household, the stated size of a "family" may be no more than a rough indicator of fertility. What anthropologists term the "nuclear family," or a married couple and their minor children living together apart from other kin, was until recently taken to be the universal norm in Western societies. Variations resulting from different patterns of marriage and remarriage, or from the adoption of children, or from sharing the residence with other kin, boarders, or servants, were regarded as aberrations or extensions of the standard. In recent publications, reflecting a shift in cultural norms, the Bureau of the Census has defined a family as any two or more members of a household who are related by blood, marriage, or adoption—a definition that has little relation to the earlier notion that the institution, comprising two parents and their children, was the key to measuring fertility. This statistical imprecision has been aggravated by pressure to include in the concept such anomalous types as one-person households, single mothers and their children, and two homosexuals sharing a residence.

The Adult and the Old

Relations between generations partly depend, of course, on how age groups are defined. Physiology sets a sequence of periods in the human life cycle, but it is difficult to decide at what ages the most important transitions take place. For example, the American psychologist Daniel Levinson approximated the stages with overlapping ages: childhood (ages 0-22), early adulthood (17-45), middle adulthood (40-65), late adulthood (60-85), and very late adulthood (80-?).[8] The American demographer Jacob Siegel divided those at or close to retirement into several subclasses, often with markedly different physical and social characteristics: "the older population" (60 and over), "the elderly" (65 and over), "the aged" (75 and over), and "the extreme aged" (85 and over).[9] As defined by various criteria, "maturity" has often been postponed long beyond what it is either by physiological criteria or by the cultures of most less developed countries. Of 25-year-olds in the United States at a recent date, more than one-fifth lived with their parents. About four out of ten young men, having once left their parents' home, returned to it. Many were free to spend their wages on themselves and pay no rent. "Children may become adults anywhere between 12 and 25 years, [depending on whether] a person can drive or rent a car, vote, be drafted, drink or purchase alcohol, get married, have an abortion without parental consent."[10]

The convention among demographers is to divide the whole age range into three sectors—persons aged, respectively, 0-14, 15-64, and 65 and over. Thus, the dependency ratio, or dependents compared with producers, is defined as those aged 0-14 plus those aged 65 and over, compared with those aged 15-64. In the United States (assuming unrealistically that all persons between 15 and 64 were in the labor force), every three persons who were working in 1980 supported two persons either below or above those productive ages. As the boom babies (those born in the surge of high birth rates in the late 1940s and most of the 1950s) move into retirement, this relatively comfortable ratio will be cut substantially. The precise ratio will depend on the average age of retirement and other mutable factors, but at best the age structure will present the producers in the population with sharpening dilemmas.

In most countries of the West the two types of dependency have moved in opposite directions, with fewer dependent children and somewhat more dependent aged. Every one of the fifteen countries of the European Union, in spite of the many significant differences among them, is undergoing a rise in the median age, and an extrapolation to the year 2020 suggests that the trend will continue.[11] Despite such programs as the former Aid to Families with Dependent Children and school lunches, most American children are cared for privately in a family setting. Most elderly persons receive at least partial governmental care, ranging from Social Security and Medicare as a minimum to public institutionalization. Put another way, the taxes used to provide for the old partly determine the size of after-tax incomes, and this remnant is one factor in potential parents' decisions about how many children they will have.

This hypothesis is often framed in reverse, that in less developed countries, which typically have few or no social-security programs, parents depend on their children to care for them in their old age and therefore have a strong motive to propagate lavishly. Analyses of both classes of economies are often based on a cross-national study of "the value of children."[12] In an interesting article, the authors argue that indices of welfare based only on consumption goods are misleading, for they ignore the contribution of coresidence. Of all unmarried elderly in the United States, 11 percent lived at above-poverty levels only because they shared the home of their family members. Among disabled unmarried elderly, the proportion was almost a third. These data, the authors argue, suggest that fertility differences by social-economic factors (or by race) may well be significantly affected by the less affluent parents' anticipation that their old age will be more bearable with their children's help.[13]

In a primitive society one way of dealing with the unproductive aged is politely labeled geronticide, whether by killing off infirm old people or exposing them to the elements. The custom was reportedly so well established among Eskimos that a person too old to contribute to the always precarious economy of the household took off himself (or herself) to die and thus gave the remaining family members a better chance of surviving.

In advanced civilizations before the modern age, on the other hand, often the elderly were revered. In *Japanese Things*, a delightful account of nineteenth-century Japan, Basil Hall Chamberlain summarized an ethical primer, "Four and Twenty Paragons of Filial Piety," that was used in both that country and China to train the young in the proper respect for the old.[14] One Paragon slept uncovered so that any mosquitoes would attack him and leave his parents undisturbed; another, though 70 years old, crawled about in baby's clothes in order to delude his 90-year-old parents into believing that they could not be so old after all. In a society with a relatively unchanging culture whose traditions are held in great esteem, it is appropriate that the old exercise great authority. Granting them special deference and honor, moreover, entails relatively little sacrifice, for in such a society the proportion who survive to anything approaching three score and ten is always very small.

Problems of the old are concentrated among those aged 85 and over. In the United States as in other developed countries, data concerning them are poor. Their ages as reported in the census are notoriously inaccurate, and statistics on income, health, and other conditions of life are certainly no better. The number of the oldest old is estimated at 2.6 million, or only 1 percent of the population; and even if that sector of the population doubles in the next few years, which is quite likely, this roughly 2 percent of the population will not in itself constitute a serious burden. The problem arises by a changing ratio between the proportion of the population in the labor force and the proportion that has retired from it.

In 1889, when as chancellor of Germany Otto von Bismarck introduced the world's first state pension, he opened a Pandora's box that neither he nor any of his contemporaries had dreamt of. This was the beginning of the welfare state. When Bismarck opened the floodgates, life expectancy was 45 years; today, in the countries of the OECD, it is 76 and rising. Yet state pensions in all these countries can still be claimed at 65, the age originally set, or in some countries at a lower age. "Moreover, social insurance in its present form was designed for a world in which men went out to work, women stayed at home, and few people got divorced. Jobs were plentiful, and unemployment carried a strong social stigma."[15]

In developed societies generally, the elderly are viewed as a social problem. One of the many translations of population structure into popular folklore is the familiar "conflict of generations," of which the most critical facet is what Germans call the *Rentenberg*, the mountain of taxes that in every Western country young adults (among others) have to climb in order to fund welfare programs for the old.

The problem first became acute in France: the country's perennially low fertility, by reducing the percentage of children in the population, had increased that of the elderly. Moreover, many workers retired in late middle age, wanting no more than a modest home in a village and the opportunity to spend their evenings playing cards at the local café. As Alfred Sauvy, the principal French demographer of the past generation, once remarked, in his country the class conflict between capitalists and workers was being supplanted by one between those in the labor force and the growing number who had retired from it.[16]

In the United States the American Association of Retired Persons (AARP) conducts one of the most powerful and effective lobbies in the national capital. Its Washington headquarters is ten stories high and almost a block long. The annual budget of half a billion dollars pays for a video production room, a well-stocked research center with many *young* researchers, legions of lawyers and policy analysts. Only one member of Congress, Alan Simpson, a Republican senator from Wyoming who was about to retire, has dared attack this "eight-hundred-pound gorilla," as the AARP is known among members of Congress. The hearings that Simpson conducted in 1995 concentrated on the well based allegation that many of AARP's activities are commercial and that its tax-exempt status is therefore fraudulent.[17]

Countering the AARP is the first lobbying group to represent young adults, a tiny organization called Americans for Generational Equity (AGE). A David opposed to the Goliath of the AARP, AGE has championed "the long-term welfare of younger and future generations of Americans" through such reforms as a means test for Social Security benefits, the balancing of the national budget, and tax incentives to induce persons to buy private retirement programs.

Though most members of Congress hesitated long before attacking an organization with 32 million members, in the mid-1990s for the first time Washington dared to cut back "entitlements," long deemed to be untouchable by any federal politician who wanted to remain in office. While most older citizens were satisfied with the status quo, younger ones were beginning to find the steep tax burden too onerous to be sustained, particularly since the trend in the age structure suggested that retirement benefits might no longer be available when their turn came to receive them.

In 1998 the largest annual cohort among the American baby boomers (4.6 million persons) had its fortieth birthday. More American adults are putting away childish things and concentrating on such prosaic matters as job security, family stability, the safety of their home and children, the taxes on their incomes and property. The maturing of the baby-boom generation has meant also that input to the Social Security system, based on the number of persons in the labor force, is adequate for the present. However, from 1980 to 1996 the number of Americans aged 15 to 19 fell off by about 2.5 million, or 12 percent; as these cohorts of the so-called baby bust move into the labor force, their smaller numbers will start a crunch in the funding of the system. With minor differences, this is also the status of old-age pensions in other industrial countries.

In some instances a difference by age among migrants can have a significant effect on the residual population. With the growth of cities in times past, those departing from the countryside were typically young men and women seeking new opportunities, and in extreme cases only the old remained in rural areas. The same is true of small islands; when Greeks from Ithaca left to go to America, leaving behind their elderly parents, the island's population declined by almost half from 1896 to 1951. So many young adults have moved away from Pittsburgh that the few remaining "live like kings." A local booster society lamented that without creative young people, we don't have a future; and a beginning lawyer, as a typical example, has been invited to join the boards of a dozen associations.[18]

At first, the aging of Western populations was mainly the result of declining birth rates, but in the last several decades the trend has been reinforced by successful therapies for some of the diseases from which old people are most likely to die. It is worth stressing such contrary instances to counter the persistent emphasis on such ailments as

Alzheimer's disease, which brings about a loss of organic functions and intellectual acuity. When serious gerontological studies began a generation or two ago, researchers looking for subjects typically used those conveniently assembled in "old people's homes." This subsector, though quite atypical of the whole age group, was long used to characterize the old, and we are still in the process of correcting the false impressions we were all taught.

As late as the 1950s, more than a third of the elderly in the United States were living in poverty, but since 1982 the poverty rate of the older population has been under that of the general population. Today the age bracket of Americans with the greatest wealth per capita, those aged 55 to 64, is followed by the next older, those aged 65 and over. Those who retire with a private pension and Social Security generally maintain the same level of living as when they were working; more than 90 percent live either alone or with a spouse. According to recurrent Harris polls, most older people report that they are better off than the country believes them to be.

3

Population Composition

A population's distribution by age and sex is called its structure; one by other characteristics, its composition. Apart from very rare anomalies, sex is fixed and immediately discernible, and age, though often misstated, is also unambiguous. In contrast, most other characteristics differ according to how they are defined, how much care is taken to gather data on them, and other extraneous factors.

Take ethnicity as an example. In a democratic society groups that are defined by an ethnic characteristic—religion, race, language, nationality, or some combination of these—typically have a structure that defies precise demarcation. A usually small proportion form a committed nucleus, group members in every respect. Around that core is a larger periphery, contingent members who are in or out depending on the circumstances. And further removed are sympathetic quasi-members who may choose to include themselves only if the classification is loose enough. Even the most painstaking effort to classify a population by ethnic characteristics, thus, will not generally reproduce the actual contours.

Religion is generally regarded as a characteristic difficult to define in official data. Indeed, the enumerator can ask each respondent what his religion is, but what the answer signifies is subject to wide and often contentious interpretation. Some denominations (e.g., Mormons) refuse to be counted; others (e.g., many Jews) see enumeration as a prelude to discrimination. The mainstream Protestant churches have changed radically over the past two generations, and to label a person a

Methodist or a Lutheran, for instance, tells us nothing even about beliefs and practices ordinarily associated with a faith.[1]

How complicated religious identity has become in the United States is suggested by three responses to a query on that matter: "I'm an Episcopalian, and I think of myself as a practicing non-Jew"; "I'm a Mennonite hyphen Unitarian Universalist who practices Zen meditation"; "I call myself a Christian Buddhist, but sort of tongue-in-cheek." The article continues: "Jews flirt with Hinduism, Catholics study Taoism, and Methodists discuss whether to make Passover seder an official part of worship....The melding of Judaism with Buddhism has become so commonplace that marketers who sell spiritual books, videotapes and lecture series have a name for it: 'JewBu.'"[2]

Moreover, the significance of a religious label can differ enormously from one country to another. A generation ago the church-state relations in Ireland and Italy, for instance, were poles apart, though both were labeled Catholic countries. When I lived in the Netherlands several decades ago, it was routine for a new acquaintance to inquire what your faith was, for this set the parameters of any further association. Americans, on the contrary, generally regard religion as a private matter, and persons with good manners are likely to avoid talking about it altogether.

In the United States, apart from one or two forays into this contentious topic, the Bureau of the Census has abstained from asking about Americans' religious affiliation. As an example of how great a difference this lacuna can make, take the record on Irish immigrants. The common picture of the Irish American is a Catholic, mired in the working or lower-middle class, of low to medium income. Underlying this image, however, has been an amalgam of Catholic Irish and the Protestant Scots-Irish; many of the latter live in the Appalachian region at close to the poverty level. Using data on religion gathered by the private National Opinion Research Center, Andrew Greeley was able to show that as early as the 1950s and 1960s Irish Catholics had risen far and, thus, that the typical representation from official statistics had been grossly misleading.[3]

What is a "Race"?

Of the various criteria of ethnicity, race is in many respects the most significant; the characteristics of the body, that most palpable element of one's persona, have been used throughout history to define the most pervasive type of group identity. The word "ethnic" derives via Latin from the Greek *ethnikos*, the adjectival form of *ethnos*, a nation or race. "Nation" comes from Latin via French; its ultimate source is *nasci*, to be born. The biological association suggested by these etymologies was long retained in English, and when the meaning of these terms broadened to include cultural characteristics and political structures, neither shift was consistent. Many American writers distinguish "racial" from "ethnic" minorities, the former being blacks, Asians, and other "nonwhites," and the latter the European nationalities. The distinction could be useful but for the confusion in real life between physiological and cultural criteria. A racial minority is often set off from the majority also by cultural characteristics, and whether particular attributes are labeled hereditary or environmental is very often controversial. I use "ethnic" to include both types of characteristics and "racial" to designate a biological one.

Defining the term "race" became more complicated following the Nazi program of genocide. A common response to the racist doctrine of National Socialists has been to accept, in effect, their underlying premises and argue simply that Jews do not constitute a race, or—to settle the issue once and for all--that races do not exist. However, if one understands "race" to be a group with a relatively high probability of inherited characteristics, one finds certain genetic diseases more common among Ashkenazi Jews than among either Gentiles or other Jews.[4] To argue thus means, it is true, that one must abandon the nineteenth-century concept of race as a prototype and substitute the probabilistic aggregate that modern biologists and anthropologists use.

The notion that only "pure" categories may exist in a classification of populations is rather bizarre, for it follows from the theory of evolution itself that all biological divisions, from phylum through subspecies, are always in the process of change, so that there is almost never a sharp and permanent boundary setting off one unit from the adjoining one. Whether a category is defined by a cultural or a physiological attribute, it is generally made up—to repeat—of a core, a periphery, and an outer rim; and this composite structure means that any statistical aggregate cannot accurately depict the reality it is intended to represent.

If "race" is expunged from our vocabulary, how shall we designate a category that is now so labeled? The American anthropologist Ashley

Montagu, who has argued most vociferously that the word be abolished, suggested that "ethnic group" be substituted for "race,"[5] but the consequent confusion of biological and cultural characteristics, paradoxically, is usually regarded as a hallmark of racism. Others define "race" as "a group that is *socially* defined but on the basis of *physical* criteria,"[6] a nuance that is sometimes indicated by the compound term "social race." A more effective route to eliminating racist doctrine is to differentiate cultural groups within each race. Thomas Sowell has written a fascinating essay on "Three Black Histories," documenting the significant dissimilarities between slaves, the former slaves who became free men before general emancipation, and immigrants from the West Indies.[7]

What are National Stocks?

That the federal government has included questions on race in every census derives from the fact that the original purpose of the census, to set the stage for the periodic apportionment, was complicated by the anomalous status of slaves and Indians. The South wanted slaves counted as part of the states' populations, and by an eventual compromise each was counted as three-fifths of a free person, with free blacks enumerated separately. Indians, similarly, were classified into two categories, those who paid taxes—that is, were living in the general civil community—and those who did not. This method of setting apportionment built into the census a tradition of differentiating three races: whites, blacks, and Indians.

The classification by national origins began as part of a distinction between citizens and foreign-born residents. It became especially important in the 1920s, when nativist groups tried to limit the number of immigrants from Southern and Eastern Europe.[8] Their exclusion had first been sought indirectly, by setting literacy as a prerequisite for admission to the United States, but the law kept out fewer "inferior" immigrants than had been anticipated. A succession of stopgap measures culminated in a law setting immigration quotas according to the "national origins" of the entire white population.

What these were was not easy to calculate. The frequent and untraceable marriages across ethnic lines made it impossible to divide the 1920 population itself into distinct ethnic groups, and instead an attempt was made to classify the total white gene pool by national stocks, based on (1) family names listed in the 1790 census; plus (2) immigration data, such as they were; and—for lack of any statistical breakdown by ethnic groups—(3) the rate of natural increase of the whole population. These national quotas, enacted in 1929, were gradually eroded by ad hoc laws permitting refugees and others to immigrate outside the stipulated limits; and the whole system was abandoned in a new law that went into effect in mid-1968. During these nearly four decades, various interest groups classified persons of European stocks by a formula that was laughably inaccurate.

Most recently a principal use of nationality or race data has been to allocate special benefits under the several forms of affirmative action. There was thus a 180-degree shift in policy, from discrimination against certain minorities to granting them special advantages; but with both sets of laws it was necessary to classify the population by ethnic criteria.

Added to such procedural problems are several ideological blocks. Several decades ago American anthropologists developed a doctrine of cultural relativism—namely, that one may legitimately judge the worth of any culture only by the criteria embedded in that culture's own value system. This has become a mainstay of present-day liberal beliefs; at one time such organizations as the ACLU tried to have ethnic identifications removed from all public documents. But if all those entitled to special benefits are essentially equivalent to the rest of the population, what can be the significance of any ethnic classification? There is also a widely held opinion that such social data constitute the government's invasion of individuals' privacy, that they are often used to reinforce stereotypes and prejudices, and thus that persons so labeled may suffer from discrimination. In other words, a statistical bureau that compiles an ethnic classification is faced with ideological as well as procedural hurdles.

Measurement of Ethnicity

That race and nationality are difficult to define precisely obviously means that classifying a population by either characteristic is problematic. In order to guarantee a minimum of consistency among the various federal agencies that collect ethnic data, a directive was issued to prescribe how all statistical data were to be structured.[9] As a minimum, any such classification was to include four racial groups (American Indian or Alaska Native, Asian or Pacific Islander, black, and white) and one ethnic group (Hispanic).

In general, the Census Bureau has followed this directive. The 1990 schedule had fourteen categories: white, black or Negro, Indian (Amer.), Eskimo, Aleut, ten Asian and Pacific Islander nationalities (including a miscellaneous "Other API"), and a residual "Other race." Census officials have become increasingly aware that this list has a number of faults, and there has been a continuous effort to develop a better classification. A convenient way of following these discussions is to arrange the problems seriatim.

Aggregation

As I have noted,[10] deciding how to combine units into categories is a recurrent problem in fashioning any data on population. Because ethnic groups, defined by the characteristics of their core sector, also include persons at the periphery, it is difficult to set appropriate boundaries to them. Every one of the races or ethnic groups included in the 1990 schedule is subject to reasonable challenge.

"White" and "black" categories include persons who so label themselves but would be put elsewhere if a criterion other than self-identification were used. When enumerators' judgments set how race was reported, so-called blacks ranged in skin color from persons in a clearly distinct racial group to those that no one could distinguish from whites. Walter White, head of the NAACP from 1931 until his death in 1955, passed as a white man when he traveled about the South gathering evidence on lynch mobs; his very life depended on his light skin and blue eyes. Others who, like him, were officially classified as black if they had "any trace of black blood," passed into white society altogether. An enumerator, thus, often recorded such a person's race not by a biological attribute but, for example, by the segregated residence of whites or blacks.

The composite structure of "blacks or Negroes" used in the 1990 census is a remnant of the succession of official or quasi-official names assigned to those so classified.[11] "Colored," the standard polite term until after the Civil War, probably would have disappeared altogether except for its retention in the name of the NAACP. The designation "black" became taboo in the first decades of this century, with "negro" (which is Spanish for *black*) and eventually "Negro" substituted for it. Then the more radical members of the group insisted first on "black" (or "Black") and then "Afro-American" or "African American." Each change was insisted on with great fervor, and it was recurrently regarded an insult not to keep up with the continual revision.

For a period (now past), the two labels used in the 1990 census schedule were not merely alternative ways of designating the same sector of the population. It would have been interesting to associate each of these self-designations with a subgroup. While the campaign to introduce "black" was in full swing, Roy Wilkins, long head of the NAACP, wrote in his syndicated column that he would continue to call himself a "Negro." If in the 2000 census all blacks are once again recorded as a single category, they will include quite diverse subgroups, ranging from those with middle-class characteristics to those below the poverty level. Thus, a graph showing all blacks by such an attribute as income, for instance, would form a U-shaped curve, with most persons at either end and a rather small proportion in the middle, which by the usual interpretation of statistics is how the whole race is characterized.

Geographical Units

Americans of Asian stocks are not only combined into a single unit but have as a weird addendum persons from the Pacific Islands. Not even natives of the most significant country, Chinese, are unitary: the various spoken dialects of Chinese are mutually unintelligible. Filipinos are divided by language and other cultural attributes into eight groupings; those who have immigrated to the United States have formed three somewhat antagonistic language communities. Asian Indians seemingly have no great attachment to either India or the United States; of the more than 100,000 who immigrated during the years 1965 through 1976, only 8,500 acquired citizenship. They are mainly loyal to one or another of the many ethnic subdivisions of India's heterogeneous population. The 1990 census schedule was translated into thirty-two different languages, including Chinese, Korean, Vietnamese, Cambodian, Laotian, three Philippine languages, and Samoan—all for members of the Census-begotten API, the Asians and Pacific Islanders. By children ever born per woman, API nationalities ranged from 6.215 (Hmong) to

1.615 (Japanese), by median family income from $49,309 (Asian Indian) to $14,327 (Hmong), by proportion below the poverty level from 7.0 percent (Japanese) to 64.9 (Hmong). True, many Americans are unable to discern many differences among the components of this diverse category, but is that a reason for a governmental statistical agency to imitate such ignorance or bias?

Hispanics

"Attempts to form national alliances of Mexican Americans," according to the American sociologist Ralph Guzmán, "have failed over the question, 'What do we call ourselves?'"[12] The dispute over what might seem to be so minor a matter has been sharper than the parallel one among blacks, and the latent hostility between "Mexican Americans" and "Chicanos" is only the beginning of the disparity among all "Hispanics"—or, as some insist on calling themselves, "Latinos." Again, the range was wide between Cubans and Puerto Ricans in median family income (respectively, $31,015 and $20,301) or in the percent below the poverty level (respectively, 15.2 and 32.5).

One important motive of the Census Bureau in constructing a category encompassing a congeries of quite different units, one can assume, was for its convenience in presenting data in summary tables. This proved to be an illusion. Groups set up to advise on procedures for the 1990 count had more than the usual difficulty with Hispanics; there were three subcommittees dealing, respectively, with (1) Race and Spanish Origin; (2) Ancestry, Place of Birth, Citizenship, and Year of Entry; and (3) Language. Those designated as in the Hispanic ethnic group may be of any race, and this overlap between the two broad defining characteristics was cumbersome at best. Persons of Hispanic origin were listed in separate tables marked "of any race," and there were two sets of racial categories, totals and then of persons "not of Hispanic origin."

"Self-enumeration"?

Ostensibly respondents in the last few censuses themselves defined their ethnic identity. This freedom of action was restricted, in part, by the limited and quirky range in the list that the Census Bureau supplied.

Respondents were asked to name the one race with which they most closely identified, with each person's own perception of "race" as the only overall guide. In 1990, when for the first time the Bureau included a category labeled "Other race," about 10 million persons put themselves in that miscellaneous bracket. Write-in entries included such synonyms of "mixed" as multiracial, multiethnic, interracial, and Wesort (one designation for white-black-Indian groupings), as well as such specifications of "Hispanic" as Mexican and Puerto Rican.

Seemingly, however, respondents were discouraged from identifying themselves as having more than one set of ancestors. In a special 1990 census file, those with mixed self-identities were reassigned to one of the monoracial categories, in order, Bureau officials stated, to reduce incompatibilities with classifications used by other federal agencies. Persons who identified themselves as "Chinese-white" or "white-Chinese" were assigned to the race first mentioned. If in direct interviews respondents said they could not specify one race, the mother's race was suggested as the appropriate answer.

Inconsistent and False Responses

Even if the data the Census Bureau collected on race and ethnicity have little relation to real life, they might be of some use in measuring the relative changes from one count to the next. That supposition, however, depends on a hope that persons respond consistently and avoid either intentional or inadvertent misstatements. In spite of preliminary testing in various areas, some of the queries were misunderstood. Asked whether they were "Mexican-Amer.," some persons interpreted this to mean whether they were one or the other and responded "American." Some foreign-born "Asian-Indians" so reported themselves, but identified their native-born children as "American-Indian." Other "Asian Indians" consider themselves to be "Indian-Americans" and therefore did not include themselves in the census-specified category.

The number of "American Indians," to cite the most egregious example, increased by 72 percent between 1970 and 1980 and by 38 percent in the following decade. The principal reason for this enormous growth was not an excess of births over deaths, nor successful efforts to reach a larger proportion of this grouping, but rather a trend of formerly self-identified whites to report themselves as Indians.[13] It is perfectly feasible for the same individual both to be and not to be an Indian, depending on whether on a particular occasion he wants to avoid discrimination or to receive various special benefits.

Counts by Different Agencies

The counts of ethnic minorities by the Census Bureau are used as the denominators in the calculation of rates of fertility, mortality, and morbidity. Not only are deficiencies of the census classification thus carried over to significant indicators of general welfare, but important differences in the way ethnicity is measured aggravate the shortcomings.

Even though, as I have noted, an attempt was made to set uniformity in the way that all federal agencies define ethnic sectors of the population, there are critical disparities. By the usage of several federal agencies, the same person may be classified in various categories. In 1970, when the Census Bureau compared its self-identification with enumerators' classification carried out by other federal bureaus, it found differences ranging from about 5 percent (whites and blacks) to 27 percent (Asians and American Indians).[14] More than half of the race/ethnicity reported in the 1980s on infants' death certificates differed from that reported by the parents.[15] According to a brochure distributed by the Bureau of Indian Affairs, "There is no one Federal or tribal definition that establishes a person's identity as Indian. Government agencies [as well as tribes] use different criteria for determining who is an Indian."[16] Such discrepancies, one should emphasize, are not the consequence of respondents' misunderstanding or other errors, but flow directly from the officially prescribed mode of denoting the make-up of the American population.

Mixed-Race Persons

In the 1990 count the possibility of denoting oneself of a race not among those listed was often used by those who considered themselves to be of mixed race—and did not choose to bow to the implicit pressure to designate only one of them. Tiger Woods, known throughout the country as a black golf champion, gave his background to the press as one-quarter black, one-quarter Chinese, one-quarter Thai, one-eighth white, and one-eighth American Indian.[17] He is hardly alone among the population of American Negroes, the majority of whom have some white and/or Indian forebears. For most of American history it has been official policy to ignore any intermingling and to label all persons with some black progenitors as "black," but the Census Bureau has been considering adding a mixed-race category in the 2000 count.

At one time interracial marriage was prohibited in most states, and until recently public opinion approved of this ban. From 1968 to 1994, the percent of respondents who spoke favorably of marriages between blacks and whites rose from 48 to 68 among blacks and from 17 to 45 among whites. Among first marriages by blacks, the percentage of exogamous rose from 0.7 in 1963 to 12.1 in 1993. These figures, moreover, understate the trend, for the five states with the largest concentration of interracial couples in 1990 do not provide such information to the National Center for Health Statistics.[18] The same trend toward a melting pot in a literal sense is also apparent among Hispanics, many Asians, not to say the already thoroughly mixed Hawaiian population.

If the Census Bureau accedes to the demand of some that their mixed ancestry be reported more accurately, much will change not only in how racial/ethnic statistics are compiled but also in interracial relations. Organizations that claim to represent the interests of blacks, Latinos, and other minorities are not enthusiastic about the possibility that many of their members may soon have the possibility of identifying themselves as nonblack, non-Latino, and so on. The extraordinarily complex mixture of the American gene pool may come to be reflected in attitudes and behavior, possibly with a sharp lessening of interracial antipathies.

Whatever changes the Census Bureau may adopt, however much they may improve the 2000 count, the result will not be satisfactory. The compromise between an objective classification by race/ethnicity and serial accommodations to self-appointed ethnic spokesmen has undermined the validity of the data:

> Ethnic identity cannot be established by objective criteria, at least in large-scale self-administered surveys. We therefore accept that an individual's ethnicity is whatever he says it is. The Bureau's job is to...group responses into recognizable categories that (a) are mandated for federal civil rights enforcement, (b) satisfy the more vocal ethnic lobbies, and (c) provide enough continuity with past statistics to satisfy social scientists engaged in longitudinal research. However, the Bureau's success in balancing the claims of constituencies was achieved at the expense of its fundamental mission: gathering valid and reliable information about the population of the United States.[19]

4

From Fecundity to Fertility

In the jargon of demographers fecundity, the physiological ability to reproduce, is distinguished from fertility, the realization of that potential, the actual birth performance as measured by the number of offspring. The two terms were long used synonymously, and it was only in 1934 that the Population Association of America officially endorsed a differentiation that had been developing. The lay public and many physicians, however, still use the two terms indifferently with either meaning.

However important the distinction is conceptually, empirically it is often difficult to separate cultural from biological factors. The main general theory of demography, Malthus's principle of population, presented man both as an animal, subject to the biological drives of sex and hunger, and as a member of human society, motivated to control those appetites and somewhat able to do so.

A Note on the Physiology of Reproduction

In recent decades, particularly in the analysis of fertility, demographic writings have acquired a large admixture of physiological and medical concepts and terms. Various factors, though introduced as part of social analyses, are essentially biological, and even a very slight grounding in the relevant portions of biology can help assess them better.

During the years of a woman's sexual maturity, the ova produced during each monthly cycle pass slowly from the ovaries down the fallopian tubes, where they remain viable for only a very short time. Each spermatozoon, the male reproductive organ, is shaped like a tiny tadpole, with a head and a very long tail that waves to propel it up one of the tubes to a receptive egg. If sexual intercourse takes place during the perhaps one or two days that an ovum can be fertilized, and if one of the spermatozoa breaks through the wall of an egg, the fertilized ovum becomes what is called a zygote, a single cell that time and again divides in two. It is termed a blastocyst during the first six or seven days; an embryo until it has implanted itself in the lining of the uterus; then, until birth takes place, a fetus; and finally an infant after it is completely outside the mother's body.

If no impregnation has taken place, the subsequent menstruation is in effect a symptom of biological failure. The menstrual flow takes place even in the absence of ovulation; the two processes occur discretely, triggered separately by two of the hormonal controls that regulate the process. Amenorrhea (or the lack of a menstrual flow) is not a reliable indicator of whether or not there has been an ovulation or an impregnation[1]; and the contrary assumption in many demographic works strongly suggests how important elementary physiology is as a background to a social analysis of population.

With impregnation, the genetic characteristics of the two parents are transmitted to the offspring. Threadlike strands in the nucleus of cells that carry the genes, the units of hereditary information, are called chromosomes. The 46 chromosomes in a human somatic cell comprise 23 homologous pairs, of which one is inherited from each parent and transmitted to each child. Of the 23 pairs, 22 are alike in sons and daughters. The sex chromosomes differ: females have two so-called X-chromosomes, and males have one X-chromosome, inherited from the mother and passed on to daughters, and a smaller Y-chromosome, inherited from the father and passed on to sons.[2]

Age and Fertility

Biologically and culturally, life after birth is divided into phases. Puberty marks the age at which, under the stimulus of increased flows of several hormones, secondary sex characteristics develop and, later, the reproductive organs become operative. According to one estimate, American males complete their testicular growth between the ages of

14.5 and 18, and the range of other indices of beginning adolescence is about the same.[3]

In the female the menarche, or the first menstruation, is conventionally taken to define her puberty. Seemingly the crucial determinants of when this takes place are not, as was once thought, race or climate, but rather genetic heritage, nutrition, and the girl's health. Since nutrition and health typically vary with the level of economic development, the average age differs accordingly: in the West below 14 years; in Africa above 14 years, and in Asia somewhere between the two.[4] In the West the age has gone down with the improvement in the level of living. The longest record was kept in Norway, where the age fell from about 17.1 years in 1850 to 13.6 in 1950. In Western Europe as a whole the age at menarche fell by four months per decade between 1850 and 1960. In the United States today the average age at menarche is estimated to be 12.7 years. In the opinion of one American sociologist, the increased sexual permissiveness among adolescents in the United States, to the degree that it has not been a factitious consequence of a greater candor about the subject, has been caused mainly by this earlier biological maturation.[5]

Every culture sets a conventional age at marriage, which over the period for which there are records has varied worldwide from a high in Ireland to a low in India. The actual age at marriage may fluctuate around this norm in response to a poor harvest or a rise in unemployment, for example, but generally such short-term variations are less significant than the benchmark itself.

Children have been born to a mother of 6.5 years at one extreme and to one of 59 or possibly even 63 years at the other.[6] Such anomalies are amazing, but the more important datum is the general pattern. In all human populations the age schedules of normal fertility rise smoothly from zero in the early teens to a single peak in the 20s or early 30s, then fall to near zero in the 40s and to zero at a bit higher than 50 years. Following an extensive survey, the American demographer Ansley Coale commented:

> The lowest mean age [of mothers] I have found is a little less than 26 years (in recent years in Hungary); the highest a little over 33 years (in nineteenth-century Sweden). In all but a few fertility schedules, 75 percent of total fertility occurs within a span of 16 years, and in every case I have examined within a span of 20 years.[7]

Adolescent males are less likely than mature men to produce healthy sperm in the quantity needed to impregnate an egg. In the female, the development of healthy ova usually begins some time after the menarche. "Anovular menstruation [that is, a menstrual flow with no prior production of eggs] is the rule rather than the exception during puberty and early adolescence."[8] At the start of her fecund years a female has some 200,000 to 400,000 oocytes, as immature ova are called. Most of these potential eggs decompose at an early stage, and during her entire reproductive life perhaps as few as 400 become ova.

Corresponding to the rise of fecundity during adolescence, there is a decline from middle adulthood on. The male's ability to reproduce declines with age, but the waning is more gradual and varies more from one man to another than among females. In the female the menopause, or the cessation of menstruation, marks the approximate end of her fecundity. One of the two ages conventionally used by demographers to mark the end of the female's fecund period, 44 years, is too low; and the other, 49 years, though higher than past surveys would suggest, is approximately the 50 years that most gynecologists designate as now typical of American women's menopause.

The so-called rhythm method of birth control depends on a correct timing of the ovulation that takes place each month. On an average ovulation occurs about 14 days *before* the subsequent menstruation, but few women are able to time even their menstruations precisely. When some 2,000 American women were queried twice about their menstrual history, a third of them gave significantly different responses on the two occasions.[9] After denoting a period of 21-35 days, with 2-6 days of flow, as a rather indefinite "normal menstrual cycle," a standard work in gynecology remarked that this applies to only two-thirds of adult women and to a still smaller proportion of females shortly after menarche or around the time of menopause.[10] A lifetime total of one practitioner's 3,500 patients had menstrual intervals of 26 to 34 days, with an average of 28.6 days and a good deal of irregularity. "The absolutely regular cycle," the author remarked, "is so rare as to be either a myth or a medical curiosity."[11]

Human Beings as Mammals

Participants in the very long debate about the relative importance of nature and nurture can sometimes find suggestive clues by observing biological determinants in other animals. Such nonprimate mammals as the rabbit, squirrel, ferret, and mink ovulate only following sexual excitation or even coitus. In other mammalian species, the estrous and ovulation cycles overlap, so that hormones drive the female to seek a mate at precisely those times when conception is most likely. Among nonhuman primates, ovulation is usually overtly signaled, sometimes by a swelling or reddening of the female's sexual organs, sometimes by an aroma of so-called pheromones, either of which attracts males. But in some primate species the link between estrus and ovulation is looser. Gibbons, orangutans, and gorillas show few external signs of ovulation; rhesus monkeys and chimpanzees are sometimes sexually receptive during anestrus; langurs have a sham estrus.[12]

Human females show no external sign of ovulation at all, and they can respond to males' advances at any time in the ovulation cycle. Seemingly sexual urge in human females is not closely related to the ovulation cycle. In one study wives of men away from home for extended periods (such as seamen or traveling salesmen) kept a record of the strength of their libido; it turned out to be most intense just before and just after menstruation, when impregnation is normally impossible.[13] It would seem that in humans the effect of hormonal flow on sexual craving is so weak that it can be offset by nonbiological stimuli.

The function of a permanent rather than cyclical sexual attraction is not merely to reproduce physically but also, it has been hypothesized, to hold the male to a relatively stable association. The human family is bound together by two strong physiological bonds. The sexual drive of the two partners is concentrated on one another, but since it may wander off to other couplings, in virtually all societies this tie is reinforced by cultural norms and institutions. There is also a biological bond between mother and infant: in humans as in other mammals, the woman's breasts become painful if the pressure of milk is not relieved by suckling, and regular feeding develops an emotional attachment between infant and mother.

The link between father and child, however, is cultural, what the British anthropologist Bronislaw Malinowski called "the principle of legitimacy." In every society, he held, an adult male—usually but not necessarily the "genitor" (or biological begetter)—is designated as the "pater" (or social father), responsible for the care and training of the children assigned to him by this rule.[14] Since human offspring, compared with those of most other species, take very long to mature, it requires a two-adult team to care most efficiently for children during their years of relatively helpless dependence.

It has been argued, however, that Malinowski overstated this thesis. According to one interpretation, his asseveration that legitimacy is a prerequisite to societal survival was "far too drastic," for "in reality it was the rule of respectability, of praise and blame for people's conduct, which were at play for the most part during the comparative history of bastardy, rather than rules for survival."[15] Praise or blame is, of course, a typical instrument by which any cultural standard is enforced; and if the norm that reproduction should take place only within marriage has not been an absolute precondition of a group's physical survival, this does not mean that illegitimacy has no effect on the well-being of the progeny. Though peoples or ethnic groups have indeed persisted without the principle of legitimacy to protect their nuclear family, typically they have suffered from this lack. According to an important study of an American sample, "our data indicate that despite a decrease in the degree of stigma attached to illegitimacy and the proliferation of services and programs for illegitimate children and their mothers, these children do not begin life on an equal footing with legitimate children, and their handicaps persist beyond the hazards of infancy."[16]

Lactation and Fecundity

It is widely presumed that breastfeeding one child inhibits for a period the production of another, but much of the sizable body of writings on breastfeeding has come in ideological wrappings. At the height of the French Revolution, its leaders "sermonized on the sanctity of motherhood and the importance of breastfeeding."[17] When American firms tried to market baby food in less developed countries, this commercial venture soon became one more occasion for condemning the United States. La Leche League, which advocates breastfeeding on both health and moral grounds, admits of no exception to its dogma that every mother can and should use her own milk to nourish all her infants.[18] What one author called "nature's contraceptive" has in his judgment "served us well for the last two million years," and he reinforced this appraisal with a citation from the papal encyclical *Humanae Vitae*.[19]

The physiological effect of breastfeeding varies with how the activity is carried out. In one study based on thirty-two mothers who for two years postpartum kept records on their nursing routine, the duration of amenorrhea depended not only on breastfeeding per se but on its frequency, on whether any supplements were introduced in the infant's diet, and on whether at least one hour of night nursing was maintained after the beginning of weaning.[20]

That is to say, the mere citation of "breastfeeding" as the causal factor in avoiding pregnancy can lead to imprecise conclusions. One medical team set definitions to distinguish one type from another. "Exclusive" and "almost exclusive" breastfeeding were specified with detailed descriptions; together they made up "full breastfeeding," which for mothers not wanting to become pregnant was recommended for five to six months, plus a gradually reduced proportion of the infant's nutrition into the second year. Those regimens not in accord with this schedule were labeled "partial" or "token" breastfeeding. Up to six months after the birth, the mother typically needs no contraceptive to avoid another pregnancy; thereafter, her risk depends in part on the number of feedings per twenty-four hours.[21]

Apart from the evidence from medical research, the association between breastfeeding and anovulation was indicated when historical demographers noted that when an infant died it was followed more quickly than otherwise by another birth, but what caused the difference has remained an issue in the discipline.[22]

The considerable body of writings by anthropologists can be illustrated, *pars pro toto*, by those about the !Kung, who live in the Kalahari desert in southern Africa. They have no permanent homes, and each time a group migrates to a new area the women have to carry not only household goods and food but also any children too young to walk. Every !Kung mother, therefore, is strongly motivated to space her children at least three years apart, and supposedly this child spacing is achieved by several years of breastfeeding. Allegedly the system has worked: according to a retrospective analysis, women had an average total of only five births per mother.[23]

Though reportedly no other factors helped inhibit fertility, seemingly it may have been cut especially by infanticide, which apparently the women practiced "when in their opinion it is necessary: in all cases of birth defects; [to remove] one of each pair of twins; and sometimes when one birth follows another too closely and the baby would drink the milk of his older brother or sister; or when the woman feels she is too old to produce milk for another baby."[24] Of 500 live births, however, only six were followed by a *reported* infanticide. When asked about the practice, none of the respondents admitted to killing any of their own children, but they all knew that "sometimes a woman had to do this."

> I did not have the fortitude to learn more....When they talked about it with me, they never once spoke concretely or directly of the act itself but had much to say about the necessity for it.[25]

Disease may have been another factor. Some respondents, who believed that they had had gonorrhea, reported a total fertility only half that of women who described themselves as uninfected.

Lactation, in short, has a moderate and temporary contraceptive effect of low reliability. In a sizable proportion of cases reported, the mother stopped breastfeeding because she had already become pregnant. In some societies the physiological effect is confounded by the custom of avoiding coitus so long as a woman is nursing a child.

Structural Factors in Fertility

Persons living in modern societies tend to classify reproduction into two types, either controlled by contraception or what is often labeled "unprotected." If the couple does not intervene, such a contrast implies, the unprotected process has a more or less uniform result: deviations from the overall average family size of noncontraceptors, it is suggested, can be the consequence mainly (or only) of physiological defects. The fertility of virtually all populations, however, has been checked in many more ways than by the couples' conscious control.

This fact can be forcefully exemplified by the norms of classical China, which in Western texts is often termed a "familial society." The abstract ideal, indeed, was a family large enough to guarantee continuity in the male line; but faced with a legal system lacking primogeniture, peasants also had to consider the consequence of a repeated subdivision of family plots. According to the authoritative estimate by the American sinologist Chung-li Chang, the gentry family averaged just under three children.[26]

Marital coitus has been regarded in the Chinese culture as inauspicious or dangerous on the 1st, 7th, 15th, 21st, 28th, and 29th days of each lunar month; on the 16th day of the fifth month; during solar or lunar eclipses, the days of equinoxes and solstices; when there was an earthquake, rain, thunder and lightning, great heat, or great cold; after washing the hair, a long trip, heavy drinking or eating; when the man is tired, very excited, or old; during the woman's menstruation, for one month following the birth of a child, and after the woman has reached age 40; during 27 months following the death of a parent; permanently after the birth of a grandchild. Both books and astrological calendars denoting auspicious and inauspicious days were circulating in Taiwan (and possibly also in Mainland China) then. If all the basic rules were observed, intercourse was sanctioned on only about a hundred days per year to parents who were trying to realize the goal of this familistic culture, to bring forth healthy and lucky sons.[27]

In an influential paper, the British demographer John Hajnal described what he called "the European marriage pattern," characterized by a uniquely high age at marriage and a significant proportion who never married at all.[28] When this norm began to develop is not known precisely, but an analyst has traced it back to the fourth century.[29] One interesting bit of evidence is etymological: The word *husband* derived from two words meaning "house" and "own"; its original meaning was a householder, a man who had a home. The Middle English word for an unmarried man was *anilepiman*. These two terms, one referring to the management of property and the other to marital status, gradually became associated as opposites, *anilepiman* coming to mean a man who had no living and therefore could not marry, and *husband*, a man who was able to care for a family and therefore could get (or, eventually, was) married.[30]

In Western countries the relation between social class and fertility has long been the contrary of what one might expect: the less able a couple was to care for their children materially, the more children they typically produced. This seeming anomaly was analyzed in a study of Victorian Britain. It was becoming the world's wealthiest nation, and in its social hierarchy the urban middle class ranked second only to the wealthiest of the landed nobility. To move into that favored position was possible for many, but aspirants had to set and maintain an appropriate pattern of expenditure: a comfortable home in a suitable neighborhood, one (or, better, three) full-time servants, a carriage, an annual holiday, boarding schools for children, and so on. Competition for favored positions in the expanding economy exerted pressure to reduce family expenditures, especially any that would not damage the requisite appearance of affluence; and this paring was effected first of all by a postponement of marriage. Among the clergymen, doctors, lawyers, members of the aristocracy, merchants, bankers, manufacturers, and others of the gentleman class who married between 1840 and 1870, the average age was a shade under thirty years.[31] Eventually such persons shifted to a less burdensome control of procreation with contraceptives, and their example was gradually followed by most of the rest of English society. The same pattern evolved also in the rest of Western Europe.[32]

Though the decline in English fertility was largely the consequence of institutional constraints on family size, it is generally ascribed rather to the rise of neo-Malthusianism. Actually, this movement was less effective than the typically laudatory accounts have reported it to be. Most of the noisy advocates of birth control were all-round dissidents. Charles Bradlaugh was a notorious atheist, a lonely voice in a religious age. Annie Besant, his co-defendant in the two famous trials in which they were charged with distributing a pamphlet on contraception, also began as an atheist and then advocated the hardly more popular causes of theosophy and Indian nationalism. The respectable barristers and businessmen who led the nation to begetting smaller families would hardly have been attracted to their writings. Yet the neo-Malthusian movement, which indeed took off from the Bradlaugh-Besant trials, did affect our ideas about birth limitation—in particular, by its enormous emphasis on the means, contraception, rather than the goal, family responsibility.

Contraception and Sterilization

It has always been possible to avoid having children, if by no other means then by infanticide. Some analysts believe that prehistoric man used various primitive means of contraception. One writer concluded from an ancient piece of sculpture that the couple was engaging in heterosexual anal intercourse in order to avoid pregnancy.[33] The range of contraceptives that have been used is far wider than most people could imagine. In the United States Frederick Hollick's *The Marriage Guide*, first published in 1850, went through over 300 printings, with a total sale of over a million copies. The methods discussed included a rhythm method based on an inaccurate timing of ovulation, intercourse without ejaculation, coitus interruptus, condoms, "womb veils" (as diaphragms were called), sponges, douches, and abortions. Also recommended by one or another promoter of contraception were such chemicals and extracts as ergot, cotton root, aloes, savin, tansy, opium, iodine, lemon juice, vinegar, prussic or sulfuric acid, and Lysol! The more startling items on this list were proffered by quacks, but in the middle of the nineteenth century the best doctors knew little even of the physiology of reproduction.[34]

Among the variety of today's contraceptives, none—especially as used by fallible humans—is fully effective. The estimated proportions of unplanned pregnancies per 100 American women using various contraceptive means have been as follows:[35]

Table 4.1

Method	Perfect Use	Actual Use
Oral contraceptives	0.1-0.5%	6.2%
Condom	2	14.2
Diaphragm	3	15.6
Spermicides	3-8	26.3
Periodic abstinence	2-10	16.2

In 1993 a new type of contraceptive called Depo-Provera was put on the market. Though little known to older, wealthier, or married women, "the shot," as it is known by those who use it, became a hit among unmarried teenagers, especially blacks. Many of these young women had used "the pill," which was effective only if they remembered to take it. In contrast, the shot requires only a visit to a clinic every three months, and many clinics notify their clients to tell them when the next one is due. According to the National Center for Health Statistics, by 1997 the birth rate among unmarried black women had fallen to the lowest level in years, mainly because of this shift to the new method of controlling births.[36] Of 108 patients reviewed in one study, none had become pregnant.[37]

Infertility and Sterility

The ability to have children is a characteristic not merely of the female but of both partners together. A barren marriage may be of two persons of low fecundity, each of whom may prove to be fecund when mated with another person. A typical example is an elderly widower who takes a younger woman as his second wife and starts begetting again.

According to the usual estimate, the male is responsible for 40 percent of all cases of subfecundity and the female for 40 to 50 percent, with the remainder of 10 to 20 percent indeterminate. "The examination of the husband's semen should be the first diagnostic step" in determining the cause of a couple's failure to reproduce.[38] If the sperm count is too small, or if the spermatozoa do not maintain motility for the normal period of from three to twenty-four hours, the probability of conception is very low. Impotence, or a male's inability to have an erection, may be due to damage to the nerves controlling the blood vessels leading to the penis or to some other physical disorder, but among young men the cause in perhaps 95 percent of the cases is psychosomatic.

In the 1990s the marketing of Viagra, a therapy for impotence, became something of a sensation. For most of the thousands who regained a youthful vigor, it was a gratifying miracle, but not all the consequences were salutary. Newly rejuvenated men sometimes ignored their wives and sought out mates as young as they now felt. Men with heart disease began to risk the death that can come from the physical exertion of sexual intercourse. On balance, the demonstrated effectiveness of the new drug brought Pfizer Inc., its manufacturer, extraordinary profits during the first months of the drug's availability, and other firms tried to develop competing medicines, one even investigating the possible effectiveness of such Chinese potions as tiger-penis soup.

The innate ability to reproduce is influenced by the relative fecundity of one's forebears. Such a physiological determinant is generally hard to estimate, however, for whenever children remain in the same social-economic setting as their parents—which is the typical case—a similar family size in the two generations may be due merely to the continuing influence of the relatively unchanged social environment. It is only at the two extremes of its range that hereditary influence on fecundity is clearly perceptible. On the one hand, low fecundity can result from defects in the sexual organs, and a predisposition toward some of those impediments is genetic. Multiple births are relatively rare in the human species except when they are stimulated by hormones administered as a therapy for infertility. That a high level of fecundity may be inherited is suggested by the fact that the proportion of multiple births differs significantly both by family line and by race. In one notable case with no hormone injection, when one of a set of quadruplets married one of a pair of twins, they had thirty-two children in eleven pregnancies.[39]

According to one informed estimate, infertility affects about 10 to 15 percent of American couples in the reproductive ages, or about one American couple in six.[40] Based on the fact that more infertile women were observed in 1995 than had been forecast some years before, a new projection raised the number in the year 2025 to somewhere between 5.4 and 7.7 million, with the likeliest figure just under 6.5 million. However, the larger number in 1995, which was the basis of the revised projection, may have been due mainly or only to an increased awareness of infertility among both physicians and the public, the consequence of new techniques in countering it and the wide publicity they have been given.[41]

Of currently married women in the United States who had had one or more children, roughly one-third of the wives or their husbands had been sterilized as a means of birth control. Even this most drastic method of avoiding pregnancy has a failure rate of 0.5 percent. In the United States the total number of vasectomies (male sterilizations by a removal of part or all the vas deferens) has been about 500,000 a year, and some 5 to 10 percent of the men subsequently want to reverse the effect of the operation. One physician recommended detailed counseling before a vasectomy is performed to inform the patient that the chances are slight that his fecundity may be restored.[42] According to a nationwide survey in 1982 (later data are for a smaller portion of the population), American couples were divided as follows:[43]

Table 4.2

Sterile		27.0%
By contraceptive operation	17.5%	
By noncontraceptive operation	7.8	
Nonsurgical	1.7	
Subfecund		6.6
By medical indications	5.6	
By lack of pregnancy	1.0	
Fecund (residual)		66.4

The rise in the proportion of Americans' infertile marriages in the 1960s and 1970s was partly due to the increase of sexually transmitted disease. In one decade, from 1965 to 1975, the number of reported cases of gonorrhea tripled; and after it leveled off, there was a probable increase in chlamydia, another venereal disease on which there are no national data but with an incidence estimated at a quarter of all venereal cases. Less complete data from subsequent years suggest that there has been little change in this pattern.

Since the improvement in obstetrics has been largely limited to the West, the risk of childbearing differs greatly between industrial and less developed countries. The contrast is sharpest with black Africa, where the primitive hygiene and poor health facilities are aggravated by a high incidence of sexually transmitted diseases. Of the considerable body of writings on this subject, some of the most detailed and impressive have been by Anne Retel-Laurentin, a French ethnologist and physician,[44] whose studies were amplified in two publications by Odile Frank.[45]

The disease that in the recent past has affected African fecundity most is gonorrhea, which seldom causes sterility in males but in females results in a tubal occlusion that blocks a normal impregnation. In black Africa perhaps one woman in eight remains childless, with proportions ranging from 32 percent in Gabon to 4 percent in Senegal. Gonorrhea is not life-threatening, and there have been few official efforts to combat it. In one province of Ethiopia, where more than 25,000 cases had been treated annually with privately purchased antibiotics, the bewildering contribution of the Communist government was to prohibit the sale of the drug.[46] By Odile Frank's estimate, the total fertility rate would have risen by some 15 percent if gonorrhea had been eliminated.

Since that was written there has been an explosive rise in the incidence of AIDS, which according to a United Nations survey in 1998 has reached pandemic proportions in several sub-Saharan nations. According to an estimate by two international agencies, more than 30 million people there are infected with the HIV virus. In Botswana, the hardest hit of these countries, in only 5 years the estimated life expectancy fell from 61 to 47 years, and it was projected to decline to 41 years over the next decade. In Zimbabwe, where one in every five adults is infected with HIV, the estimated rate of population growth fell from 3.3 percent in 1980-83 to a current 1.4 percent, and it is projected to drop to <1 percent in 2000.[47]

It makes good biological sense to suppose that a well fed, healthy animal is more likely than a malnourished one to reproduce itself. That families of Western industrial countries have typically been much smaller than those of less developed countries might suggest that, on the contrary, better diets lessen the ability to procreate, a thesis widely propagated in the 1950s by the Brazilian physician-publicist Josué de Castro. His two main works, *Geography of Hunger: Hunger in Brazil* (first Portuguese edition, 1946) and *The Geopolitics of Hunger: An Essay on the Problems of Nutrition and Population in the World* (first Portuguese edition, 1951), were translated into many languages and had a worldwide impact. It is not excess population that may cause famine, he asserted, but famine that creates overpopulation.

Even when a food shortage verges on starvation, it is not easy to link it with a loss of procreative power.[48] For example, of 300 severely undernourished male prisoners of war, only 15 lost both sexual desire and their potency. A full-scale famine generally does not leave behind statistics that can be analyzed in order to distinguish precisely between excess mortality, a fall in fertility, and the typical surge in emigration. Analyses of nineteenth-century Ireland, for instance, are inconclusive.[49] Possibly the only place where records are good enough to draw a firm conclusion is the Netherlands during the last two years of the Nazi occupation. A careful study concluded that there was no perceptible effect from "exposure to famine" on age at menarche or several other indices of reproductive difficulties. The one exception was that children of pregnant women lacking adequate nutrition had a higher incidence of perinatal deaths.[50]

Of cases of subfecundity associated with the female, tubal pathology may be the consequence, among other causes, of venereal disease or an inept abortion. A relatively common abnormality is an adhesion that impedes, or prevents, the passage of both ova and sperm. If the flow of a fertilized egg into the uterus is not completed, the result may be an ectopic (from the Greek for "out of place") pregnancy, which rarely if ever results in a normal birth. In 1989 (the latest figures available), in the United States there were 16 ectopic pregnancies per 1,000 pregnancies reported, and they caused about 15 percent of all maternal deaths. The rate had increased by five times over that in 1970.[51]

In the mid-1990s about 5.3 million Americans of childbearing ages, or one in every six couples, have experienced difficulties in producing a child. Perhaps as many as 10 to 15 percent of couples in the reproductive ages fail to produce a conception within a year of regular intercourse. Roughly one in three of those subfecund couples has sought therapy, at a total cost of more than $1 billion annually. "Between 1968 and 1984, the number of office visits for infertility increased by nearly threefold—to the level [in 1984] of 1.6 million annually."[52] One woman spoke for a sizable portion of her generation: "Like many baby boomers I pursued my career with gusto and zest, never considering children. But now you can't get a parking space at the fertility clinic."[53]

The larger number of couples unable to have a child by normal procedures has resulted in enhanced efforts to repair low fecundity. The prolonged diagnostic examinations are expensive and bothersome. The most remarkable of these ameliorative measures is fertilization in vitro, which costs between $4,000 and $6,500. The woman is injected with a hormone that greatly stimulates the production of ova, several of which are retrieved surgically and joined in a laboratory with the man's sperm. Then, three or four of the fertilized eggs are reinserted into the uterus.[54] The first "test-tube baby" was Louise Brown, born on 25 July 1978, in Oldham, England.

"In the 1990s," according to one practitioner, "this procedure has clearly come of age. In experienced hands it is highly successful and cost-effective."[55] In fact, it is successful in only about one time out of five. Because the expensive process has such poor results, some physicians have suggested that they should offer a money-back guarantee, but the suggestion has hardly won unanimous support.[56] Sometimes more than one egg is fertilized, and the birth of triplets or more infants at once can mean increased danger to both the mother and her offspring. Obstetricians may recommend that there be a "multifetal reduction"—that is, an abortion of one or more of the several fetuses, and some mothers find it disturbing to have to choose whether to consent to this procedure.[57]

The legal complications that artificial fertilization can produce are suggested by a case in California. A couple used in vitro fertilization with donor eggs, donor sperm, and an unrelated surrogate mother. Before the child was born, the couple separated, and the man wanted nothing to do with the infant. Who were the legal parents—the genetic parents, the gestational mother and her husband, or the adoptive parents? In a court case the judge ruled that the child was parentless, and though his remarkable decision was reversed on appeal, the six adults involved all had to pay in time and money to avoid the responsibility that eventually rested only with the separated prospective adoptive couple.[58]

In a book published in 1978 the author alleged that a wealthy man, identified only as "Max," had himself cloned.[59] Later some doubt was raised about whether the account had been a hoax; in any case, it got enough attention from a wide range of ethicists and politicians to bring the cloning of human beings to the fore. The near consensus was that, after the cloning of one mammal it was possible to repeat the procedure with any other mammalian species, but that it should be prohibited in the case of Homo sapiens. Obviously the case is not closed, and the cloning of a human Dolly is likely within the next several decades. Would-be parents unable to conceive a child by conventional means would have another possible mode of reproduction—in a literal sense.

Another escape from the consequences of infertility that has become common with American couples is to adopt a child. In non-Western societies adoption has many functions; nineteenth-century Japan had no less than ten categories of adopted persons, and a Latin American peasant might attain greater security or move up socially by being adopted into an upper-class family. But in the United States almost the sole purpose of adoption is to transfer the legal status of an unwanted child, who becomes a family member with an infertile couple. Under terms of a federal law passed in 1980, states that institute an adoption-assistance program receive federal funds to facilitate the placement of children with "special needs"—particularly older, handicapped, or minority children.[60] The complex process, which varies considerably from state to state, is generally supervised by social workers, charged with protecting the rights of the children involved but sometimes enforcing counterproductive regulations. There are so-called black-market adoptions to evade these rules, as well as a flourishing business of "search experts" to help prospective adoptive parents try to follow them.[61]

However tragic subfecundity or sterility may be for the individuals concerned, the overall effect of such impairments is typically less than some demographers and health professionals have suggested. Because most of such cases result from either low fecundity or the couple's advanced ages, many of the families in either circumstance include several children who had been born before the couple became infertile. That point was illustrated by a fascinating 1965 survey in New Orleans. Of a sample of ever-married or ever-pregnant white women aged 15 to 44 years, the one-third diagnosed as currently subfecund or sterile had an average of 2.54 children, and the two-thirds diagnosed as fecund had families with an average of 2.55 children.[62] The near identity of the two figures is coincidental, but not the implication of the research. These data, though gathered in a single city, are probably close to typical of white Americans, a population in which impairments to fecundity generally have about as much effect on the birth rate as does contraception. In other words, sterility is likely to be a significant depressant of overall fertility only in populations with few potential parents who control the size of their families by other means.

Maximum Fertility

From puberty to menopause, a woman is fecund for approximately thirty years. In a society where people are married for the whole of this period and do not use contraceptives, how fast would the population grow?

Such a society is approximated by the Hutterites, an Anabaptist sect in the United States and Canada whose members still follow the dictates of its sixteenth-century founder.[63] They have maintained a communal life, are pacifists, and do not practice birth control. Their average of 10.4 births per couple, the world's highest recorded fertility, even so reflects some slippage. Consider a woman who married at age 15 and remained alive and with her husband throughout her fecund years: if in each age interval she gave birth to the same number of children that Hutterites do, she would bear an average of 12.6 children during her lifetime. Ansley Coale used this extrapolation from Hutterite childbearing to construct an elegant new measure, the index of overall fertility. Taking the 12.6 children that, with its age-specific fertility rates, would be born to members of that sect over the whole of the female's fecund years, Coale denoted this as the maximum reproduction feasible for the average couple in any society. He then used this maximum, as compared with the total fertility of less prolific peoples, to devise a measure that denotes immediately how each society ranks in begetting.[64]

Demographers use a term to designate all the factors that affect fertility—physiological, cultural, and other, omitting only birth control and the bearing of a child. Fecundability, coined by the Italian demographer Corrado Gini, is defined as the probability that a woman having regular sexual intercourse will conceive during one menstrual cycle in the absence of any attempt to prevent conception. The mean value for women aged 20-29, according to one estimate, is about 0.3; that is, during their most fecund years women will conceive in one menstrual cycle out of three during which they have regular sexual intercourse.[65] Or, according to another estimate derived from a study of nonsterile American couples, fecundability increases with the wife's age to about 21 and then declines slowly and more or less linearly to about age 40. For the whole fecund period the overall figure is 0.15, or half the estimate for just women in their 20s.[66] Other estimates have differed from these two, depending on the quality of the data, the variables included, and the method of estimation.

Essentially the same idea is encompassed in the phrase natural fertility, which was brought into demographic terminology by the French demographer Louis Henry.[67] At that time he was interested mainly in analyzing past populations, particularly in specifying how the so-called fertility transition took place. It is impossible to determine from documentary evidence when a particular society started using such an early control of conception as, for instance, coitus interruptus. Henry estimated the date by recording the length of intervals between births: so long as the couple had fewer children than they wanted, the spacing between the offspring would remain more or less constant (or would fall slowly as a consequence of aging), but when the family reached the size it desired, some kind of contraception, even though not completely effective, would result in longer intervals between births. Using this device, the American demographer John Knodel tried to determine when inhabitants of a sample of German villages replaced natural fertility by family planning; he found that the transition extended over the whole of the nineteenth century.[68]

Optimum Age of Mothers

What are the best ages for childbearing? Data on the deaths of mothers, fetuses, newborns, and infants all show that the risks rise on either side of an optimum age range, but authorities differ on what that range is.

The rates of neonatal, postneonatal, and infant mortality, when plotted against the age of the mother, all show a U-shaped curve, with a high point a <15 years, falling to a low in the 20s, rising in the 30s to a new high at >45. These data, though a generation old, were regarded as better than any later statistics, because they were based on a national sample. Rates similar to these "are found in study after study despite differences in overall levels of mortality."[69]

Over the past several decades the trend in the United States has been marked by a growing incidence of first births to teenagers and to women in their late 30s and early 40s, both of which may well represent departures from the optimum. The designation "teenager," of course, is not specific: a child of 13 is always ill equipped physiologically and otherwise to have her own offspring, but this need not be true of a young woman of 19. Where is the dividing line? According to some studies, mothers in their late teens do not suffer disproportionately from premature births or neonatal mortality; others hold that the deleterious effect, though reduced, persists at least up to 20 years.[70] One pair of researchers concluded that risks to girls above age 15 were the consequence not of immaturity but rather of their typical social-economic circumstances.[71]

Consider a woman who works outside the home to age 30 or 35 and then wants to start a family. Will she probably be able to bear one or more healthy children? All of a woman's oocytes, the reproductive units that eventually develop into eggs, had been formed when she was a fetus. As the stock is depleted, the chances increase that too few of the smaller number will evolve into sound ova, viable fetuses, and healthy children. The average number of oocytes remaining at ages 39-45 is of the order of 1.5 percent of the original store, and when all the oocytes are gone, the woman is sterile.

According to many authorities, the age range with the smallest incidence of all types of reproductive mortality is the 20s. Only with respect to higher birth orders, because of the increased danger from closely spaced births, does the optimum age rise to the mid-30s. A mother 5 years older than the optimum runs increased risks of 5-19 percent; one 10 years older, 21-77 percent; and one 15 years older, more than 100 percent.[72]

One indication of the effect of American women's age on their fertility is given in the *Statistical Abstract of the United States, 1997*, summarizing data from the National Center for Health Statistics. If one compares for various age groups the number of pregnancies with the number and percent of fetal losses (not including induced abortions), the figures are suggestive:

Table 4.3

Age of Mother	Pregnancies (-000)	Fetal Losses	
		Number (-000)	Percent
Total	3,964	556	14.0
<15	8	1	12.5
15-19	489	75	15.3
20-24	1,007	107	10.6
25-29	1,145	148	12.9
30-34	884	138	15.6
35-39	368	76	20.7
40+	63	11	17.5

Among nulliparous French women (that is, with no prior births of viable children) who sought therapeutic services from an institution called CECOS, 2,193 were artificially inseminated with donor sperm. Their mean success rate per ovulation cycle fell with increasing age, and the study indicated that the critical cutoff is at 30 years.[73] These data have been challenged, and particularly the conclusion drawn from them--that women who want children would be well advised to have them early and adjust their career aspirations accordingly.

Two papers— "Infertility after Age 30: A False Alarm" and "Age and Fertility: How Late Can You Wait?" by, respectively, John Bongaarts of the Population Council and Jane Menken in a presidential address to the Population Association of America—offered most of the counter arguments that have been made in a large number of subsequent papers.[74]

The French women who were given semen from donors, Bongaarts pointed out, were presumably less fecund than the average, and therefore inferences drawn from their experience would be inconclusive concerning a general population (*a reasonable argument*). In any case, the rate of impregnation with artificial insemination is lower, age for age, than with natural sex relations. (*This contention was convincingly challenged in another paper.*[75]) Since we do not know how many involuntarily childless women there are in modern populations, Bongaarts continued, we must depend on findings from historical demography, which indicate the following relation between age and fecundity:

70   From Birth to Death

20-24 years	95.9 percent fecund
25-29	94.5
30-34	90.6
35-39	80.3

(The rise in apparent absolute sterility from about 4 percent to almost 20 percent would seem to be quite significant, contrary to the point that Bongaarts was making.)

To follow the argument further from Menken's address: In the past, allegedly attention was concentrated on reducing the effects of what was seen as hyperfecundity, and estimates of past infertility may therefore be below actuality. *(The tragedy of a barren woman, on the contrary, was probably far greater when being a mother-housewife was virtually the only respectable female role.)* At the present time, a postponement of marriage and childbearing often implies, according to Menken, an earlier promiscuity, but seemingly the only significant effect of these multiple matings is the spread of pelvic inflammatory disease (PID). "PID is treatable; aging is not." *(On the same page Menken noted that the general treatment of infertility has improved, but she failed to note that only about half the cases of PID can be cured. PID is not a specific disease but a composite term for various sexually transmitted infections. Therapy is sought with a "broad spectrum" of medications. PID can develop into a tubo-ovarian abscess, which requires surgery in about a quarter of the cases.[76])*

Many women have wanted both to be mothers and to compete fully as workers, employees, professionals, or business executives; and some have succeeded against considerable (though lessening) prejudice and other formidable barriers. According to a careful study by the American sociologist Valerie Oppenheimer, women's rising level of employment in the United States has not affected the age distribution of marriage; contrary indications were based on an aberrant stretch of time.[77] However, many of these married women may well have had fewer children than they would have had as housewives. That the dual goal should be partly frustrated by biological limitations may be galling, but it does not help to dismiss the decline in fecundity with advancing years as a myth. The available data, however, are poor enough to encourage a variety of interpretations.

To accept uncritically either the conclusions of the French [CECOS] study or those of Bongaarts [and Menken] is to draw a conclusion from an inadequate base of reliable data. Either conclusion may be misleading to women who are trying to balance career and childbearing goals.[78]

The prolongation of females' lives has provided a possible—though, to many women, not very attractive—means of squaring the circle. If we take 45 years as the age of menopause and 75 years as the life expectation of Western women, then the 30 years of postreproductive life are about equal to the fecund period, much of which the typical woman once used for reproduction. "One is tempted to observe that the long postreproductive period provides the human female with a lengthened opportunity to transmit a cultural rather than a genetic heritage to the next generation, a point of view that suggests that rational fertility is compatible with natural development."[79] Many of the women who have left behind them their major family responsibilities do indeed take on such tasks, often as part-time volunteers. But is it not fanciful to suppose that in general an ambitious young woman would find this a resolution of her dilemma?

5

Mortality

Paradoxically, it is to some degree arbitrary where one divides what is called fertility from what is called mortality. For example, in the mid-1990s a dispute developed over a bill that Congress had passed and President Clinton vetoed; it banned so-called partial-birth abortions, and the controversy focused on whether this procedure is tantamount to infanticide.

It was only with the development of international statistics in the last decades of the nineteenth century that the two processes of birth and death became more precise; and until the meanings of the relevant terms were standardized internationally, one country's data, even if satisfactorily accurate and complete by themselves, could give a totally false picture when compared with those of another.

Fetal and Infant Mortality

The term *birth*, which is defined in a medical dictionary as simply "the act or process of being born," would seem to be unambiguous; but indeterminacy can arise from setting a boundary between a "live birth" and a "stillbirth." If a fetus is expelled "alive" by one criterion but expires shortly after the trauma of being born, should one state that a "live" birth has taken place? Jurisdictions have not been consistent. In 1950 the World Health Organization tried to set a standard by proposing a precise definition of fetal death as one prior to the complete expulsion or extraction from its mother of a product of conception, irrespective of the duration of the pregnancy; after the separation, the fetus does not breathe, its heart does not beat, the umbilical cord does not pulsate, the voluntary muscles do not move. In the United States the National Center for Health Statistics, which compiles data sent in from the fifty states, adopted this definition and revised the recommended registration form, but only about half of the states were prompt in changing their official definition. In any case, the registration of fetal deaths, particularly of those early in the gestation period, is everywhere far from complete. The record pertains mainly to deaths at twenty weeks or more, which in the United States are the only ones that the laws of some states require officials to register.

Comparisons of infant mortality in developed and less developed countries are often taken as one of the most significant of international contrasts in well-being. According to the 1990 edition of the UNICEF's annual report, "infant mortality is known to have risen in parts of Latin America and Africa south of the Sahara."[1] But according to the U.N.'s *Demographic Yearbook*, only fourteen less developed countries or territories registered 90 percent or more of their infant mortality. "Thus, for countries comprising well more than 95 percent of the estimated population of the third world, it is not immediately apparent how one would go about documenting recent year-by-year changes in infant mortality rates."[2]

A Historical Note

According to historical analyses of several regions of France, the expectation of life during the period 1680-1720 was about 25 years. This does not mean, of course, that everyone died by that age, but rather that the large proportion of deaths early in life, when balanced against the relatively few who survived to old age, averaged out at 25 years. Taking these studies as a base, the French economist Jean Fourastié spelled out the kind of life people led at that time.[3]

He invited the reader to consider an average family head, a man who had married for the first time at age 27. Born into a family of five children, of whom only two or three reached age 15, he also, like his father, had five children, of whom again only two or three were still alive when he died. Living to be 52, this man moved into the venerable elite, for only one in five males reached that advanced age. In his immediate family (not to speak of uncles and aunts, nephews and nieces, and first cousins), he survived an average of nine persons: one of his grandparents (the other three having died before his birth), his two parents, three siblings, and three of his children. He had lived through two or three famines as well as three or four periods of poor harvests and high grain prices, which recurred every decade or so. He had lived also through sicknesses of his brothers and sisters, his children, his wife (or successive wives), his parents and himself, having survived two or three epidemics as well as such more or less endemic diseases as whooping cough, scarlet fever, and diphtheria. He had often suffered from toothaches and slow-healing wounds. Death was the center of life, just as the cemetery was the center of the village. This was a representation of life not only in France of that time but also in the rest of Europe and, until its transformation started after the Second World War, in much of the less developed world.

A century or so later, by about 1800, in the West expectation of life from birth had risen to around 35 or 40 years, half of what it is today. In spite of the fact that life had been extended by 10 years or more, existence was still similar to Fourastié's reconstruction: out of every five children born, one would still die before his fifth birthday and another before he reached maturity.

In industrial countries a major breakthrough to the modern control of death took place between the last decades of the nineteenth century and the First World War. Infections that attack mainly infants were checked; babies survived who a few years earlier would have died, and as a direct consequence, for several generations population in industrial nations grew by unprecedented proportions.

For a period the historic improvement in death control was restricted to the West, but from the 1940s on it spread to the rest of the world. The most startling early instance of a new pattern was in Ceylon (subsequently Sri Lanka), where the estimated expectation of life at birth rose from 43 years in 1946 to 52 a year later. In most Western countries the 9 years of longer life realized in those 12 months had taken half a century to achieve. This amazing decline in mortality seemingly derived mainly from one factor--DDT, an insecticide that had been developed during the Second World War. When sprayed from airplanes over low-lying areas, it all but eliminated malaria, the principal cause of death in Ceylon, by killing the mosquitoes that carry the protozoa of the genus Plasmodium that occasions it.[4]

Soon the same control was applied elsewhere—in India, Mauritius, portions of the Near East—wherever Anopheles mosquitoes bred in large numbers. Before the Second World War, malaria had been the most potent single cause of sickness and death, and within a few years the World Health Organization instituted a campaign to eliminate it altogether. The project did not succeed, mainly because mosquitoes became resistant to the insecticides being used, but also because an offensive was instituted against the use of DDT. Most of a special issue of the *WHO Chronicle* (May 1971) was devoted to the consequences of a zealots' crusade to ban its use. In the opinion of a wide range of health experts, the cost of withdrawing DDT before the development of an equally effective substitute would have been a disastrous worldwide resurgence of malaria.

Today the disease has been brought somewhat under control by the drainage of swamps, education of affected populations on the use of screens, various insect repellents, and insecticide-treated bednets, which cost as little as $2.50 each and reduce deaths from the disease by almost a third. In 1998 researchers at Johns Hopkins University discovered that feeding zinc or vitamin A to children, who are the most susceptible to the disease, seemingly raises their immunity to malaria. There are also more effective drugs, such as mefloquine, but they are too expensive to be distributed wholesale in less developed countries.[5] Meanwhile every year victims of the disease number in the millions.

Other ailments were brought under control by sulfa drugs, antibiotics, and subsequent new remedies. Mass vaccinations so much reduced the threat of smallpox, a scourge for centuries, that in the mid-1970s several countries repealed their laws requiring everyone to be vaccinated. All these measures, one should emphasize, were applied to the whole populations of less developed countries with no more than a passive participation by the people affected. Expensive antibiotics and other supplies, as well as medical and administrative personnel, were furnished mainly by Western taxpayers through the funding of international agencies and bilateral relief programs. Persons all over the world who knew nothing of modern medicine in any other sense became quite familiar with penicillin. As before, the main effect was on infant and child mortality, and its decline was again equivalent to a rise in the birth rate--a rise, moreover, unaccompanied by any change in the social structure, the country's technical equipment, familial values, or any other of the supposed determinants of the fertility level.

Eventually mortality fell in less developed countries to levels more or less the same as those in nations with the best health systems. Crude death rates (the number of deaths in a year per thousand persons in the affected population) are not the best measure of mortality, and the vital statistics of many less developed countries are not to be trusted. But for a comparison between a few examples of each category in the mid-1990s, the measure is sufficiently precise to be revealing:

Table 5.1

Industrial Countries		Less Developed Countries	
Australia	6.88	Algeria	5.9
Denmark	10.42	Bangladesh	11.21
Germany	12.21	China	6.92
Japan	7.71	Egypt	8.7
Sweden	11.43	India	9.61
United States	8.8	Mexico	4.58

This near parity has developed in spite of a continuing sharp contrast in infant mortality. Many infant deaths in less developed countries, such as those caused by food contamination, have been the result of infections not easily controlled in the aggregate. But because of the population structure, relatively few persons in those countries have died of heart disease, stroke, and cancers, which attack mainly the old and are therefore the main causes of death in developed countries.

In other words, the most publicized population problem of recent decades, the explosion of people in the Third World, has been the result principally of the successful application of the life-saving techniques of Western medicine, together with the medical personnel, all furnished at great cost and with the best intentions mainly by the United States and other Western powers.

What is Death?

One important consequence of the remarkable advances in medicine has become an unexpected confusion of what the word "death" means. The traditional definition given in *Black's Law Dictionary*, which has been frequently cited in American law cases, is "the cessation of life,...a total stoppage of the circulation of the blood and a cessation of the animal and vital functions consequent thereon, such as respiration, pulsation, etc." In fact, that simple definition may have become too simple.

Today patients are subject to seemingly endless medical intervention with antibiotics, intravenous feeding, artificial respiration, artificial heartbeats. In 1968, a committee of the Harvard Medical School faculty proposed a new criterion of death: irreversible coma as inferred from a flat electroencephalogram.[6] One important reason for their proposal was that adopting this new criterion would make available for transplants a large number of hearts, kidneys. lungs, and eventually also possibly other organs.

The suggested new definition set off an extensive debate in medical and legal journals. How the state designates death is not a trivial affair, for dependent on it are such matters, among others, as homicide, inheritance, and religious services marking the end of life. With the Harvard proposal adopted by some jurisdictions but not by others, a person could be "dead" by one criterion but "alive" by another, and doctors faced the dilemma whether to apply life-saving procedures while not sure whether there was "life" to preserve. In 1969-70 Kansas passed the country's first statutory definition of death and then another one, the first based on the traditional whole-body criterion and the second on the new brain-oriented one. As a commentator remarked, in that state there were two ways of dying. In a new law passed in New Mexico, the term "human being" was substituted for "person," suggesting that human life is not merely biological.[7]

In 1971 the Institute of Society, Ethics, and the Life Sciences in Hastings-on-Hudson, N.Y., presented a symposium on "Problems in the Meaning of Death." Two of the papers, later printed in *Science*, are as interesting an exploration of the issues as one can find. Robert S. Morison, a professor at Cornell University, argued that "life" and "death" had been reified as events when in fact both are processes.[8] Just as the debate about abortion revolved around the unanswerable question of when life begins, so also using a specific criterion to define the series of changes in a person undergoing death, he argued, is erroneous biologically, medically, legally, and morally. Whether to withhold the extraordinary measures that keep some patients alive, whether to accelerate the death of others, are not questions to which a single response is appropriate: "We must shoulder the responsibility of deciding to act in such a way as to hasten the declining trajectories of some lives, while doing our best to slow down the decline of others." Western values require that the decision be made for the benefit of the patient, but society as a whole will also gain from a more rational use of scarce medical resources.

In the second paper, Leon R. Kass of the National Research Council rejected Morison's conception of death as a process and insisted that it is correctly regarded as an event.[9] What dies is the organism as a whole. It is this death, the death of the individual human being, that is important for physicians and for the community, and not the "death" of organs or cells, which are mere parts. Whether a person is "dead," he argued, must be judged not on social-moral grounds, as Morison did in Kass's view, but by medical-scientific criteria as judged by a physician. A person does not "die" when his life is judged to be not worth living. Defining the event of dying is difficult, but not impossible; and the definition must be restricted to the condition of the dying person, not contaminated by the interests of relatives, potential transplant recipients, or society as a whole.

Early Deaths

One obvious determinant of the probability of dying is age. Infant mortality is high relative to that of other ages for two reasons—because a baby, if barely born alive, may not be able to remain so very long, and because any baby, even if born healthy, is especially susceptible to disease and accident. The two types of causes are termed, respectively, endogenous, referring to what might be considered a postponed fetal death, and exogenous, referring to a death that differs from general mortality only in the age of the person. In the *International Classification of Diseases*, causes of death in the first category include immaturity, birth injuries, congenital malformation, and "ill defined diseases peculiar to early infancy"; and those in the second category, certain parasitic diseases; pneumonia, influenza, and other infectious diseases; gastroenteritis and diarrhea; and accidents. The same distinction can be approximated by dividing the deaths of infants between neonatal mortality, or those during the first month of life, and postneonatal mortality, or those during the rest of the first year.

Thus, one can distinguish three main stages of development from the time of conception: a viable fetus, birth, and a time after birth when endogenous causes of death are no longer important. The timing of the three stages must be somewhat arbitrary, for the empirical distribution from any average is large, and the stages depend in part on how advanced medical practice is.

According to a summary of sixteen studies of primitive societies in various parts of the world, a generation ago the proportion recorded as dying under one year of age ranged between 10 and 35 percent, that under 5 years between 30 and 70 percent.[10] Other studies suggest that in Europe of the seventeenth and eighteenth centuries one child in four died during its first year.[11] By the beginning of the twentieth century the international range was great, with infant mortality rates (deaths during the first year of life per 1,000 births) around 100 in advanced Western countries and well over 200 in the worst of the less developed countries that had usable statistics. In the most recent period the difference has been still wider—below 30 in countries with the best records, and probably still well over 200 in those with the least control but also the poorest data.[12]

The probability of a newborn's survival depends in large measure on whether the length of the pregnancy approximates the normal duration of 38 to 42 weeks. The reported period of gestation is imprecise for two reasons: it is based on the woman's recollection of when her last menstruation took place, and her memory may be faulty; and it is assumed that the follicular phase of every cycle (that is, the period between a menstrual flow and the following ovulation) is exactly 14 days, which in some instances is not the case.[13] Because the time from conception is often difficult to estimate, whether a pregnancy has proceeded to term is usually estimated by the size and particularly the weight of the newborn.

In 1888, the Paris gynecologist Pierre-Constant Budin set a birth weight of less than 2,500 grams (or about 5.5 pounds) as the criterion of "prematurity," or the condition of an infant born before term. It took until 1935 for the American Academy of Pediatrics to adopt the definition, and it was only in 1950 that the World Health Organization endorsed it. As American obstetricians now define "term," a normal gestation is one that results in an infant at birth of more than 19 inches in length and 6 pounds in weight.[14]

Recently ultrasound waves have been used to establish the approximate age of the fetus. When passed through the soft tissue of a pregnant woman's belly, the waves are reflected back when they hit the higher-density tissues comprising the fetus's body. These reflected waves are amplified and displayed on a screen, showing any fetal abnormalities that are there. With serial sonar techniques, it is also possible to estimate the maturity of the placenta; and such a series, adjusted for the probable size of the newborn infant, correlates well with the duration of the pregnancy as estimated by other means.

Much has been written about prematurity, and the consensus among physicians is that the shorter the gestation, the greater the risk to the infant. In 1950, to give a typical range in the United States, during the first month of life more than 870 per 1,000 died of those weighing 1,000 grams or less, but fewer than 6 of those weighing 3,501 to 4,000 grams. At that time infant mortality was significantly higher in the United States than in several countries of Western Europe, and it was typically supposed that the reason was the superior medical care available through state-run institutions, as contrasted with the American mixture of private and socialized medicine.

A more important reason, it turned out, was that in other countries many of the premature newborn were classified as stillbirths and thus excluded from statistics on infant mortality. American obstetricians typically tried to save more of those born before term, and as a consequence the proportion of births in the United States that were premature increased from 7.7 percent in 1959 to 8.2 percent in 1974. In Great Britain over the same period, the proportion remained constant at 6.6 or 6.7 percent, and in other comparable countries, which then kept no records on weight at birth, unofficial estimates of the percentages were as low as 5.5 (Netherlands) or even 5.04 percent (Sweden).[15]

In the United States the significantly higher proportion of premature births that were judged to be potentially viable raised the risk of death during the first month of life by more than a hundredfold. Compared with Sweden or the Netherlands, at that time the two countries with the best *recorded* control of infant mortality, the attempts of American obstetricians to save more infants with a dangerously low birth weight accounted for 85 to 90 percent of the difference in deaths during the first month of life. The partly successful efforts to improve obstetrical techniques, it is worth repeating, showed up in statistics—and thus in interpretations by reputed authorities—as proof that the American health system was inefficient. Moreover, "although infants born before 28 weeks account for fewer than one percent of live births, careful recording of births and deaths and inclusion in national statistics penalize the countries that have the best reporting."[16]

Differences by Age and Sex

For a population lacking modern medicine, if we plot the percentage of all deaths against the ages at which they take place, we typically find a U-shaped curve, with very high rates in infancy and early childhood declining to a low point in early maturity and then gradually increasing as the age rises. Over the history of Western countries, as the incidence of infant mortality declined, the U lost most of its left leg, changing into a J-shaped curve.

It was once conventional to set the life span (or the maximum duration of human life under optimum conditions) at fourscore and ten; now one authority has estimated it to be 114 years.[17] A number of biologists and demographers have collaborated in a book that tries, from various points of view, to answer the question of how to interpret the secular rise in longevity.[18] Every year records show that the human life span has increased; what is the limit? Or has the once utopian view that there is no limit, with the possibility of altering man's genetic make-up, now developed a genuine feasibility?[19]

The capacity of self-renewal and the ability to reproduce the species, the main characteristics that set living beings apart from inert matter, both decline with advancing age—as do also the amount of work one can do, the speed of nerve conduction, the amount of acid secreted by the stomach's mucous membranes, the maximum filtration rate of the kidney, the cardiac output, the maximum rate at which one can breathe.

Though, as measured by any of these indicators, aging varies considerably from person to person, eventually we all reach an age when, lacking any other cause, we die simply of debility. However, old age is never listed among the causes of death:

> In its obsessive tidiness, the Report [issued annually by the U.S. National Center for Health Statistics] assigns the specific clinical category of some fatal pathology to every octo- and nonagenarian in its neat columns....Everybody is required to die of a named entity....Everywhere in the world, it is illegal to die of old age.[20]

There is also a difference in the typical mortality of the two sexes. A good review of how the main causes of death have changed over time is especially detailed on differences between the sexes. In an interesting study designed to distinguish between biological and environmental factors, the American sociologist Francis Madigan compared two Catholic teaching orders, one of monks and the other of nuns; under their more or less equivalent conditions of life, the average female lived longer.[21]

In a society without modern medicine, the greatest danger for females is associated with pregnancy and childbirth, but in industrial countries the significant progress in obstetrics, especially during the past several decades, has greatly reduced this prime risk. Other contrasts are based, for instance, on the comparatively greater progress in controlling cancers that mainly affect, respectively, men or women. Causes of death that affect males appreciably more than females were led by heart disease, followed by accidents, violence, and lung cancer.[22]

As a result of all these factors, the difference between men's and women's life expectation has widened throughout the West. As reported in the *Statistical Abstract of the United States, 1997*, the expectations of life by sex, with projections to the year 2010, are shown in Table 5.2:

Table 5.2

	Total	Males	Females	Difference
1970	70.8	67.1	74.7	7.6
1980	73.7	70.0	77.4	7.4
1990	75.4	71.8	78.8	7.0
1995	75.8	72.6	78.9	6.3
2000	NA	73.0	79.7	6.7
2010	NA	74.1	80.6	6.5

According to the same source, moreover, the difference in age between grooms and brides is substantial, particularly in the frequent second or later marriages. The median ages at marriage of the groom and bride are shown in Table 5.3:

Table 5.3

		Groom	Bride	Difference
First marriage	1970	22.5	20.6	1.9
	1990	25.9	24.0	1.9
Later marriage				
Divorced	1970	34.5	30.1	4.4
	1990	37.4	34.2	3.2
Widowed	1970	58.7	51.2	7.5
	1990	63.1	54.0	9.1

These two differences by sex, in the ages at marriage and at death, have resulted in a vast production of widows, whose number in the United States rose over the past generation from fewer than 6 million to more than 10 million, while the far smaller number of widowers declined. In 1996, according to the same source, the proportions of widowers and of widows were markedly divergent, particularly in higher age groups:

Table 5.4

		Male	Female
Aged	40-44	0.5%	1.5%
	45-54	0.8	4.3
	55-64	3.0	12.6
	65-74	9.6	32.8
	75+	22.9	63.6
Total		2.7	11.0

Cause and Effect in Mortality

There has always been a tendency to ascribe a single agent as the cause of each disease, and it is often difficult to test the validity of such a hypothesis. The word *malaria*, for instance, derives from *mala aria*, Italian for "bad air." The close association between fetid effusions from a swamp and the incidence of the disease, a matter of common knowledge in all malarial regions, was evident from the very high correlation between the two variables. Moreover, a project to control the disease, if it happened to concentrate on draining the swamp, might have "proved" that the correlation indicates a valid causal relation. Indeed, when the French drained swamps in Algeria, military deaths from malaria fell by 61 percent from 1846-48 to 1862-66, and presumably the unrecorded decline among civilians was of the same order.

In what is called a spurious correlation, the assumed independent variable (in that case, the quality of the air) and a dependent one (the prevalence of the disease) are, in fact, both effects of a factor antecedent to both (the presence of a swamp in which mosquitoes breed). This is a very common pattern; the mammoth transformations termed economic development and modernization resulted in millions of independent changes, any two of which are likely to have a high correlation. Let us say that we are able to show that in Massachusetts during the fifty years prior to the First World War, as telegraph poles were erected the birth rate declined. By a Freudian interpretation (as credible as some others that have been proffered), a phallic symbol was gradually being substituted for a phallus.

Or, to take a genuine case, as Massachusetts was converted from a rural-mercantile to an urban-industrial state, the proportion of the population institutionalized for serious mental illness increased. It was (perhaps one should say it *is*) widely believed that it was the rise of civilization, the departure from man's "natural state," that generated this greater prevalence of psychic disturbances. But when the rates of first admissions to Massachusetts institutions were broken down by age, there was virtually no change over the century in the state's records. In any population psychosis is more frequent among those of advanced age; and because of the large number of immigrants (most of whom were born into the society, as it were, as adults), the gradual decline in the birth rate, and the decline in mortality at advanced ages, the proportion of old people increased. However, there was "no long-term increase during the last century in the incidence of psychoses of early and middle life."[23] An elaborate theory had been concocted for a relation that disappeared when tested by even so obvious a control as age.[24]

A case more familiar in epidemiology is John Snow's famous analysis linking cholera to drinking water. According to Dr. Wade Hampton Frost, who trained a whole generation of twentieth-century British epidemiologists, Snow's assessment was "a nearly perfect model," "a masterpiece in the ordering and analysis of evidence."[25] Since that seems to be a general appraisal, it is worthwhile looking at the original study to check how warranted this judgment is.

The first sections of *On the Mode Of Communication of Cholera* (1854) cite a number of cases of the disease, each of which seems to have been linked to prior instances. These facts "prove that cholera is communicated from person to person."[26] No series of such anecdotes, however, can prove anything. Indeed, this is the typical manner of confirming a stereotype: a person who believes, for example, that women are poor drivers will cite a number of episodes in which gender and maladroitness are indubitably linked, ending with such an observation as "it would be easy...to quote as many cases similar to the above as would fill a volume."[27]

Snow's initial proposition was that, because persons in frequent contact fell sick from cholera, therefore the disease is infectious. Consider the case of pellagra, which was judged by not only most of the public but also the American Medical Association to be an infectious disease. Indeed, a commission of physicians pointed out that pellagra had spread most rapidly where sewage disposal was not in accord with recommended practices. In other words, evidence of the same kind and quality was used not only to designate pellagra as a contagious (rather than a food-deficiency) disease but even to suggest that the mode of transportation might be by an infected water supply.

To return to Snow: In ten days there had been more than 500 fatal cholera attacks within 250 yards of the spot in central London where Cambridge Street joins Broad Street, and Snow suspected that the public pump at the junction of the two streets might be the source of an infection. A map that he made showed a decided clustering of deaths around the Broad Street pump, but also a number of puzzling deviations. The outbreak rose with frightening rapidity to a high point of 143 fatal attacks on September 1, thereafter subsiding to only 12 on September 8, the day that the handle of the pump was removed to prevent persons from drinking its water. Some of the deaths on Snow's spot map were far closer to other public pumps; that is, persons died whose link to the fatal pump, since it was not mere proximity, had to be presumed from alternative hypotheses. Reportedly pubs, restaurants, and coffeehouses used water from the Broad Street pump, and thus their patrons may have consumed it no matter where they lived.

Moreover, some patients, removed to hospitals, left no record of their prior addresses.

In short, there was not entirely a one-to-one relation between the suspected source of contamination and the range of the disease. Cases that did not fit the hypothesis were sometimes ignored, sometimes explained away; for, as Snow explained, "if the locality of the few additional cases could be ascertained, they would probably be distributed over the district of the outbreak in the same proportion as the large number which are known."[28] This is not, by present-day standards, part of "a nearly perfect model" of epidemiological analysis. Certainty had to wait until the identification of the responsible microorganism, the cholera vibrio. Then it turned out that Snow had been right, unlike the nameless analyst who linked malaria to fetid air.

It is almost irresistible to interpret a high correlation as a cause-effect relation, and one would think that the most fundamental element in the training of epidemiologists would be to correct this all but universal intuitive impulse. It is startling to find, on the contrary, that the authors of one standard text instruct their students that "the stronger the association between two categories of events,...the more likely it is that the association is causal."[29] It would be difficult to put it less well. Even a perfect correlation between two variables is not a necessary indication that one causes the other; and, on the other hand, an actual cause-effect relation may show a total lack of correlation, which may have been completely masked by an intervening variable. When a high correlation stimulates the interest of a researcher, he should test the association in every way that his experience and imagination suggest, in order to reach the—still tentative—conclusion that indeed one factor caused the other.

Whenever an American dies, a physician or coroner fills out a death certificate, which includes his judgment on the "immediate cause," "due to, or as a consequence of" one or two factors, and "other significant conditions." The certificates are compiled by the National Center for Health Statistics into national mortality statistics, which refer only to the immediate cause. A partial list of the major causes of death in 1995, as given in the *Statistical Abstract of the United States, 1997*, follows:

Table 5.5

	Deaths (-000)	Rate per 100,000 Population
All causes	2,312.2	880.0
Major cardiovascular diseases	952.5	362.5
Malignancies	538.0	204.7
Accidents	89.7	34.1
Chronic pulmonary diseases	104.8	39.9
Pneumonia and influenza	83.5	31.8
Diabetes mellitus	59.1	22.5
Suicide	30.9	11.8
Chronic liver diseases and cirrhosis	24.8	9.5
Other infectious and parasitic diseases	49.6	18.9
Homicide and execution	21.6	8.2
Nutritional deficiencies	3.5	1.3

Social Disorder as a Cause of Death[30]

If ever it becomes possible to reduce significantly the mortality from cancers and degenerative diseases, then the main causes of death would be those that can be loosely categorized as the consequences of social disorder. Their common characteristic is that at least part of their etiology lies well outside the conventional limits of medicine. A substantial proportion of both morbidity and mortality during recent decades cannot be classified as purely medical phenomena, for the behavioral component is both too important and too obvious. Some malfunctioning of social institutions, some deviance from what everyone knows should be done to maintain optimum health, often an infraction of some law, riots that may develop into civil wars—these are not matters to which a physician's expertise is particularly pertinent. Though the afflictions may be infectious (e.g., venereal diseases) or chronic (e.g., addictions), even in these instances a narrowly medical analysis is incomplete. In short, we may not be exaggerating greatly if we predict that some time in the relatively near future homicides, accidents, addictions, and the like may, in the aggregate, be the most important cause of death.

The World Bank has tried to compile a worldwide list of diseases, including such violence-related phenomena as automobile accidents, falls, homicide, suicide, and war. There were enough flaws in the data to excite a good deal of criticism, but there has also been a near consensus that, in the words of the director general of the World Health Organization, violence has become a neglected epidemic that may soon surpass infectious diseases as the principal causes of morbidity and premature mortality worldwide. In a recent issue the *Journal of the American Medical Association* called for more papers on "violence, a neglected epidemic."[31]

As noted in Table 5.5, in 1995 there were 89,700 deaths from accidents in the United States. The principal site of serious accidents used to be the workplace, but over three decades these were cut in half, mainly because of the sizable shift of workers from factory to office jobs, partly because of more effective enforcement of safety standards. However, the data are typically flawed, and they have been made more difficult to interpret by such new or augmented factors as computers, revised regulations, campaigns by labor unions, medical specialties, marketing of diagnostic and therapeutic devices, and employers' resistance to the classification of diseases as "occupational." A recent work examined the consequent complex interaction with respect to three allegedly work-induced ailments: carpal tunnel syndrome, back pain, and hearing loss.[32] The conclusion is the same as in a broader analysis of how occupational diseases are measured by the several persons and institutions involved in determining the benefits to be awarded—namely, that any statistical conclusion can be made only with built-in and sometimes arbitrary interpretations.[33]

The list of causes of death in 1995 includes 30,900 suicides. In the vast body of writings on this act, the recurrent themes are the poor data, the sizable differences from one culture to another, and the psychological or social reasons for taking one's life. Even one who knows all the circumstances may often find it hard to really know whether a fatal end is a suicide or an accident.

In one of the classics of sociology, the French pioneer in the discipline Émile Durkheim noted that the suicide rate was consistently lower among Catholics than among Protestants, Jews, or atheists; and he explained the contrast by the stronger cohesion of members of the Catholic Church and thus their greater insulation from "suicide-generating currents."[34] Another likely—more likely?—interpretation is that because suicide is a greater sin for Catholics, their families took greater care to disguise it as a consequence of an accident, perhaps enlisting the support of sympathetic doctors and even coroners in what all are prone to see as a white lie.

On the other hand, Durkheim's hypothesis was partly confirmed by one report. The suicide rates of Denmark and Sweden are among the world's highest, Norway's among the lowest. According to a joint study by the Scandinavian nations, Norwegians have far stronger ties to family, neighborhood, social clubs, and church; like the Catholics in Durkheim's analysis, their social integration is stronger.[35]

What are the characteristics of Americans who reportedly have killed themselves?[36]
- Three times more men than women.
- Higher percentage of whites than of blacks.
- Higher rates with advancing age, especially after 60.
- Divorced men more than single men.

Such gross patterns are not very informative concerning the probable risk of any person; that in the United States two-thirds of suicides are white males is hardly a clue about how a particular white male is likely to behave.

In the context of demography, the most relevant aspect of suicide is the ambiguity of the statistics. Why have suicides in Scotland been consistently less frequent than in England and Wales? One author concluded that the contrast is a factitious result of juridical procedures; another, that if those procedures influenced reported data at all, it may have been to raise the Scottish rate relative to the English one.[37] A yet more indicative instance was a comparison of two official counts of self-inflicted deaths by military personnel in 1975-76, one by the surgeon general and the other by the adjutant general. The suicide rate per 100,000 population ranged from 8.4 (the medical count), through 11.0 (the legal one), to 16.3 (the author's independent estimate based on the same two sets of data).[38]

When a physician assists a dying patient to take his life, the doctor is subject to censure or worse. As noted earlier, advances in medicine have been so great that persons who a few decades ago would have died are now often kept "alive," though in many instances with few of the qualities of normal life. The consequence has been a campaign for the right to die and what is called PAS, for physician-assisted suicide.

In the United States the campaign for this reform was led by the Hemlock Society, which sought a legal remedy, first unsuccessfully in Washington State and California, then with passage of a Death with Dignity Act (1997) in Oregon. The opposition was mostly from churches; the state medical association stayed neutral. About $5 million was spent by both sides, but with little effect. A poll that the U.S. Catholic Conference conducted after the vote confirmed that some 60 percent had supported the measure but also that 83 percent had decided to do so before the final weeks of the campaign.[39]

> The Oregon laws, we think, has it just right. The physician must discuss depression with the patient, and if the possibility of it exists, ask the patient to see a psychiatric worker. If the patient refuses, then the physician can decline to help.[40]

In 1995, as listed in Table 5.5, there were 21,600 deaths due to homicide or what the official record calls "legal intervention" (that is, execution). During the 1990s the overall crime rate of the United States declined, and types of violence shifted in part to such new felonies as carjacking, bombings, and gang murders. The number of murder victims under the age of 18 increased from 1,573 in 1985 to 2,428 in 1995, and the consequent rising fear was focused on the welfare of children. According to the Fordham Institute for Social Policy, which regularly tracks sixteen indicators of national well-being, their Index of Social Health fell from a 1973 peak of 74 points (out of a possible 100) to 40 in the late 1990s. However, homicides of persons aged 15 through 24 reached a peak in 1993 and then declined. At the annual meeting of the American Society of Criminologists in 1998, one member designated two probable causes: an abatement of the demand for crack cocaine and the many jobs available even to unskilled youth. Others emphasized police efforts, such as in New York City, to remove illegal guns from potential criminals.

Addictions

In the early years of the twentieth century "drug addiction" meant no more than the illicit use of "drugs," without any implication concerning patterns of usage or what drug was taken. In the early 1930s a distinction was made between "addiction," involving a physical dependence and a consequent compulsion to continue using drugs, and "habituation," involving a psychological attachment and no more than an emotional distress (rather than withdrawal symptoms) if the use was suspended. In 1965 the World Health Organization recommended a new term, "drug dependence," which it defined as "a state, psychic and sometimes also physical,...always includ[ing] a compulsion to take the drug...and sometimes to avoid the discomfort of its absence."[41]

Not only is there confusion among the terms denoting patterns of use, but what is meant by "drug" has been ambiguous. A distinction is made between heroin or cocaine, for instance, and the usual substances that a physician prescribes and a "drugstore" sells, but many substances may be classified as either. Alcohol or marijuana may be in or out of the category set by terms like "drug dependence"; sedatives and stimulants are usually not included. The confusion affects also what sectors of the population are defined as drug users. Black males have long been defined as a prominent proportion of addicts, particularly since the early 1980s, when crack cocaine (that is, cocaine that can be imbibed by smoking) was introduced.[42]

The recorded number of addicts who die from drug use may be understated. In an especially careful study in 1970, the authors compared the deaths reported to the chief medical examiner of Maryland over the years 1951-66 with the names listed in that state's drug-abuse register. There were 386 fatalities not assigned to drug abuse that in their view were in fact so caused; of these, almost 60 percent had been reported as suicides, 20 percent as accidents, and 20 percent as of unknown cause. One reason for the misclassification, it would seem, was the stereotype of a young male, often black, dying of heroin use. A slight majority of those whose deaths were misclassified were female; most were 40 years and over; a vast majority were white; and the typical drug used was a barbiturate.[43]

One of a series of books presenting opposing points of view on various social issues is on drug abuse.[44] The contributions suggest how little agreement there is among those involved with the matter: "Drug abuse is a serious problem" ("may be exaggerated"). "Increased heroin use is a serious problem" ("evidence is inconclusive"). "Cocaine abuse is a serious problem" ("is not"). "The war on drugs should be prosecuted more" ("should be abandoned"). "Random drug testing in the workplace is fair" ("unfair"). "Increased regulation of prescription drugs is necessary" ("unnecessary"). "Legalization would reduce the drug problem" ("would not"). And so on.

The number of active drug addicts in the United States as counted in federal, state, and local records has been compiled each year from 1956 by the U.S. Commission on Narcotic Drugs. From that base year to 1969, the reported number roughly doubled. Americans who reported using any illicit drug during the past year were estimated to have fallen from 16.3 percent in 1985 to 10.8 percent in 1993. This overall change in the exaggeratedly large population surveyed (Americans aged 12 years or more), however, masked a rising proportion of teenagers who reported that they had ever used an illicit drug. Even eighth-graders who said they had used any drug rose from 12.9 percent in 1992 to 23.6 percent in 1996. Though these statistics are probably not very precise, they do suggest that there has been a rise in Americans' use of drugs, and not merely marijuana, and that this epidemic has spread to school children.

Alcohol used in moderation is not only not harmful but beneficial, and alcoholism is notoriously difficult to define, either medically or legally. In 1862 Sir Francis Anstie in England set 12 ounces of absolute alcohol per day as the upper limit of safe drinking. This standard, still often used today in the United States as an overall guide, translates into four 8-ounce containers of beer, a half-bottle of wine, or three 1-ounce shots of 100-proof liquor. The best index of the prevalence of alcoholism, according to several authorities, is the number of deaths from associated ailments.[45] In 1995 there were 24,800 deaths from chronic liver disease or cirrhosis, and many of these were caused by the consumption of too much alcohol.

Prohibition radically changed Americans' attitudes toward excessive drinking; Edmund Wilson delightedly listed the 300 terms added to American English to denote various degrees of drunkenness.[46] Some of those who learned to drink during that period became alcoholics, but of course there are no statistics to indicate what proportion.

Future Medical Advances

From prehistory to the Middle Ages the human life span doubled, and then it remained almost static until the nineteenth century. The increase from roughly 18 to between 35 and 40 years was due mainly to the consolidation of large areas in which powerful states maintained effective social order. The second doubling, from about 35 to more than 70 years, can be ascribed to technical improvements in agriculture, medicine, and public health. Remarkably, the successful application of the most recent innovations in death control is almost completely independent of whether or not the affected societies are able to effect concomitant rises in social welfare. The determinants of mortality, in short, have been reduced more and more to the single decisive one, whether the fruits of modern Western science are available.

Demographic analysis has played a large part in improving our understanding of mortality. The key instrument has been to compare death rates or life expectancies of various social groups and infer from the differences the probable causes of mortality. From 1960 to 1990, for example, the advantage of whites over blacks, and of females over males, both remained almost constant at about seven years greater life expectancy at birth. Such gross contrasts, however, often raise more questions than they answer. Is the difference due to physiological differences between the races and the sexes, or to dissimilar lifestyles—or, to carry the analysis further, to variation in social support as measured by religious participation (among other factors), to degrees of stress in various occupations, or to contrasts in the availability and actual use of health-care facilities? One important path to a resolution of some of these puzzles is to break down mortality differences by cause of death. An important task for future demographic analysis, according to an interesting article, is to move beyond documentation of social-economic differences in measures of mortality and concentrate on developing and testing theories to explain these differences.[47]

A crucial example of recent medical progress is the rise of a concept, immunity, and its application to patients. A young child, the son of an Air Force officer, was admitted to Washington's Walter Reed Hospital nineteen times over four years, suffering from one serious infection after another. His blood was unable to produce gamma globulins, or antibodies, and the affliction stopped when this protein was regularly injected. In 1952, when Dr. Ogden C. Bruton published a paper on the case, it was the first reported instance of disease due to a defect in the body's immune system.[48] The concept of a body's ability to resist infection was subsequently expanded to power to combat anything that the body recognizes as alien, such as transplanted skin or organs or a substance that causes allergies or nonviral cancers. A further step is the manipulation of hereditary faults, so as to bring about, according to one account, "life without disease."[49]

An interesting book by Roy Porter, an English professor of medical history, sums up the past with the declaration that "the breakthroughs of the last fifty years have saved more lives than those of any epoch since medicine began."[50] Major elements of this transformation included new drugs developed in a "pharmacological revolution," new technology like CAT and PETT scans, heavy investment in research by both public and private sources, the elimination, as major threats to life, of such diseases as tuberculosis, tetanus, syphilis, rheumatic fever, pneumonia, meningitis, polio, and septicemia.

A National Roundtable on Health Care Quality, convened by the Institute of Medicine of the National Academy of Sciences, met six times in 1996-98 to discuss changes under way in American health care and the implications for its quality. Its conclusions were anything but an endorsement of the profession:

> Serious and widespread quality problems...may be classified as underuse, overuse, or misuse, occur in small and large communities alike, in all parts of the country, and with approximately equal frequency in managed care and fee-for-service systems of care. Very large numbers of Americans are harmed as a direct result.[51]

All the wonders of the recent past led Porter, similarly, to a rather pessimistic view of the near future. Overwhelming the unequivocal progress, in his opinion, are new problems. The populations of the West live longer, and this longevity in itself multiplies medical costs and quandaries. After a certain degree of senility has been reached, death may be not a fearful event but rather a release from a life no longer worth living:[52]

> William Osler [the author of America's first great textbook of medicine in 1892] was of two minds about pneumonia in the elderly. In the first of fourteen editions of *The Principles and Practice of Medicine*, he called it "the special enemy of old age," elsewhere . . . "the friend of the aged." Taken off by it in an acute, short, not often painful illness, the old escape those "cold gradations of decay."[53]

6

Health

As I noted in the last chapter, during the past several decades the apparently obvious meaning of "death" has become ambiguous. While physicians and lawyers were trying to cope with this—still unresolved—confusion, they were also seeking a more precise meaning of the term "health." In the past health had generally been understood as a correlate of the death rate or life expectation: a population in which fewer persons died was defined as healthier. And this definition, of course, has not altogether disappeared. When the U.S. surgeon general began *Healthy People*, his 1979 report, with the assertion, "The health of the American people has never been better," the principal evidence he offered was a decline in mortality. Not surprisingly, this meaning is found also in the word's etymology. The Old English word for "whole" generated a number of words related to physical well-being: "hale," "heal," "wholesome," and "health."[1]

As mortality declined in the modern era, however, the notion that every live person is "healthy" became more and more unsatisfactory.[2] Some diseases are disabling without affecting the death rate significantly. One important medical advance after another kept patients alive but with a weakened constitution, perhaps "healthy," perhaps not. Moreover, morbidity data in records collected from doctors and hospitals depend, of course, on the existence of those persons and institutions, so that the more medical facilities are available, the lower in general would be the indicated level of health.

A supposed route out of the quandary was suggested by the World Health Organization, which took as its long-term objective the universal establishment of "positive health," which it defined as "a state of complete physical, mental, and social well-being, and not merely as the absence of disease or infirmity." Such a utopian goal, it needs no stressing, hardly relates to actual problems in the real world. Nor is it satisfactory to identify health as what biologists call "Darwinian fitness," or a successful adaptation to a particular environment. For instance, sickle-cell anemia sometimes develops in populations living near mosquito-breeding areas, where it provides a partial protection against malaria; but that does not warrant our labeling this local adaptation, when it persists in another habitat, an indication of general good health.

Although "healthy" is commonly used in both an instrumental and a descriptive sense, it is useful to retain the differentiation between an "unhealthful food," habit, or environment and the higher proportion of "unhealthy" persons that may be the result. Some dictionaries have not helped in establishing the distinction, which was assigned to the two terms only in the 1880s and can still be dismissed by citing references from "distinguished speakers and writers of English."[3] The point rather is that the differentiation is useful, and ignoring it can muddle a discussion.

Varieties of Sickness and Therapies

If "health" were to be understood as the opposite of "sickness," one must reckon with the fact that the latter term also has no precise definition. If one surveys what various primitive peoples have considered to be an ailment or, within larger societies, how disease has been defined in various ethnic groups or at successive times, it becomes evident that the concept varies along several dimensions. Among food-gathering bands sickness and immunity are typically interpreted as the acts of, respectively, hostile and protective spirits.[4] Supposed cures are based mainly on magic of diverse kinds, including scarification, massage, and the application or ingestion of (sometimes possibly effective) plant substances.

After the Second World War, as colonies successively attained their independence, whatever progress had been realized in health care often came to be seen as one more characteristic of the former imperialist culture, which, like all other such intrusions, had to be subordinated to its native counterpart. Now a bibliography on folk medicine can be titled *Resources for Third World Health Planners*.[5] According to a

World Health Organization report, "African traditional medicine is one of the pillars of the cultural heritage of the Region....An integration of the two systems (traditional and Western), without compromise of principle yet with full understanding on both sides, should enable the sorely underprivileged population to benefit from one of the fundamental human rights: the right to health."[6] "South Africa to bring traditional healers into mainstream medicine," according to an article in the English medical journal *Lancet*.[7]

Similarly, India has its followers of Ayurveda, a work of one hundred chapters, each of one hundred stanzas, that was handed down to mankind by Brahma, creator of the universe. From its origin around 4000 B.C., the exegeses that have accumulated include, as a striking example, hymns to cure specified diseases. One of the more recent ingredients, homeopathy, was added in the mid-nineteenth century by a German practitioner.[8] After India acquired independence, a movement was started to foster Shuddha (that is, pure) Ayurveda, purged of alien influences and essentially hostile to Western science. The consequent mixture of the two traditions, one can reasonably contend, has not been in the best interest of India's people.

Chinese medicine in its traditional form comprises such elements as a variety of herbs, acupuncture, and moxa (a mass of wormwood leaves burnt on the skin as a cautery). According to Chinese accounts, this mode of therapy dates from the third millennium B.C., reaching a kind of apex in codification during the Han dynasty (206 B.C.-A.D. 220). In the words of an early Western authority, it consists of "a far-reaching and interlocking relationship of the practices of medicine with superstition and religious practices, magic, divination, sorcery, astrology, alchemy, palmistry, geomancy, physiognomy, necromancy, spiritism, demonology, fortune telling, etc."[9]

The Chinese Communist regime has subsidized native treatments in various ways, partly out of nationalist pride, partly as an accommodation to what is reportedly the masses' preference, and partly as an expedient by which "barefoot doctors" could be put in the field after only six months of training. A strange amalgam of traditional and Western medicine is reflected in a 1,200-page compendium titled *Peasant Village Physician's Handbook*.[10]

Chinese medicine has spread to a sizable number of practitioners in the West, especially in France but also in the United States. A good example of Americans' fascination with this exotic treatment is given in an article on herbs. It begins with an account of Misha Cohen of San Francisco, an "Oriental Medical Doctor," whose patients were cured after "Western medicine" had failed them. Of the 5,767 different substances used, most are first treated in various ways--fried, dipped in honey, boiled, or baked. Green tea has "some anticancer properties" (a claim that has been validated). Zheng Gu Sui "relieves pain from bruises, fractures, sprains, and torn ligaments."[11] When consumers of China's medical lore swallow not only possible therapies but patent nonsense, is it as with Chinese peasants, because of their ignorance, or rather because their bounteous education has inculcated a preference for progressive views? It may be partly because of this link to radical politics, but certainly also because it fits in with a broader trend toward what is termed holistic medicine.

In a work appropriately titled *The Complete Medicinal Herbal*, the range is extraordinarily wide, beginning with Galen's four humors (blood, phlegm, black bile, and yellow bile) and Hippocrates's four qualities (hot, cold, dry, and damp), going through India's Ayurveda and China's Yin, Yang, and Qi (energy), before touching on medieval Europe's use of urine as a medicine. These introductory remarks set a pattern throughout the book, in accordance with the book's premise that ancient medicine is the basis of modern practice.[12]

The body of the book consists of a list (alphabetical by the Latin names) of plants and their supposed uses. Take the various species of the rose as an example. The Chinese, we are informed, use both rosehips and flowers to stimulate Qi. The French essential oil is known as an aphrodisiac. The Bulgarian type, on the other hand, can combat depression and anxiety, as well as problems with the skin or digestion.[13] Perhaps the most interesting item is an "Important Notice" in the introductory section: "Neither the author nor the publishers can be held responsible for claims arising from...the inappropriate use of any remedy....Always seek medical advice if symptoms persist."

It is a token of the widespread multicultural tolerance that standard medical institutions have at least partly accepted some varieties of alternative medicine. In the United States, medical schools teach it, hospitals and HMOs offer it, some states require health plans to cover it. A more combative stance would begin with an appropriate definition of "alternative medicine": namely, therapies that are not tested, as required by the Food and Drug Administration, to demonstrate their safety and efficacy, but rely instead on anecdotes and venerable theories:

In 1992, Congress established...an Office of Alternative Medicine to evaluate alternative remedies....Of the 30 research grants the office awarded in 1993, 28 have resulted in "final reports" . . . [but] only 9 in published papers. Five [of these] were in two journals not included among the 3,500 journal titles in the Countway Library of Medicine's collection. Of the other four studies, none was a controlled clinical trial that would allow any conclusions to be drawn about efficacy.[14]

Medicines of the nineteenth century, the efficacy of which was judged mainly on the basis of anecdotes, have given way to today's fantastically efficient pharmacopoeia, certified by randomized, controlled clinical trials that measure their effectiveness and safety. That with no such scientific foundation the alternatives to this stockpile of successful medicaments are achieving popular acceptance is incomprehensible. On the other hand, it may well be that some traditional therapies are efficacious and safe; the obvious resolution of the dilemma is to subject them to the same procedures that are used to test Western medicines.

A twelve-member panel representing various types of relevant expertise undertook to provide a responsible assessment of acupuncture. The conclusion was that the procedure is effective in adult postoperative and chemotherapy nausea and in postoperative dental pain, and that it may be useful as an adjunct or even alternative treatment of a list of specific ailments. In short, "there is sufficient evidence of acupuncture's value to expand its use into conventional medicine and to encourage further studies of its physiology and clinical value."[15]

In the last years of the nineteenth century D. D. Palmer, a grocer in Davenport, Iowa, developed chiropractic as a school of therapy, and his son successfully promoted it. According to its main thesis, virtually all illness results from "subluxations," or slight dislocations of the spinal column, and thus originally all treatment consisted of the manipulation of this part of the body. Since 1974 chiropractors have been licensed in all states, and this partial respectability has spread. The opposition of the American Medical Association to what it once termed an "unscientific cult" ended in 1987, when five chiropractors won a suit charging the AMA with restraint of trade. In 1994, a federal health agency, after reviewing 4,000 studies of low back pain, concluded that spinal manipulation can provide temporary relief. A research team at the University of Washington compared the effects of this treatment with those of exercises recommended by physical therapists, with inconclusive results. Low back pain is a very common complaint, and a publication of the Harvard Medical School, after reviewing this record, offered a somewhat equivocal and limited recommendation.[16]

Some ethnic minorities in the United States have their own medical beliefs. According to a survey in a Texas town, five illnesses there were confined to Mexican Americans: *caída de la mollera* (fallen fontanel, or the displacement of the top of an infant's cranium), *empacho* (blockage of food in the intestinal tract), *mal ojo* (evil eye), *susto* (shock, which is treated with blessed water on which herbs and palm leaves are floating), and *mal puesto* (sorcery).[17]

The sizable body of writings on nostrums to treat such ailments generally at least implies a contrast with the informed and rational middle classes of the modern West. If there are general accounts of the comparable superstitions of intellectuals, supposedly the best informed sector of the middle class, they have escaped my search for them. Consider the coterie around Wilhelm Reich, who held that the universe is permeated by a primal, mass-free "orgone energy." When humans fail to liberate this energy through a sexual release, the consequence may be not only individual neuroses but social disorder. Because of his "proletarian sexual politics," Reich was in effect expelled from both the International Psychoanalytic Association and the German Communist Party. In the mid-1930s rumors circulated among psychoanalysts that he was mad, and from the details in the generally favorable biography by his widow, the allegations were well based. Articles opposing his opinions, in his view, were part of a Moscow-directed plot. When U.S. federal prosecutors charged him with fraud for selling the so-called orgone boxes that he had invented, the reason, he averred, was that Communist infiltrators in the Food and Drug Administration were conspiring against him. Diagnosed as paranoid, he died in prison--of heart failure aggravated by his refusal to accept treatment from physicians who he believed were also trying to kill him.[18] The Reich cult was never large, but it included both some distinguished psychiatrists and such prototypical intellectuals as Paul Goodman, Norman Mailer, William Steig, and Herbert Marcuse.

Following the development of the atomic bomb, a number of intellectuals trailed after the *Bulletin of the Atomic Scientists* in condemning not only that weapon but nuclear power and, in some instances, even diagnostic tests that involved X-rays. In Boulder, when I was on the faculty of the University of Colorado, a dentist refused to accept me as a new patient until I had signed a statement giving him the right to

X-ray my teeth! He had had so much trouble with some of my colleagues, especially those in the humanities and social disciplines, that he decided to weed out in advance any prospective patients who would not accept his professional guidance.

One is what One Eats

As recently as a generation ago, a physician trained in the best American medical schools received virtually no training in nutrition. The word *vitamin* entered our vocabulary only in 1912, when the first one, thiamin or B_1, was isolated; and over the following decades knowledge gradually accumulated about how the other twelve vitamins, various minerals, and the most recently identified phytochemicals contribute to our health. A special board of the National Academy of Sciences devised a Recommended Dietary Allowance, listing the amounts of nutrients that healthy persons, classified by sex and height, should consume daily. Its figures are updated every five to ten years.

The wide dissemination of a typically half-realized nutritional science has brought about an almost chaotic confusion. Advice from medical and commercial sources urges everyone to eat so and so much (with amounts constantly revised) of each food class, and a flourishing business has developed to provide supplementary pills for those who fail to maintain the currently prescribed diet. Most nutritionists hold that, if one eats "properly," these are unnecessary, and all agree that ingesting too large quantities can be dangerous. In 1994 Congress passed a "pill bill," which empowers the Food and Drug Administration to bar health claims on the labels of nutritional supplements and herbal products unless they have been approved by reputable scientific bodies.

With the rapid development of this field of knowledge, a new vocabulary was introduced to the populace. Many in the general public know that they should distinguish HDL ("good" cholesterol) from LDL ("bad" cholesterol)[19]; they have a picture of the food-guide pyramid in their minds. Not only do many cookbooks now include information on such matters, but publishers have found it profitable to offer the general reader a *Nutrition Bible* or a *Wellness Encyclopedia*, among a number of similar competitors.[20] There are shelffuls of books that, though often written by physicians, might strike the layman as more than a bit dubious. Dr. Ronald Klatz, president of an "American Academy of

Anti-Aging Medicine," tells us how to *Grow Young with HGH* (human growth hormone).[21] The book has the characteristics of both a research-based report and a con man's spiel, and a cautious reader might well vacillate between enthusiasm and mistrust.

The tendency to overeat has many of the characteristics of what is ordinarily defined as an addiction. A distinction is made between "overweight," which means an excess of body weight consisting of muscle, bone, and fat, and "obesity," which means an excess accumulation of body fat. A well-muscled athlete might be overweight but not obese, but in general the two go together. Either condition is difficult to gauge accurately, and the usual approximate measure is the body mass index, defined as the weight in kilograms divided by the square of the height in meters.

According to data based on a physical examination of samples of the civilian population, the proportion of Americans aged 20 to 74 who were graded as overweight rose from a quarter in 1976-80 to a third in 1988-91. More females than males are overweight, and among black and Hispanic women the proportion is a full half. The condition is a significant factor in a number of ailments; nearly 70 percent of cardiovascular disease are caused in part by obesity.

That at least has been the consensus until recently. But in its January 1998 issue the *New England Journal of Medicine* published an article titled "Losing Weight—An Ill-Fated New Year's Resolution." According to the editors of that highly respected professional journal, "the cure for obesity may be worse than the condition." Worry about overweight has been exaggerated, the article stated, and in any case efforts to lose weight are generally futile. Five months later, the government issued new guidelines that lowered the threshold the agency defined as "overweight," so that some 30 million more Americans were so labeled. In one attempt to resolve the difference, the editors of *Consumer Reports* gave both sides points:

> Obese people, with a BMI [body mass index] of 30 or more, clearly need to lose weight. So do those with lots of belly fat, regardless of their BMI. There's no definitive proof that losing weight helps people who are only moderately overweight, with a BMI of 25 to 30,...[but] virtually all moderately heavy people should at least consider losing weight.[22]

Food fads common in the United States differ in both type and range. Only the well-to-do can afford some of the more esoteric diets.

Weight-reducing regimens include sometimes dangerous appetite-reducing pills or other outlandish means of slimming. The penchant for "natural" or "organic" food is often symptomatic of a much more expansive yearning for a pseudosimple life. Michael Fumento, a qualified and respected popularizer of scientific data, wrote a book called *Science under Siege*, a detailed account of several case studies of calamities that had been fabricated by various categories of zealots:

> We pump death-dealing chemicals into our water, air, food, and soil. Our personal computers are as deadly as they are useful. The very energy that makes modern man's life so much easier than that of previous generations...is pumping cancer into the bodies of his children.[23]

It is a commonplace of journalism that manufacturers have a vested interest in pronouncing their products to be safe. Fumento makes the point that the self-anointed defenders of "the public interest" derive their money and power from publicizing highly sensational charges. Neither side has a monopoly on the truth.

Dimensions of Wellness

If we think of whatever today's physicians treat as a "disease," there is hardly any limit to the concept. Not merely mental illness but depression and even moodiness are conquered with pills.[24] Surgeons treat not only broken bones and ailing tissues but also ugliness and aging.[25] Not only obesity but any deviation from the prescribed weight is a medical condition. Peering into the future, one wonders whether there is any attribute of humans that, if it deviates from a sometimes arbitrary norm, will not be defined as an ailment:

> The fundamental problem stems from uncertainty about the limits of our health potential. How long a life can we live?...How much pain and suffering can and should we be ready to endure?...How much fitness do we require?...We have defined our unlimited hopes to transcend our mortality as our needs, and we have created a medical enterprise that engineers the transformation.[26]

The theme of a recent book, *The Therapeutic State*, is that government agencies try to gain support for their programs by emphasizing their healing function. Courts accept emotional stress as a basis for tort claims. The directors of educational or welfare programs use psychological criteria as a measure of their success. President Clinton's most often repeated appeal to the public may well be "I feel your pain." According to the book's thesis, therapy has become the dominant concept to define the duties that in the United States those who govern owe the governed.[27]

A telling symptom of this expansion of medical functions is the resurrection of a word, "wellness," to mean "good physical and mental health, especially when maintained by proper diet, exercise, and habits;...fitness and emotional well-being." Though recorded as early as 1654, it had never been accepted as fully as its antonym, "illness." That 68 percent of the so-called Usage Panel of the *American Heritage Dictionary* found the word unacceptable in its ordinary modern sense may suggest less a lexical decision than a distaste for the movement associated with the term.[28]

A more significant indicator of both current interest and a prospective future is the rise of a new discipline called biodemography, together with the application of its methods and concepts to the puzzles of aging. In a recent book, *Between Zeus and the Salmon: The Biodemography of Longevity*, the range set in the title is between an immortal god and a fish that dies shortly after it reproduces. Members of all species proceed to senescence before they die, and with the notable increases in human longevity scientists in a half-dozen fields have studied the problem of what in the genetic structure sets this pattern. In what has been called the biology of the life table, one finds fascinating nuggets of information: after age 85 the probability of dying within the next year decreases progressively; menopause, a routine biological event in human females, is seldom encountered by creatures in the wild, where survival beyond the reproductive years is exceptional.[29]

On the Reconceptualization of Pain

The understanding of pain, by both doctors and the lay public, used to be that it is a symptom of ill health, and this is probably still the typical perception. A widely used reference work restricts its description to this function: "the excessive stimulation of nerve endings during pain is attributed to tissue damage, and in this sense pain has protective value, serving as a danger signal of disease."[30] However, it was never considered to be merely a warning to patient and physician that something was amiss; severe internal lesions may lack entirely any accompanying subjective distress, and such normal processes as teething, menstruation, and childbirth can be quite painful.

Some years ago, when I was trying to add to demographers' slight understanding of how American couples decide whether or not to have another child, I suggested to a doctor with whom I was acquainted that one factor might be how much pain the woman had experienced during the birth of a prior child. I got a short lecture on what were even then medical axioms—that pain is largely subjective, and that in any case it cannot be reliably measured. My tentative project never got off the ground.

The expanded definition of pain is reflected in a comment by Allan I. Basbaum, professor of anatomy and physiology at the University of California, San Francisco:

> Pain is not just a stimulus that is transmitted over specific pathways but rather a complex perception, the nature of which depends not only on the intensity of the stimulus but on the situation in which it is experienced and, most importantly, on the affective or emotional state of the individual.[31]

Around 1960 the new way of conceptualizing pain evolved into an unprecedented institution, the pain clinic, where pain is seen as a malady to be treated, having been almost wholly transformed from symptom to ailment. Some specialists in its treatment developed a new theory: what they termed "benign chronic intractable pain syndrome" may be initiated by an injury anywhere in the body, but its persistence is due not to "peripheral" but rather "central" (that is, in the brain) disturbances.[32] This view, calling for a complete change in therapy, has not been accepted by the whole profession.

Where is Medicine Headed?

One point made in this chapter is that several of the concepts used in medicine are far less precise than laymen or even many physicians had supposed. That "health" and "sickness" are understood differently in various cultures and subcultures may mean that sometimes "therapy" must also adapt to specific human environments, and that mind-body relations may be far more significant than traditional Western medicine

The momentous improvement in all branches of medicine over the past half-century led a number of knowledgeable writers to forecast an imminent conquest of all disease. In 1996 life expectation in the United

States rose to new and record heights: total population, 75.9 years; males, 72.8 years; and females, 79.0 years.[33] Yet the optimism that such figures would once have engendered has largely vanished, for two reasons. As threats to life are successively conquered, the appetite for a still longer and less burdened span grows. The extension of life's span has resulted in higher proportions of old people, who, as they approach their demise, greatly raise the incidence of heart disease and cancer. Moreover, ailments once thought to have been conquered have reappeared in force (for example, tuberculosis[34]), and brand new diseases have emerged (for example, AIDS[35]). In what one must assume is an ironic piece, one author suggested that AIDS has become a way of controlling population growth.[36]

Of new medical treatments the most promising would seem to be gene therapy. The ability of a bacterium or virus to evolve very rapidly and thus to evade the human body's immune system can be countered, if geneticists are correct, by a corresponding adjustment of that immunity. This vision, if it is realized, is both awesome and, to many commentators, frightening. In one work after another, we are warned that man must not attempt to play God. An English journalist recalled the title of the dystopia that Aldous Huxley described with an account of the genetic future titled *Brave New Worlds*.[37] Has any significant advance in human welfare been realized without a chorus of Cassandras?

In a book written jointly by a biologist and a moral philosopher, the point is made that the breeding of animals or the artificial pollination of plants is essentially a cruder kind of engineering, which with little or no opposition from anyone has resulted in innumerable benefits to mankind. This introductory remark is followed by the biologist's straightforward description of techniques and the philosopher's convoluted commentary on "morals" and "ethics," "extrinsic" and "intrinsic" concerns, "natural" and "unnatural." The contrast between science and philosophy is striking: the first offers facts, the second mainly questions.[38]

Early in the next century, when the Human Genome Project will have recorded all the information stored in human DNA, which of the fantastic possibilities that journalists now imagine will then be realized? Trying to look into the future reminds one of the Chinese curse: "May you live in interesting times!"

7

Prehistoric and Primitive Populations

Analysts of present-day populations of developed countries—as if alluding to a sort of base reference—occasionally discuss the way that population grows in primitive societies and, by inference, also in prehistoric times. Whether this link between prehistoric and primitive is legitimate has been a controversial topic.

When early investigators described contemporary tribes as "living fossils," their conclusions were sometimes denounced as racist. Some of those who work back from the present as a guide to research on man's forebears have changed the term "ethnographic analogy" to "ethnoarchaeology," which at least temporarily may satisfy the demands of political correctness.

The data at the base of archaeology are so thin and tenuous that to someone outside the discipline it seems overmeticulous to object to a careful extrapolation from present-day primitive to past prehistoric populations, and there are indications that this view is gaining support. Of the more than twenty volumes that emerged from the World Archaeological Congress in 1986, one pertains to the "conflict in the archaeology of living traditions." Many of the papers describe the contentions in the United States or Australia over whether it should be permitted to exhumed the bones of ancient natives, but a few others discussed how it might be possible to synchronize data on prehistoric with those on living primitives. For example, a Canadian proposed that archaeological findings on the Eskimos might be coordinated with their own oral "history," for "evidence about the past need not limit perception and interpretation of the evidence to material analogies."[1]

Beginning in the 1960s the American archaeologist Lewis Binford started a movement toward what is called "processual archaeology." As one important reform, he recommended that his colleagues should abandon the more or less random search of sites and substitute for it research based on general principles, which could be tested against empirical data. In order to understand the relation between material artifacts and the general culture, for instance, he thought it important to study present-day hunter-gatherer societies in detail, seeking clues on how tools, weapons, or animal foods reveal the way people behave.[2] A paleontologist came to the same conclusion on how to upgrade his perception of fossils: namely, to improve his understanding of prehistoric plants and animals by closely observing particular habitats: both the ecology and the organism's manner of coping with it should be as close as possible to the fossil's.[3] When Binford gave a series of lectures in Britain and Scandinavia, he found that many of his colleagues there were indifferent to the ethnographic literature on contemporary hunting-gathering societies. He regarded his lectures, thus, as "a kind of missionary work, pointing to some of the interesting problems of inferential method that arise in dealing with hunters and gatherers."[4]

How Reliable are Data on Primitives?

In an analysis of population, however, stretching the plausibility by using ethnographic analogy does not carry one very far, for typically the record of present-day primitives lacks solid demographic statistics and analyses. In my undoubtedly prejudiced opinion as a demographer, an anthropologist's field work could not begin in a more fruitful fashion than by conducting a census. With counts of the two sexes, the several main age groups, the families, the number of persons with specific social, economic, and cultural traits, the analyst would have a map to guide him to whatever topic he desires, with many of the links and patterns already suggested. Yet until recently, apart from some works in such adjacent fields as physical anthropology and human genetics, most anthropologists have found the study of population an unfamiliar and treacherous field. From the body of information accumulated, we know more about primitives' kin structure than about their family size, more about beliefs in the afterworld than about life expectancy.

Moreover, how much faith is warranted in accounts by strangers from a totally alien culture, trying to make sense of exotic and bizarre customs, not to say numerical data? Robert Schmitt, at the time State Statistician of Hawaii, wrote a devastating résumé of the garbled population estimates of Central Polynesia, which typify numerous reports about how many persons are to be found in primitive societies. He began his essay by citing the statement of one authority that when Captain James Cook discovered Tahiti in 1769, he estimated its population at 240,000 souls. "Yet Wallis, not Cook, discovered Tahiti; Cook made his estimate in 1774, not 1769; and his figure was 204,000, not 240,000."

> The original estimates of the population of Central Polynesia by early visitors are...inconsistent, unrealistic, and misleading. It is thus doubly regrettable that they should be made more so by subsequent mistranslation, incorrect ascription, and misinterpretation.[5]

The lacks in ethnography, moreover, are not limited to travelers' accounts from a century or more ago, or to the uses that subsequent scholars made of their sometimes haphazard notations. Most works on primitive peoples are written by a single investigator and then accepted without any on-the-spot check by another ethnographer. A famous exception to this norm, a personal review by another anthropologist of a classic work, is suggestive.

Margaret Mead's 1928 book on Samoa is possibly the most influential exposition in American anthropology.[6] It was systematically reviewed by Derek Freeman, an anthropologist who spent years in Samoa, spoke the language fluently, was adopted into a Samoan family. In two devastating books, the first based on interviews with some of Mead's informants and the second on a detailed analysis of Mead's notes and diary as preserved in various archives, Freeman analyzed in detail how this work came to be written.[7] As Mead's defenders discovered, however reluctantly, a contrast between the two authors leaves her in an embarrassing position.

Coming of Age in Samoa was written by a 23-year-old doctoral candidate. At Barnard College Margaret Mead took an undergraduate course from Franz Boas, whom she described as "the greatest mind she had ever encountered." With a background of only two semesters of undergraduate anthropology, he accepted Mead as a doctoral student. She became one of his most gifted disciples, who in the 1920s included most of the discipline's major figures.

Mead intended to do her dissertation on American Indians, but under Boas's direction she had to shift to Polynesia. Also under his guidance, she set her proposed research "to throw light on the problem of which phenomena of adolescence are culturally and which physiologically determined." Before she arrived in Pago Pago, her father arranged for a supportive reception by the heads of the U.S. naval detachment who were in charge of the island. She lived in a comfortable room in a hotel and for a period took beginning lessons in Samoan from a naval nurse. She began her research on male tattooing, which reflected her own interest rather than the topic that Boas had assigned her. For data on adolescent behavior, she decided the best locale was several of the minor islands. There she lived mainly with the only American family on Ta'u, for she regarded boiled taro, the Samoan staple, as "so much putty-tasting, soap-textured grey matter." Her communication with Samoans was principally through a young woman who, as she put it, "spoke a little English." Her principal informants were 25 girls, aged 14 to 20. Among Samoans, she was told, premarital sex was a "pastime par excellence," girls deferred marriage "through as many years of casual lovemaking as possible." Mead ignored the facts that most of the people were primly Christian and that the brothers of young girls took seriously their duty to protect them from sexual encounters. Her book includes mind-boggling contradictions: that, for example, in a society that placed enormous value on a bride's virginity, premarital sex among adolescents was not only permitted but expected. Such disparities, in her view, represented nothing more than a widespread hypocrisy embedded in the culture. Freeman's well-documented explanation is quite different:

> In Samoa...it is not acceptable in ordinary conversation to discuss sexual matters publicly... [Mead's informants] blandly agreed with all she had suggested to them, telling her with due embellishment that they, like other young women and adolescent girls, regularly spent their nights with members of the opposite sex. In so doing, they were...engaging in...recreational lying,...a custom that is very much a part of Samoan culture.[8]

As a conclusion from this research, Mead saw her work as an empirical proof of the theory that her faculty sponsor, Franz Boas, had proposed as a deduction from his cardinal theoretical contribution, that cultural rather than biological inheritance is decisive in determining the characteristics of human societies.

If it is proved [Mead wrote] that adolescence is not necessarily a specially difficult period in a girl's life--and proved it is if we can find any society in which that is so--then what accounts for the presence of storm and stress in American adolescents? First, we may say quite simply that there must be something in the two civilizations to account for the difference. If the same process takes a different form in the two different environments, we cannot make any explanation in terms of the process, for that is the same in both cases.[9]

Mead's predisposition to document preconceived notions about Samoa was reinforced by her slipshod field work. In the introduction to *Coming of Age*, she announced her conviction that a trained Western student can "master the fundamental structure of a primitive society in a few months." By Freeman's calculation, her field work lasted for twenty-one weeks, of which she spent seven on other issues that interested her more than her assigned doctoral topic. She had two bouts of tonsillitis, during which she was confined to her bed, and her interviews with adolescents were interrupted by a hurricane. It was mainly during a period of four weeks, by Freeman's reconstruction of her field work, that she collected information on individual girls.

In his foreword to the book that Mead wrote from her field notes, Boas commended her "painstaking investigation." In the endless scholarly debate on nature versus nurture, Mead's work seemingly confirmed his strong opinion that cultural environment was in all cases far more influential than biology in determining human behavior.

How Many Food-Gatherers?

In most discussions of modern populations, the analyst passes over the most basic question: what entity is being measured. Those residing in a national state or one of its subdivisions is its "population," and complications in defining the concept need not be considered. As a telling example of the difficulties encountered by both archaeologists and ethnographers, consider the estimated number of aborigines of the Western Hemisphere.

What was the pre-Columbian population of the Americas? Estimates rose prodigiously from A. L. Kroeber's 8.4 million in 1939, to Ángel Rosenblatt's 13.4 million in 1945, to Henry F. Dobyns's 90-112 million in 1966.[10] And these three prominent instances are a small portion of the range cited in a work by Russell Thornton, the most thorough exposition on the subject.[11] Obviously the basic data are poor enough to allow very much latitude in interpretation.

The not very legible record, moreover, was recently made more confusing by supposed evidence that the New World was first inhabited not about 12,000 years ago, as has been the orthodox view, but something like 40,000 years ago. These very first Americans derived, some researchers now believe, from four lineages, whose prior homelands were very loosely located in Eurasia, Siberia generally, the Baikal region of Siberia, and the east Asian coast.[12]

All estimates of prehistoric populations start from some relatively recent date and work back through accounts of massacres, epidemics, and other causes of extraordinary mortality to a presumed pre-contact number. Of the causes of population losses, violence and hardships are generally interpreted to have been far less significant than various infectious diseases, which would have been deadly among a people that had not developed a relative immunity to them. In some instances yet more important was the disappearance not through death but through race mixture and reclassification. Throughout Latin America persons of mixed white-Indian-Negro antecedents comprise so large and complex a sector of the population that eventually the early efforts of most of the region's countries to assign a separate label to each combination were abandoned. Data based on so flimsy a classification hardly facilitate an attempt to reconstruct pre-Columbian numbers.

According to Thornton's estimate, the number of inhabitants of the Western Hemisphere, 72+ million in 1492, declined over several centuries to about 4 to 4.5 million. Europeans brought smallpox, measles, the bubonic plague, cholera, typhoid, pleurisy, mumps, whooping cough, colds, the venereal diseases gonorrhea and chancroid, pneumonia and some other respiratory diseases, quite probably typhus and venereal syphilis, and only remotely possibly, tuberculosis. From Africa came the arthropod-borne diseases malaria and yellow fever and, some say, probably dysentery.[13]

According to an 1894 guess by census officials, before the founding of the United States more than 5,000 whites and more than 8,500 Indians died in warfare.[14] Many Indians died also from the trauma of mass removal and the arbitrary attacks by whites that Thornton labels "genocide," as well as from the destruction of much of the underpinning of their way of life.

The difficulties in estimating the current aboriginal population of the Americas can be exemplified by the various definitions of "Indian" in the United States.[15] As I have noted, even in federal law there is no single definition of an Indian.[16] Each legal definition—enrollment in a tribe, tribal membership, adoption (e.g., of a wholly white person)—has its own background of legislation and court decisions, which varies also from tribe to tribe. Especially after the number of mixed-race Indians grew, the definition based on race was amended: "Indians were defined as those who lived in tribal relations with other Indians."[17]

It is often not only convenient but possible for a single individual, depending on the context, both to be and not to be an Indian. According to a report in the *New York Times* (21 March 1976), a presumably authentic Mohawk commented that one consequence of federal aid programs had been a large-scale production of "instant Indians." This offhand remark was spelled out in elaborate detail in a book edited by an American anthropologist, James Clifton, with the appropriate title *The Invented Indian*.[18]

In 1850, for the first time, the federal statistical agency tried to include all Indians in its decennial enumeration; but it was not until 1890 that a serious, and still only partially successful, count was attempted.[19] Subsequently the numbers rose and fell erratically, as though there were a series of catastrophes and rapid recoveries. In 1910 a special effort was made to include everyone who might be classified as Indian, for it was anticipated that the small minority would disappear into the general population and that, therefore, the census in that year was a last chance to make a full count. The consequence, according to the Bureau's own account, was probably an "enumeration as Indian of a considerable number of persons who would have been reported as white in earlier censuses."[20] Similarly, the Bureau warned those using the 1990 enumeration to do so "with caution," for, among other reasons, "8 percent of the 1.8 million people who identified themselves as American Indians then said they belonged to these tribes: Haitian, Polish, African American, Hispanic, or Arab."[21] More money is spent per Indian enumerated, one can assume, than in counting any other sector of the American population, for there has been a more elaborate procedure in defining, counting, collating, and printing the data. Yet the statistics are so ill based they are virtually worthless. And it is from this base that estimates of the pre-Columbian population of the United States area are mainly derived.

Prehistoric Populations

Estimating prehistoric populations presents a different set of dilemmas, of which one of the most important is timing. The first system of dating was simple: a stratum of rock laid down on top of another was defined as later in time. This method afforded no more than relative dating, and fixing absolute times to each of the periods set by stratigraphy has been central to archaeology's development as a discipline. The first technique, based on the fact that each year trees grow by a different amount, depends on counting and measuring the resultant rings observable on a crosscut.

Willard F. Libby (1908-80), an American chemist who had worked on the project that developed the atomic bomb, subsequently devised radiocarbon dating. Every organic substance produces C_{14} (carbon-14), an isotope of carbon that gradually decays and is dispersed into the atmosphere. After years of calculating, Libby concluded that it takes 5,568 years for half of the C_{14} in any sample to decay. Having established this invariable half-life, he offered archaeologists a technique for calculating the absolute date of any artifact derived from plants or animals. This became the standard tool in the discipline, and in 1960 Libby won the Nobel Prize in chemistry for his radiocarbon research.[22]

After the initial euphoria, some serious faults were found with radiocarbon dating. Most of the subsequent corrections pushed back the specified times considerably, so that both the origins of mankind in eastern Africa and many of the later developments were dated earlier than originally supposed. According to one account, "archaeologists can now get absolute dates for pottery manufacture, the use of hearths, the making of obsidian tools, and even the production of rock art. The adequate dating of materials is now scarcely ever an insuperable problem."[23]

Because time and money are typically not sufficient to enable an archaeologist to investigate a whole site, a dig very often includes only a portion, and generalizations from the known segment to the whole necessarily results in some slippage. Were all the houses inhabited at the same time, or do they represent a number of successive generations? In Central Mexico, for example, "sites may represent those segments of a living community which have been abandoned during normal community operations."[24] Dwellings occupied seriatim may well have been constructed over perhaps a few decades, too short a period to be distinguished by any dating technique.

In the 1950s the manner of selection began to be set according to the same sampling and statistical methods used in, among other disciplines, demography. From this new start it was a short step to using computers to simulate models. For example, the subsistence economy of the Shoshone Indians as depicted in ethnographic writings was converted into a computer program, and when the food intake was varied, the model deduced the consequent behavior patterns. These predictions were then tested against the data from the dig, with a 75 percent concurrence.[25] The procedure, apart from technology, was what Binford had recommended.

In attempts to derive population figures from building sites, it has been estimated that each person in a primitive society requires from 10 to 12 square meters of living space. But among thirteen American tribes, the floor area assumed to contain a single nuclear family ranged between 119.5 and 322 square feet,[26] or about 5.8 to 29.9 square meters. Other analysts have tried to guess the size of a household from the capacity of cooking jars, from skeletal remains, even from animal bones in garbage heaps.[27] It is as though a modern demographer attempted to eke out some numerical data from an investigation of the kitchens, cemeteries, and dumps of present-day societies.

One of the more interesting innovations in the investigation of prehistoric populations is to reconstruct them by using a genetic analysis. With such techniques, the American anthropologist Henry Harpending concluded that the diverse forebears of present human groups increased substantially some 50,000 years ago.[28] Using several unlinked genetic markers, two researchers devised two new statistical tests of population growth and applied them to prehistoric Africa.[29]

An alternative tool used by some archaeologists is a site's carrying capacity, or the maximum number of people who can be supported indefinitely from a given environment. As a simple ratio, the concept implies that members of the aggregate are independent of one another, an assumption that is virtually never true of a human population. Carrying capacity is usually a function of the society's organization as well as of the resources and life conditions in a biophysical environment.[30] When migrant food-gatherers settled down and their foraging could be supplemented with agriculture and dairying, it was not only an increased food supply but also the more complex social structure accompanying sedentary life that resulted in a rapid growth of population.[31]

Contrary to earlier beliefs, the shift to farming may not have brought about an improvement in people's living conditions. A few hours of gathering per day was replaced by perhaps 10 hours of toiling in hard soil.[32] Hunter-gatherers, of all types of human societies, are most like other species of predators. They depend on the supply of food in their habitat, made available in part by the hunters' skill. This relation between carnivores and the animals they eat had been studied with a so-called predator-prey model. Using a computer, two researchers applied the model to humans living on Easter Island, with a plausible cycle of feast and famine.[33] As another example, Netsilik Eskimos, who inhabit a barren area of some 30,000 square miles north and west of Hudson Bay, have lived almost entirely on seal, caribou, and fish, supplemented only by a few berries picked during each August.[34] Their food has depended, in other words, on the day-to-day success of "man the hunter," with a life considerably more precarious than that of other primitives.

With foragers' economic base, there is little chance of a significant increase in population. One estimate of the rate of growth during the Paleolithic (roughly, from 750,000 to 15,000 years ago) was between 0.001 and less than 0.003 percent per year.[35] However sparse and dubious the data on which such guesses are based, they are basically irrefutable because, over the very long periods involved, higher rates would have resulted in impossibly large populations. One reason that Robert Malthus spent so much effort in presenting his famous arithmetic and geometric ratios is that most people find it hard to imagine how fast a base figure grows when it is increased by a fixed proportion each year. For example, if the number of people in the Middle East in 8000 B.C. was 100,000—an arbitrary estimate but not an unreasonable one—with an annual growth rate of 0.5 percent (or only a quarter of the rate at which the world's population grew in recent decades) the 100,000 would have become 46.2 trillion by 4000 B.C.

Estimating Fertility and Mortality

It was once assumed that the reason for the minuscule increments in prehistoric times is that under the assumed circumstances, the human species, just like every other plant or animal, grew in accord with the Darwinian model. Every viable species has a vast reservoir of potential procreation, most of which is never realized; among humans, as I have noted, only a tiny proportion of the spermatozoa and ova unite to form zygotes, and especially among populations lacking modern controls of early death, most zygotes fail to develop into adults capable of producing another generation. Even so, it was speculated, fertility was at least as high as mortality, so that the population growth fluctuated around a more or less stable long-run figure.

Over the past several decades a number of scholars have offered another scenario. In 1922, A. M. Carr-Saunders, an English social analyst who had been trained as a biologist, argued for a totally different kind of balance between fertility and mortality among primitive peoples.[36] Mankind has always had the ability to control the number of offspring—through infanticide, primitive forms of abortion, or prolonged abstinence from intercourse; and ample evidence existed, in his view, that primitives (and hence presumably also early man) have used such means to realize both an average family size close to what the parents desired and a total population close to an optimum relation with the resources available. Prehistoric peoples, in short, were not typically ill nourished and miserable; they enjoyed a "Stone Age affluence." When primitives came into contact with Europeans, he further alleged, these once universal controls of fertility were abandoned, either because the methods were opposed on moral or religious grounds or because an initial rise in mortality made them unnecessary. Citing the "well known and excellent study" of Carr-Saunders, the American sociologist Norman Himes began his history of contraception with the supposition that "some forms of limitation on the rate of increase are undoubtedly as old as the life history of man."[37] In another work the same allegation was extended from the prehistoric world to the Renaissance.[38]

By the 1960s, a considerable sector of anthropological doctrine had adopted something like this model. True, if a people lacks a continuous supply of plant food and thus depends virtually exclusively on hunting, it is subject to the restraints connoted in the predator-prey model. Members of what might be termed the Carr-Saunders school hold, however, that in general hunter-gatherers have not suffered from either starvation or even malnutrition; that chronic diseases have been infrequent, in part because of the small proportion of the population that reaches the most susceptible ages; that apart from snake bites, deaths from predatory animals have been a minor factor. The incidence of infectious disease has varied greatly, for ineffective therapies are countered by a low population density.[36] Accidental deaths due to drowning, burns, suffocation, exposure, and so on have been a significant cause of death among some peoples but not among others. Social mortality—cannibalism, infanticide, sacrifices, geronticide, institutionalized warfare—have largely disappeared today, sometimes supplanted by such other forms as homicide and suicide. Though the hunter-gatherer is "never perfectly adapted to the conditions in his environment, [allegedly] there is a degree of adaptive stability—of ecological conservatism—which does not exist in a modern urban setting."[40]

This sanguine view of primitive societies is not, of course, universally accepted. Its basis, according to critics, is not convincing evidence but rather the sentimental view that many anthropologists have of primitives and, by extension, of prehistoric peoples. "Unfortunately, anthropologists and demographers have been most attracted by each other's most speculative, largest-scale, and least secure evidence. Theoretical structures have grown unduly rapidly given the weakness of the evidence upon which they are based."[41] In this view, the postulate that voluntary fertility control ever prevailed in primitive societies can be accepted only if one is willing to assume that certain customs adopted to meet other social ends were intended also, or even fundamentally, as controls of population growth. For example, such critics have interpreted the widespread custom of postpartum sexual abstinence as mainly an attempt to improve the chances of child survival—and thus, in fact, to raise the rate of population growth.

From the common characteristic that defines primitive peoples, their lack of civilization, there is no reason to expect a uniform mortality among all of them, independent of their habitat, standards of sanitation, nutritional norms, patterns of violence, and therapeutic skills. There is suggestive evidence that, among the hunter-gatherers of the Pleistocene (roughly, 2 million years ago), both the dominant causes of death and the expectations of life differed widely.[42] And if we accept the postulate that population growth was close to zero among all prehistoric peoples, from the different levels of efficiency in death control we must conclude that the fertility of foragers, on which there is no direct evidence, also varied from one band to another. In other words, the commonplace in works on cultural anthropology may well be appropriate also here—that, within the range set by the lack of civilization, there is a far wider variation in the characteristics of primitive peoples than merely that shortcoming might imply.

Ethnographic data on fertility are likely to be especially flawed. The privacy of sexual matters is reinforced by a reluctance to acknowledge practices forbidden either in the culture being studied or by the researcher's Western standards. In a fertility survey in East Africa, for instance, "a man who refused to give any information to the first two investigators finally gave the names of two children to the third...[and] later admitted to ten children, but still concealed a second wife in another village."[43] An anthropologist who conducted detailed interviews of females in Ghana subsequently compared his results with those from a survey of the same small population. It was possible to see which items were falsified and thus to speculate on the reasons for the bogus responses. One motivation obviously was that the respondents wanted to appear more in accord with Western norms. Thus, in the survey women cited themselves as married when they were not, living with a husband when they had no husband, having never had an abortion when they had had as many as three, and so on. Another motive seemed to be female vanity; thus, age was understated, residence was shifted to a more prestigious place, a female servant appeared out of the imagination, and so on.[44]

The Australian anthropologist Norma McArthur summed up a paper on Polynesia with an observation on population:

> Given the generally inadequate data we have about primitive populations, it would be foolish to try to generalize about the course of primitive population change in Polynesia after its discovery. And because of the smallness of even the aggregates, none of these populations is amenable to the sort of logic that might be applied to really large populations.[45]

This conclusion, whether or not it is accepted with respect to contemporary primitives, would seem to apply a fortiori to archaeological data on prehistoric man, which are typically much thinner and even less reliable.

8

Population Theories

Like most general theories of Western civilization, those concerning population evolved first in ancient Greece. Both policies and their conceptual frameworks varied in details, but there was much consistency from one city-state to another. In Sparta legal coercion reinforced by public sentiment compelled every man to marry in order to produce many children of sound mind and body. In Athens the somewhat less uncompromising laws inhibited celibacy and promoted the fruitfulness of marriages. The typical pronatalist policies were intended not to generate a growth in numbers but rather to prevent their decline.[1] In the ideal city-state that Plato pictured in *Laws*, its population was to be kept stable at 5,040 (the product of 1 x 2 x 3 x 4 x 5 x 6 x 7) by encouraging or inhibiting fertility or by infanticide. If the number grew much beyond this optimum, the community was supposed to establish colonies. To neglect measures that would keep the population more or less fixed, according to Aristotle in *Politics*, would "bring certain poverty on the citizens, and poverty is the cause of sedition and evil."

Greek thought on population, in sum, was characterized by an overriding concern with policy and thus a relative indifference to empirical or conceptual analysis. Policy was to be applied, moreover, to aggregates ridiculously small by present-day standards. And whether the meaning of "population" was in accord with the modern sense is often not clear; in most instances the term probably referred only to citizens, thus omitting females, children, slaves, and aliens.

In its far larger arena Rome's policy was also consistently pronatalist. As imperial hegemony spread from Italy throughout the Mediterranean basin and beyond, the center was troubled by moral decay, the dissolution of the family, and a slower growth of population. Successive pronatalist measures culminated in three enacted under Augustus (63 B.C.-A.D. 14), which punished celibacy and adultery and rewarded prolific parenthood.[2] Since they had little apparent effect, the laws were repeatedly amended and finally repealed under Constantine (c.288-337).

As the empire gradually disintegrated, many came to believe that the end of the world was imminent, and sects competed with dogmas appropriate to the apocalypse. The early Christian church gradually developed its own family doctrine with a compromise between libertine and ascetic, but emphasizing the latter.[3] Catholic thought reached its apogee in the *Summa Theologica* of Thomas Aquinas (c.1224-1274). For him, a marriage between Christians was not merely a means of obeying the biblical injunction to replenish the earth but a spiritual bond, a sacrament. The function of intercourse is procreation, he wrote, and "whoever uses copulation for the delight which is in it...acts against nature."[4]

The dominant theme of the early modern period was the view that population growth is precarious and has to be fostered. Just as the mercantilist state hoarded gold, so it hoarded people, and for the same reason—to augment its economic, political, and military power: "An almost fanatical desire to increase population prevailed in all [Western] countries." If rapid population growth resulted in what was termed "overcrowding," the mercantilist solution was to ship the surplus to colonies, where the settlers and their progeny could continue to aggrandize the state's power in another quarter of the globe. In the innumerable letters back and forth concerning the young women sent to the French colonies, they were quite clearly seen simply as breeders: "In the same breath mention is made of shiploads of women, mares, and sheep, the methods of propagating human beings and cattle being regarded as roughly on the same plane."[5]

Modern demography began with the efforts of mercantilist states to keep track of their populations.[6] William Petty (1623-1687) was the first exponent of what he called "political arithmetic." John Graunt (1620-1674) constructed the first crude life table. Gregory King (1648-1712) calculated population estimates based on local enumerations, which he corrected for technical errors. On the Continent, Johann Peter Süssmilch (1707-1767) used Protestant parish records to estimate

Prussia's fertility and mortality. Richard Cantillon (c.1680-1774) held that internal migration, deaths, and especially marriages and therefore births varied according to the prevailing standard of living and the demand for labor. François Quesnay (1694-1774), who founded what was later called Physiocratic thought, analyzed the implicit limits of population growth.

The intellectuals (so-called "philosophes") of eighteenth-century France varied greatly on many issues, but most found reason to favor policies stimulating population growth. Montesquieu (1689-1755) believed that the entire world had undergone depopulation and recommended pronatalist decrees. According to Voltaire (1694-1778), a nation is fortunate if, with no official stimulus, its population increases even by as little as 5 percent per century. Louis de Saint-Just (1767-1794) held that one can usually depend on nature "never to have more children than teats," but to keep the balance in the other direction requires the state's assistance. By Saint-Just's notion of an equitable family law, as inspired by Jean Jacques Rousseau (1712-1778), marriages should be encouraged by state loans, and a couple that remained childless after several years ought to be forcibly separated.[7]

Malthus

With respect to population the climax of the philosophes' ideas came with the writings of two utopians, William Godwin (1756-1836) in England and the Marquis de Condorcet (1754-1794) in France, both of whom focused their attention on the wholly rational age they discerned just over the horizon. In a world from which diseases had been wholly eliminated, the span of life would have no assignable upper limit. People would devote themselves to more important tasks than, in Condorcet's words, "the puerile idea of filling the earth with useless and unhappy beings." In the history of population theory, the two have remained significant mainly because they became the first target of Thomas Robert Malthus (1766-1834), whom most subsequent analysts have taken to be the discipline's leading pioneer. Unfortunately, many references to "Malthusian" thought are based, at best, on the first edition of *The Essay on the Principle of Population* rather than on the much enlarged and thoroughly revised later editions—or, at worst, on a total misunderstanding of what he stood for.[8]

According to the principle of population as expounded in Malthus's *Essay*, any population, "when unchecked," doubles once every generation. Among "irrational animals" this potential may be realized, and its "superabundant effects are repressed afterwards by want of room or nourishment." But rational humans can consider the consequences of their reproductive potential and curb their natural drive. With human beings, thus, the control of population growth can be by either "preventive checks," the chaste postponement of marriage, or "positive checks," deaths consequent from too large a population relative to its subsistence. When tension arises between the number requiring nourishment and the food available, it can also have a beneficial effect: a man who postpones marrying until he is able to support a family is goaded by his sex drive to work hard, thus contributing to social progress. It was mainly for this reason that Malthus opposed contraceptives: their use permits individual sexual gratification with no benefit to society.

Through successive editions of the *Essay*, Malthus increasingly stressed the negative correlation between station in life and size of family. This in his view was the principal clue to solving what later became known as "the population problem." In order to bring the lower classes up to the self-control and social responsibility exercised by those with more money and education, Malthus asserted, the poor should also be given more money and education. "The principal circumstances" that induce prospective parents to have fewer children are "liberty, security of property, the diffusion of knowledge, and a taste for the comforts of life." And the circumstances that tend to increase procreation are "despotism and ignorance."[9]

In retrospect, the argument that upward mobility into the middle class effects a decline in fertility, though it is far less familiar than that relating population growth to available subsistence, may well be Malthus's most important contribution to demographic analysis. For many decades Malthus's reputation was far below that of lesser social analysts. Recently it has become apparent that much of present-day demography was at least partly stimulated by the discipline's founder and that those who denounced him as a false prophet had typically begun by misrepresenting his ideas.

Marx and His Followers

Still today, among the most prominent opponents of Malthusian theory are persons who identify themselves as Marxists.[10] This is in several respects rather remarkable. In the usually tangential treatment first by Marx and Engels and then by their immediate disciples, population was pictured less as a significant ingredient of the historical process than as an epiphenomenon.

According to Marx's economic theory, to which his most significant remarks on population are attached, competition under capitalism drives all entrepreneurs to increase their efficiency to the utmost by installing more and more machinery. "Accumulate, accumulate! This is the Moses and the prophets!"[11] The growing stock of capital goods gradually displaces some of the workers who were employed with less efficient equipment. "The laboring population therefore produces, along with the accumulation of capital produced by it, the means by which [it] itself is made relatively superfluous, is turned into a relative surplus population; and it does this to an always increasing extent."[12] Moreover, the capitalist "progressively replaces skilled laborers by less skilled, mature labor power by immature, male by female, that of adults by that of younger persons or children."[13]

In fact, the effects of technological advance on the size and composition of the work force has been considerably more complex than in this depiction; and the long-term consequences of the greater efficiency were a better livelihood, a shorter workweek, and the development of tertiary services.

But even if Marx's main point were to be granted—that with increasing mechanization there is a trend toward an ever larger number of unemployed--it still hardly follows that this tendency would take place "independently of the limits of actual increase in population."[14] If demographers' forecasts in the 1930s (half-repeated in the 1990s) had proved correct—that the populations of Western countries would soon begin to decline, and if the decline had been at the same rate as machines displace workers (taking the Marxist dogma as valid)—then there would have been no "industrial reserve army," no "immiseration," no Marxist model at all. Marx built his system on the unstated and therefore unexamined postulate that the rapid population growth in nineteenth-century Europe would continue indefinitely.

Moreover, according to Marx, Malthus's principle of population was merely a biological generalization, supposedly valid irrespective of the society's class relations. On the contrary, he wrote:

> Every special historical mode of production has its own special laws of population, historically valid within its limits alone. An abstract law of population exists for plants and animals only, and only in so far as man has not interfered with them.[15]

Seemingly this contrast between the human species and all other forms of life suggests that, according to Marx, humans can transgress their biological limitations, and this utopian vista was strange coming from this source. Summing up the essentials of his friend's work at his graveside, Engels held that "Marx discovered the law of evolution in human history: the simple fact, previously hidden under ideological growths, that human beings must first of all eat, drink, shelter and clothe themselves before they can turn their attention to politics, science, art, and religion."[16] In other words, Marx and Engels believed (though not consistently) that it was only the men they termed "utopian socialists" who held that with a good social system man could escape the bounds of his physiological limits.

Marx's theories related to population, such as they were, eventually became the ostensible base of various policies in the Soviet Union. We enter a different world in trying to analyze this development; theories developed in the democratic West are in many respects ill suited as a guide to parallel phenomena in such past totalitarian societies as the Soviet Union and Nazi Germany. Though their cultures differed greatly, these two countries had certain features in common, many of which related to population theory and its application:

- The Party was defined as omnipotent, able to cope with any increase in population. In the words of the first Soviet delegate to the U.N. Population Commission, thus, "I would consider it barbaric for the Commission to contemplate a limitation of marriages or of legitimate births, and this for any country whatsoever, at any period whatsoever. With an adequate social organization it is possible to face any increase in population."[17] (Compare this with the quotation from Engels in the preceding paragraph!)
- Population theory had the same purpose as any other science—to bolster the power of the Party.[18] In particular, that the totalitarian state had a constant need for workers and soldiers generated such pronatalist policies as family subsidies.
- Efforts to stimulate the birth rate, however, were hampered by the Party's hostility to the family, which by its legal and emotional links between gen-

erations helps maintain a traditional opposition to radically new ideas and practices. Both the Soviet Union and Nazi Germany tried to establish institutions that could replace the family, such as brothels in which SS-men could impregnate young women certified as racially pure, or the Soviet children's homes in which the state could convert orphans and the offspring of political dissidents into reliable instruments of the Party. Since such substitutes never produced a large enough crop, in both countries policy fluctuated between attacking the family and fostering it.

- The need for a high fertility was enhanced by the recklessness with which sectors of the population designated as hostile or inferior were killed off. The terror most closely associated with the Nazis was the mass murder of Jews. More often Communists defined their victims as class enemies, but the difference was not fundamental: antagonism to ethnic minorities was also a constant element of Soviet society. Slaughter began in different sectors of the population and sometimes was concentrated there, but in both cases it spread to the whole.[19]
- Totalitarian ideology was based on what in German is called a *Stufenlehre*, a doctrine of stages. All analysis, all planning, began not from the empirical present but from the inevitable perfect future, homogenized into a "classless" or "*Judenfrei*" (Jewless) sameness. The road to this paradise could be seen clearly only by the Party, whose function it was to move the rest of the population toward its destiny. The ruthless terror often needed was warranted by the glorious community that would ensue from it.

The Demographic Transition

In the modern era the world's population increased at an unprecedented rate to unprecedented high totals, and the basic reason for what is now almost routinely called a "population explosion" is no mystery. Mortality fell sharply, and in many areas fertility did not. As originally formulated,[20] this so-called demographic transition was conceived as taking place in three broad stages: (1) preindustrial societies, with a high fertility more or less balanced by a high mortality and a consequent low rate of natural increase; (2) societies in transition, with a continuing high fertility but declining mortality and a consequent high natural increase; and (3) modern societies, with both fertility and mortality stabilized at low levels and a consequent more or less static population.

The societies grouped together under Stage I comprise all that have not begun industrialization, from bands of hunters to great civilizations, and generalizations about them are therefore often thin and too broad. It was assumed that the mortality of all primitive peoples was very high relative to that in advanced societies today, but estimates of longevity in ancient times can hardly be very precise.[21] Whether or not pre-industrial peoples were warlike, lived in a favorable climate, developed cultural norms promoting cleanliness, and so on—such factors certainly influenced their death rates. Because in such societies the control of mortality was typically precarious, many writers at least implied that, unless fertility was close to the physiological maximum, the population would die out.

Contrary to the theory, Stage II sometimes was marked not only by a fall in mortality but also by a rise in fertility. Improved health can result in a greater physiological ability to reproduce. All societies have the means of reducing fertility,[22] and when beginning modernization undercut whatever traditional institutional checks existed, fertility was likely to rise or at least to fall less rapidly than the theory would lead one to suppose. In Tokugawa Japan (1603-1867), as an example, infanticide had been common, but under the new norms of the Meiji regime (1868-1912) it was if not impermissible then at least not genteel. If the age at marriage had been set at well past puberty, as in early modern Europe, the institutions bolstering this norm often became less effective. Religious practices or taboos unintentionally inhibiting fertility, such as prohibiting the remarriage of widows in Hindu India, sometimes dissipate. Most remarkably, family planning programs can themselves result in a rise in the birth rate, for if women are able to depend on reliable controls later in their reproductive life, some may begin childbearing at an earlier age--and then continue. In short, the effect of modernization is partly to increase fertility and partly to decrease it—a process considerably more complex and varied than the model suggests.[23]

The most significant conclusion drawn from the demographic transition has been that a rather simple history of the West could be used to predict the future of less developed countries. Even in the first expositions, and increasingly in the polemics that ensued from them, causal links were hypothesized between the three stages. Thus, past patterns in industrial countries were taken to be a reliable guide to predicting population growth in less developed countries, and policy recommendations were offered that derived from such an elaboration. But note some of the more important differences between the two: Europe was relatively empty at the beginning of the long-term rise in numbers; India, Java, and Egypt started from very high population densities. The overflow from Europe emigrated by the millions; later, immigration to virtually any country was far more restricted. The West's decline of mortality resulted from successive improvements in agriculture, sanitation, and medicine; in the less developed countries, with the most advanced methods brought in from the outside, the fall in death rates has often been many times faster.

It is true that population increase in the modern period has been faster than ever before in history and this rise has been due in large part to the imbalance between a declining mortality and a temporarily fixed fertility. But the theories to explain this broad generalization were at first too broad and have since become varied and partly self-contradictory. In a series of monographs at Princeton University on the shift in Europe's fertility, an important effort has been made to round out our incomplete and imperfect knowledge.[24]

To sum up, until modern times there was no theory as we understand the concept, but rather what is better designated one or another doctrine used to justify a population policy. If we define a "theory" as a general thesis or a set of linked propositions used to explain empirical data and, usually, to set a direction for future research, what theories have demographers today? There has been much theorizing concerning why people migrate, why the level of fertility rises or falls, how intelligence is inherited, why ethnic groups do or do not acculturate, and so on—all of which have related more or less closely to the size, growth, and composition of population. I have touched on some of these matters in other chapters, but here the main points have related to just two theories, Malthus (with an addendum concerning Marx and his followers) and the demographic transition.

Perhaps not surprisingly, demographers have often denigrated the discipline's theories, as can be exemplified with quotations from two leaders of the past generation. "The major advances in the science of population," according to Kingsley Davis, an eminent American member of the discipline, "have come from improvements in the sources of information and in techniques of analysis, rather than from their broad interpretations."[25] Another important American demographer put it even more strongly: "Much of the progress made during the past two or three decades is due to the fact that demographers at long last managed to rid themselves of preoccupations with the overarching theories which dominated so much of the nineteenth-century work in the field."[26]

It is strange to find two distinguished members of a discipline commenting with some satisfaction on the paucity of theory, which any philosopher of science would describe as a serious lack. Not only is the dearth of a general framework to which partial insights can be related in itself an important deficiency, but one prime cost has been that the near vacuum has been filled by those adept at verbalizing about "the limits of growth" and "the population bomb," which for several decades have been the principal subject matter of population studies.

Any subject which finds it necessary, or indeed possible, to consider its material divorced from a body of theory must be in trouble. This seems to be the case with demography. A book titled *The State of Population Theory: Forward from Malthus*[27] took the first steps toward remedying what all the contributors saw as a serious lack. Important issues, for instance, relate to serious challenges to Malthus's principle of population, as argued in the paper by the Danish economist Ester Boserup. Problems of scale are manifest in theories about family or ethnicity, for these are seldom coordinated with generalizations about the broader society. Indeed, the contrast between the first and subsequent editions of the *Essay on Population* followed from Malthus's recognition that he needed empirical evidence to support his theoretical presentation:

> Demography without numbers is waffle, an amiable kind of social natural history....But demographic models rarely have statistical distributions or confidence limits built into them.[28]

To a degree, what population theory can become depends on how demography is defined, and this is still an open question in the discipline.[29]

9

Forecasts and Projections

In the physical sciences there is a symmetry between explanation and prediction. Take a simple example: why does ice float on water? The response calls on a law, namely, that any solid whose density is less than that of the fluid on which it is placed floats on that liquid. Since the density of ice is less than that of water, it floats on it. If the statement is about an already floating piece of ice, we call it an explanation; if about what will happen if we place the piece on water, it is a prediction.[1]

Many in the social disciplines have expected the same degree of certainty from the generalizations that can be fashioned from data about people. To test the validity of a social theory, we are told, we must determine whether it accurately predicts the future. For example, one reason that Marxists have believed that their doctrine is superior to any alternative is that allegedly it predicts the manner by which the working of capitalism leads inevitably to its downfall. However, since knowledge in its broadest sense grows in an unpredictable manner and in the process may affect anything, the course of history cannot be properly construed as an evolutionary process. Generalizations concerning particular sets of events may constitute valid elements of the social disciplines, but laws concerning the whole cannot be discovered because they do not exist.[2]

Yet virtually all rational action is based on one or another supposition about how things will work out in the weeks or years or decades to come, and among those elements of the future one of the most important is the number of people concerned. The administrator of every level of government, the person in charge of every type of public or private institution, the entrepreneur in every kind of business, must try to adjust its operation to some supposition about how many it will serve during the next period. Every statistical bureau, therefore, is under constant pressure to provide population forecasts.

Moreover, much of demographic analysis and theorizing pertains not merely to the population today but also, and often mainly, to the one we can expect tomorrow. The core of Malthus's principle of population is that the growth in the number of people is potentially greater than the increase in the food to sustain them. Virtually the whole of the vast body of articles and books by the army of doomsayers is based not on an observed disparity between population and resources but rather on a prediction of how such a disparity, whatever its present size, will in the near future become disastrously large.

Tomorrow's Population

Essentially any prediction of a future population is made by extrapolating, by one means or another, a past trend as far into the future as the chutzpah of the would-be seer will carry him. The simplest type of projection is to continue the past growth of the total population. However, since age structure is crucial in setting the rates of change in fertility and mortality, one should not expect that a linear projection, in which the population's distribution by age and sex is ignored, could ever lead to useful results.

Yet one calculation by an American of the Revolutionary period, Elkanah Watson, set an astounding record. Noting merely that the population of the United States had increased by about a third during each of the first two decades following the 1790 census, he wrote a two-page paper calculating the growth in numbers if this decennial rate were to continue.[3] For 1840, his projected figure was a mere 0.3 percent less than the actual count; for 1850, almost 40 years after the calculation was made, his estimate was even closer to the actual, only 0.03 percent higher than the actual count. This progression, however, was a pure fluke. Until 1860 the reason that census counts increased by a regular proportion was the remarkable coincidence that each deficit in natural increase was canceled by almost exactly the same number of immigrants.

In the 1920s several statisticians proffered the S-shaped logistic curve as a law by which one could predict a future population. The American zoologist Raymond Pearl developed such a theory by analyzing the actual multiplication of fruit flies subsisting on a given amount of nutrition in a closed bottle. As the Drosophilae able to propagate increased from the original pair, their number rose at an accelerating rate until the limiting factor of the fixed food supply became relevant. Then the curve flattened out, approaching but never quite reaching the maximum set by the available subsistence.[4] One reason for the wide popularity of the logistic curve, one can presume, was that it resembled the usual caricature of Malthusian theory, with an ever-growing population set against a supply of nourishment growing more slowly or, as in this case, with no increment at all. The short popularity that the logistic curve enjoyed was again the consequence of coincidence; eventually, after repeated failures, its brief heyday ended.

In the 1930s two fertility rates devised by the British demographer R. R. Kuczynski became fashionable. A gross reproduction rate as he defined it measures whether over the next generation each woman would reproduce herself with one daughter. The second new index, the net reproduction rate, measures the natural increase, with mortality from a female life table used to deduct the proportion of females born that will not survive to the midpoint of each age group (that is, 17.5 years for those aged 15-19, 22.5 for 20-24, and so on). The measures have an attractive elegance. A rate of 1.0 means that the fertility (or natural increase) is such that over one generation the mothers would precisely reproduce their number, a rate of 2.0 that they would precisely double their number, and so on.[5]

In fact, however, the rates were deceptive--especially during the 1930s, when in all Western countries fertility was falling to a low point. During that decade the average net reproduction rate of the United States, for instance, was 0.98, or 2 percent below the replacement level of 1.0; and many writers (including sometimes even demographers) cited the figure as though it indicated that the population was in actual decline. The annual age-specific birth rates from which the reproduction rates are calculated, however, are not a good indicator of the completed family size--that is, how many children on the average that each woman eventually bears over all her fecund years. During the depression many older women, who had borne children in the 1920s, refrained—sometimes temporarily—from having more; and younger women often put off starting their families until the economy improved. What was widely interpreted as the first step toward an impending depopulation turned out to be a long but temporary aberration. Reproduction rates, as several critics pointed out, are "analogous to the speedometer on a car in that they measure the approximate speed or force of reproduction at a given time but not necessarily the actual distance being covered or the actual time required to reach the destination. The 'speed' fluctuates too much [to be a] reliable measure of distance."[6]

The reproduction rates are less used now than several decades ago, but they have been replaced by so-called intrinsic rates of birth, death, and natural increase. These are derived from a stable population—that is, the one that, after a considerable period with fixed age-specific rates of fertility and mortality, would eventually ensue. In other words, an intrinsic rate of natural increase is what would come about if the population were to continue to grow (or decline) with the base year's birth and death rates for each year of age. As calculated by the National Center for Health Statistics, the United States had the following intrinsic rates of natural increase:

```
1970 .......... 6.0
1972 .......... -2.0   First indication of a decline
1980 .......... -5.1
1983 .......... -5.8   Low point of this series
1990 .......... -0.1
1993 .......... -0.7
```

Like the reproduction rates, thus, intrinsic rates are half-disguised projections into the future. If interpreted carelessly, they also have the same major fault: an unstated assumption that the current rates of fertility and mortality will persist unchanged.

When efforts to reduce the fertility of less developed countries are evaluated, the test of their effectiveness is often flawed in the same way. A nation with a rapidly growing population develops an age structure with a high proportion currently or soon to be in the most fecund range. Suppose that a program to reduce the fertility succeeds in bringing down the number of children per family to, say, 2.1—about enough to replace the two parents and make up for sterility and early mortality.

With an age structure typical of a developing country, because of the large number of families, the population would continue to grow by about 70 percent over the next half century.[7]

Component Projections

In virtually all projections made today, the total population is not extrapolated as such but is rather divided first into its component parts, which are projected separately and reassembled at successive future dates. Childbearing, to repeat, is more or less restricted to adolescents and young adults, the same age bracket that predominates in most migrations. Deaths, on the contrary, fall from a high point during infancy and early childhood and then do not rise significantly until late maturity. In accord with these universal characteristics, a component projection is made by applying simultaneously age-specific rates of fertility, mortality, and migration to a given population in the process of gradual change in both size and structure.

The method can be illustrated by the forecasts that two American demographers, Warren S. Thompson and P. K. Whelpton, made in the 1930s.[8] As they noted, major advances in death control had cut the toll especially of infectious diseases, particularly those affecting infants and young children. They expected a decline in adults' deaths from pneumonia but little improvement in the control of other major causes. By 1980, the authors estimated, the likeliest expectations of life from birth would be 68.8 years for males and 71.2 for females. (The actual figures turned out to be, respectively, 70.0 and 77.5.) The highest fertility they anticipated was a continuation of the age-specific rates of 1930-1934, when the average woman had 2.2 children. More probable, in their opinion, would be a decline by 13 percent over 50 years, ending with a completed family size in 1980 of 1.9 children per woman. Immigration was estimated in alternative projections as either zero or a net arrival of 100,000 immigrants.

Based on the trends in fertility, mortality, and migration that the authors believed to be most likely, the projected 1940 population that Thompson and Whelpton calculated seven years before the census was more precise than the count itself before that was corrected for underenumeration! Not surprisingly, both in the United States and other Western countries demographers used this enormously successful technique with vast confidence, often predicting population declines by gargantuan proportions. The fantastic success, however, was not maintained: Thompson and Whelpton's alternative projections for 1950 ranged between 137 and 142 million, and in 1980 between 134 and 158 million, contrasted with actual census counts at those two dates of, respectively, 151 million and 227 million.

The extraordinary success of the initial component projections was based, as with Watson's simple extrapolation, on the fortuitous happenstance that the worldwide depression of the 1930s, which in large part set the social-economic context of fertility, continued for the whole decade. After the economy improved, prospective parents who had put off having children collectively took part in producing what became known as the baby boom. The grossly inaccurate guesses Thompson and Whelpton offered about future fertility, moreover, were compounded by smaller errors in the other two factors: death rates went down and immigration rates went up faster than they had anticipated. By 1950, only a decade after the census count that Thompson and Whelpton had so remarkably predicted, grossly inaccurate prognoses by demographers had become notorious.[9]

Like statistical agencies of other countries, the U.S. Bureau of the Census first stopped using the term "forecast," then began the practice of calculating several alternative future populations, and finally emphasized that its projections were merely mathematical exercises, giving the agency's patrons the figures that would result by extrapolating the recent population growth with specified demographic rates to given future dates. No predictive value was to be assumed, it was repeatedly asserted, but of course every person or institution that depended on the figures assumed that these professionals knew more than anyone else about the future growth of population.

As reported in the *Statistical Abstract of the United States, 1997*, the Bureau of the Census offered the following population projections from 1996 (in millions), with a suggestion that the "middle" estimates may be the most likely:

Table 9.1

	Lowest	Middle	Highest	
1997	267	268	269	
2000	271	275	278	
2020	289	323	358	
2050	283	394	519	

Note that between the years 2020 and 2050, according to the lowest projection, the population of the United States would begin to decline.

The crucial unknown was, and remains, fertility. The control of diseases has advanced more rapidly than most physicians would have thought possible a generation ago, and migration has been more erratic, and usually larger, than students of the subject predicted. Yet the trends in these two determinants of future populations have not been so far out of line as suppositions about how many children parents in Western countries would choose to bear, or how competently they would use the contraceptives available to them.

That population projections are flagrantly inaccurate is, of course, well known to every person associated with constructing them, as well as to most of those who use them. Why then do all statistical agencies, national and international, devote so much time and money to devising eminently fallible pictures of a future we cannot foretell? Perhaps the best answer, offered almost as a joke, was given at a professional conference by the British demographer John Hajnal. The accuracy of a projection, he contended, is irrelevant to its utility. Persons in government or business who are responsible for deciding how to conduct their affairs need some notion of how many persons the state or corporation will have to deal with, and until they are provided with an authoritative estimate of the future population, they are stymied. Once they have such a projection, they are able to act. If the estimate happens to be correct, they continue; if not, they change course. One way or the other, the forecast has served its purpose of getting them started.

Among those unhappy with this half-acceptance of false forecasts, one of the more prolific has been the American demographer Nathan Keyfitz. It is true, he wrote, that "demographers can no more be held responsible for inaccuracy in forecasting population 20 years ahead than geologists, meteorologists, or economists when they fail to announce earthquakes, cold winters, or depressions 20 years ahead." But demographers should try to give those who use their figures some notion of the probable range of error, and he suggested how this might be done.[10] In a subsequent paper, however, he concluded that an increased knowledge of how and why fertility has changed in the past can have little effect in improving population forecasts. In effect, one must fall back on merely statistical extrapolations that are both independent of any knowledge about the supposed determinants of the population growth and, thus, are based on the often false assumption that current fertility and mortality rates are fixed for the whole of the projection period.[11]

The fact that fertility is almost always the principal unknown in any population projection means that it is possible to make reasonably accurate forecasts if all of the people concerned are alive at the starting date. If there are extraordinary changes just over the horizon, so that one need look no farther ahead than 15 or 20 years, a population forecast can be quite revealing. The American demographer Nicholas Eberstadt exemplified this observation with a projection of East Asia's population to the year 2015.[12] The number of people will grow by 350 million, rather than the 480 million that had recently been anticipated. In 2015, the region will have—not the ten children under 15 for every person 65 or older, as is now the case—but only four. This aging, dramatically rapid as compared with the past history of the West, will have profound social and economic consequences. "For example, the neo-Confucian social order will be tested by a proliferation of the elderly and, presumably, a vast concomitant increase in the number of infirm and aged dependents....A region that once seemingly defined the image of surplus labor will be forced, increasingly, to confront a labor scarcity." Because of the traditional preference for male offspring (allegedly often implemented by female infanticide), the sex ratio at birth in China and North Korea may be as high as 116 males to every 100 females. In these countries, once these infants reach marrying age, one male out of every six will not be able to find a bride in his age cohort, and marriageable females younger than he will be even scarcer. With the enormous importance in these cultures of ensuring continuity of the male line, this will be "a new form of social distortion with unpredictable, and possibly far-reaching, consequences."

Another example of the possibility of accurate short-run projections comes from a completely different context. In 1987 an attempt was made to predict America's future needs of trauma centers based on the evolving population structure, and in 1998 this forecast was matched against the actual change during that period. As predicted, the sector of the population that increased fastest was persons older than 65, and the injury-related deaths independent of age fell. The population projections helped in predicting the number and type of future injuries, but it was necessary to supplement the forecasts with data on social-economic trends.[13]

Auguste Comte's aphorism that demography is destiny is sometimes all too valid.

The World's Future Population

In most instances, whatever the faults of projections in general, one made of the population of a developed country represents the best prospect for a more or less accurate future figure. In that case the recorded current population is reasonably precise, as are also the age structure and the rates of fertility, mortality, and migration. Moreover, it is possible to draw trend lines from earlier census figures, suggesting—perhaps—some indication of how the course may continue. Since none of these attributes characterize data of less developed countries, one should expect that the lamentable record of forecasts for industrial countries will be still worse when the same methods are applied elsewhere, not to say to the whole world, including large areas where every statistical datum is more a guess than a count.

In his meticulous review of "the population debate," the American demographer E. P. Hutchinson noted correctly that concern about the total size of mankind is as old as human history.[14] He surveyed the controversy in seven chapters before reaching Malthus, who is usually taken to mark the beginning of modern demography. A representative example of the early history is the three-volume work of a Prussian army chaplain, Johann Peter Shümilch, who estimated the world population in 1741 at about 1,000,000,000. He thought that food could be made available for 13,932,000,000,000,000. "The earth," Shümilch concluded, "has not yet reached the limits of its population by far, and plague or war or famine are not needed to maintain the balance [between people and food]."[15]

Contrary to such "optimistic" estimates, there was a school represented, for example, by the Scottish philosopher and historian David Hume: "Almost every man who thinks he can maintain a family will have one; and the human species, at this rate of propagation, would more than double every generation."[16] (Note that this "optimistic" view includes one element largely absent in the underclasses of today's countries: the notion that reproduction is motivated by a man's belief that he can support a family.) Malthus reconciled the opposing views into a composite theory that took both possibilities into account: there is a tendency, he wrote, for the growth in the number of people to outstrip the food needed to nourish them, but this tendency can be offset by the chaste postponement of marriage.

The debate between "optimists" and "pessimists" has continued. As measured by the publicity given to their views, especially but not exclusively in popular publications, the doomsayers have dominated the debate. A typical example of the genre was a 1972 volume sponsored by a prestigious international group of businessmen and other concerned persons called the Club of Rome, *The Limits of Growth*.[17] Its profoundly pessimistic projections were based on a rather simple fallacy: the estimated past trends of several important variables were extrapolated into the future, but with the rather silly assumption that there would be no appreciable change in the most dynamic factor of all: technology. An increasing population will require, for example, an ever increasing amount of "food" (with no suggestion of what this is likely to encompass over the period of the projection), which must have been produced on a limited area of "arable" land (the significance of this adjective changed radically almost while the authors were grinding out the message of disaster). As one notable review of *The Limits of Growth* pointed out, "In 1872 [that is, a century before the book was published] any scientist could have proved that a city the size of London was impossible, because where were Londoners going to stable all the horses and how could they avoid being asphyxiated by the manure?"[18] The Club of Rome revised its very pessimistic conclusions considerably in a second report, *Mankind at the Turning Point* (1974), which received a good deal less attention.

According to a similar report by two agencies of the United States government, "If present trends continue, the world in 2000 will be more crowded, more polluted, less stable ecologically, and more vulnerable to disruption than the world we live in now....The outlook for food and other necessities will be no better. For many it will be worse."[19]

Perhaps the best counter-voice was that of the late American economist, Julian Simon. Typical were his comments on the earth's "carrying capacity," the maximum population that is set by physical and biological limits:

> Because of increases in knowledge, the earth's "carrying capacity" has been increasing throughout the decades and centuries and millennia to such an extent that the term has by now no useful meaning. These trends strongly suggest a progressive improvement and enrichment of the earth's natural resource base, and of mankind's lot on earth.[20]

An editor of the English scientific journal *Nature*, Philip Ball, wrote an interesting book specifying one highly important area of Julian Simon's vision.[21] He discussed the new materials that are on the threshold of being created and will probably come into being during the next century. To make an engine part, a vacuum cleaner, a coat hanger, or whatever, there are today between 40,000 and 80,000 materials from which to choose; and there is every reason to expect that this enormous expansion in the elements out of which goods are manufactured will continue or even accelerate. The range of novelties in store is merely suggested: "The next revolution in information technology will dispense with the transistor and use light, not electricity, to carry information." The demand for more capacious and more compact memory devices will bring forth new kinds of light-based memories. Materials that replace machines "will lead to intelligent systems that adapt their properties to the environment." "The living world provides endless inspiration for the design of synthetic materials with sophisticated structures and functions." "Most of the human body can now be replaced with artificial parts," and "the ultimate goal is the growth of new organs."

The Concept of Chaos

In the 1960s practitioners in several of the physical sciences began to develop a new sensitivity to what had earlier been dismissed as systemic flaws too small to be bothered with. When tiny differences in input became overwhelming differences in output, as in the cause-effect relations studied in meteorology, the phenomenon was half-facetiously labeled the "butterfly effect": a butterfly stirring its wings in Canberra supposedly can transform New York's storm systems a month later. Thus, no matter how dependable the data are, meteorologists are not able to predict the weather completely accurately. In a few years the characteristics of such "chaos" were hypothesized concerning not only weather systems but the swings of a pendulum, the famous red spot on the planet Jupiter, waves in the ocean, and assorted other matters studied in several disciplines.[22]

When biologists studying such questions as how predators interact with their prey, how a change in population density affects the spread of an infectious disease, the new insights of mathematicians, physicists, and astronomers began to spread to the life sciences. It is possible to postulate a simple model describing, for example, the population growth of a species that reproduces only during a particular season; one can estimate the number of gypsy moths next spring merely from an approximation of the current population of gypsy moths. But when the Australian biologist Robert May applied this method to fish populations, he found that the logistic model (which several decades earlier Raymond Pearl and others had applied to human populations[23]) did not work. At a certain point the numbers predicted from the model oscillated between two points in alternating years. This also was "chaos."[24]

Using the computer to extrapolate series from a number of equations, the American mathematician Benoit Mandelbrot had to coin a word for the new shapes, dimensions, and geometry he was constructing. He thumbed through his son's Latin dictionary and came across the adjective *fractus*, from the verb *frangere*, to break. The neologism "fractal" evolved, standing for describing, calculating, and thinking about shapes that are irregular and fragmented, jagged and broken up.[25]

In sum, the new rationale postulates that simple systems behave in simple ways, but complex behavior implies complex causes. Different kinds of systems behave differently. For a while most physicists, mathematicians, biologists, and astronomers were hostile to the mavericks announcing a new way of looking at reality. In each of the disciplines these pioneers met, successively, "uncomprehension, resistance, anger, acceptance."[26] The diffusion of the new insights to ecologists' study of animal populations, then of epidemiologists' analysis of infectious diseases, brought the innovation closer to the domain of demographers.

In the next decade or so a mathematician interested in population, or a demographer with a far better understanding of mathematics than I, may well establish a completely new framework for population forecasting. What this will be I do not know, but what it will not be is certain: today anyone can extrapolate from a given series by a stipulated rule, but not meaningfully relate this exercise to the real world and honestly label it a "forecast." With the new mathematics associated with what has been termed chaos, it may be possible to do better.

10

State Control of Population

When attempts to predict a future population have succeeded, it has been mainly by fortuitous coincidence. Though none of the several methods devised to forecast the number of people have worked, governments all over the world have used such fallacious indications of what is in prospect as rationales for either pronatalist or antinatalist measures. Ever since the days of ancient Greece and Rome, officialdom has tried to intervene in the process of reproduction by motivating potential parents to have more or fewer children. Typically these policies, whether pronatalist or antinatalist, have made little difference in the countries' fertility.[1] Yet the efforts of governments to influence population growth have increased over the past several decades, and indeed much of recent demographic work has focused on what is termed "the population problem" and how to cope with it.

Population Optimum

Any policy set to affect the rate of population growth is obviously based on a judgment about whether the present number of people and the current increase or decrease are desirable by one yardstick or another. When things are going well, no one tries to alter them. But the criteria setting an optimum population are like population forecasts in that they are also, to put it no stronger, rather indeterminate.

A vague concept of optimum population existed for centuries before it was brought to the surface and analyzed. The modern theory of the optimum was implicit in Malthus; the best population had been achieved in several countries of Northwest Europe, where an equilibrium between people and their subsistence had been effected by fostering moral restraint through an institutionalized postponement of marriage. On the other hand, the growth of population in the American colonies, which at that time was doubling every twenty-five years, he deemed appropriate for a land so sparsely settled. For each situation, in other words, Malthus implied that there is a best rate of population growth and a best number of inhabitants.[2] Also without using the term, John Stuart Mill defined the optimum as the "degree of density sufficient to allow the principal benefits of combination of labor," after which all further increase would be "mischief so far as regards the average condition of the people."[3]

The best population, implicit in Malthus and Mill, was made explicit by the English economist Edwin Cannan.[4] This was the first formal statement of the optimum: namely, the number of inhabitants of any country that brings about the highest per capita economic return, with "return" later specified by other analysts as total production per head, or real income per head, or the point at which the marginal and the average product per laborer are equal.

To this relatively simple formulation several complicating factors were successively added. In relating people to the economy, leftish critics asked, are we discussing the actual or the optimum institutional framework—that is, the current capitalist or the future socialist economy? Others pointed out that a society has many legitimate functions, and that there is no reason to suppose that each of them is best served by the same number of people. In most situations, for instance, the population size that produces the maximum income per capita is smaller than the one best able to defend the country in war. According to one formulation, after some decades of hairsplitting, the optimum population was defined as simply "the number socially desirable."[5]

Since no consensus evolved on how to define the optimum, some rejected the concept altogether. In the words of the Swedish social analyst Gunnar Myrdal, optimum population is "one of the most sterile ideas" ever developed in economics; "its elaboration has not increased its scientific significance or practical applicability. The theory stands mainly as an excuse for, and also as an actual inhibition of, the proper posing of the problem of the economic effects of population changes."[6]

The American Association for the Advancement of Science posed the question, "Is there an optimum size of population?" to 31 knowledgeable persons; of these, 13 responded "Yes," 7 replied "No," and 11 had no answer.[7] In the several decades since that survey, no progress has been made in elucidating the term.

Yet it is hardly logical to advocate a population policy with no idea of what its goal should be. When Myrdal helped work out a pronatalist program for Sweden's government, his proposals obviously implied some notion of how large that country's population ought to be. This lack of any theory to buttress demands for corrective action has been a bizarre, but recurrent, characteristic of modern population policy. Demographers, statesmen, and do-gooders who advocate measures to realize the "best" population typically neglect to think seriously about what they mean by "good."

Pronatalist Policies

So-called population theories before the modern era pertained, in fact, less to doctrine than to policy. Long before anyone tried to understand how the number of people relates to their welfare, philosophers, theologians, and statesmen tried to set guidelines. Mercantilism, which was Europe's dominant economic creed from the fifteenth to the eighteenth century, was fanatically pronatalist. A major break with that doctrine was effected by Adam Smith, who argued that population growth depends not on official attempts to regulate it, but rather on the demand for labor and the supply of food; and this view was consistent with his general defense of personal liberty and a free market.[8] In fact, the pronatalist policies of the mercantilist era proved to be not very efficacious. The decline of Europe's fertility seemingly began in France, starting well before the revolution of 1789; by 1800 French natality was estimated to be a tenth below its traditional level. In the middle of the nineteenth century, when the marital fertility rates of Sweden, Denmark, and England and Wales were close to 0.7 of the maximum ever recorded, the French index was around 0.5 and falling rather fast.[9] Especially after the country was defeated by Prussia in the war of 1870-71, French statesmen and scholars devoted much time and effort to analyzing why their country's families were getting smaller and how the trend could be reversed. In this respect, indeed, France was seen as a precursor of the West's future, and such eminent demographers as the American Joseph Spengler and the German Hans Harmsen also wrote books, respectively in English and German, on why French fertility was so low.[10]

In the 1870s, first some of France's employers and then, following their example, the national government started to pay a supplementary wage to workers based on the number of their dependents. With support for the measures from voters endorsing three significant ideologies—Catholic, meliorative, and pronatalist—family subsidies soon moved beyond criticism. Over the years they were increased in both the total amount and the sectors of the population covered.[11] These measures culminated in a Family Code, enacted in mid-1939 and put into effect under the Nazi occupation. Within a few months after the end of the Second World War in 1945, the government established the National Institute of Demographic Studies (INED) and charged it with providing an accurate factual base for pronatalist policy. Not only has *Population*, INED's principal periodical publication, been largely devoted to this task but also a good proportion of the rest of its typically excellent publications. In a projection of France's population to the year 2075, the various alternative routes to the future had in common the assumption that the population was moving toward stability.[12]

During the 1930s countries ranging in political orientation from Sweden and Britain to Nazi Germany and the Soviet Union initiated pronatalist measures of various sorts. They can be exemplified by laws in Fascist Italy, which used virtually every conceivable device to maintain its high rate of population growth. Special taxes were imposed on both bachelors and married couples with few or no children, and taxes were cut for those with large families; the dissemination of information on abortion or contraception was forbidden; families with many children were given preference in obtaining housing; bachelors in the civil service could not advance beyond a certain low level unless they married.[13]

In the most extensive analysis at the time, the English demographer David Glass demonstrated that throughout Western Europe neither coercion nor encouragement had worked. The one possible exception was Nazi Germany, where the stringent prohibition of abortion may have raised fertility, which in his view even that country's other pronatalist policies did not.[14] In the worldwide contest between parents and the state over which shall control the number of children born into each family, parents have generally come out the winner, but not when a government uses its full power to exert a contrary will.[15]

Current Policies in Developed Countries

Some years ago, when the Dutch demographer Dirk van de Kaa reviewed Europe's birth rates, he reported that many of them had fallen to below the replacement level.[16] An actual decline in numbers had started in Denmark, West Germany, Austria, and Hungary; and an earlier stage of the same process was evident in several more countries on both sides of the former Iron Curtain. Most European countries have half-acknowledged pronatalist policies, either positive (for instance, providing family subsidies and facilitating access to housing for newly married couples) or negative (for instance, the prohibition of abortion), or both. But to date there has been no sign of a second baby boom, similar to the one that ended the similar period of low natality a generation earlier.

In the United States, on the contrary, the noisiest activity has been the campaign to bring about zero population growth. From President Eisenhower's declaration that he could not imagine anything more emphatically *not* a proper function of government than providing birth control, only ten years passed to President Nixon's complete reversal of this directive. Nixon recommended that domestic family-planning services supported out of federal funds be expanded and integrated; and as a direct consequence of his message, Congress set up a Commission on Population Growth and the American Future to lay a foundation for antinatalist programs. The membership of the Commission included senators and congressmen, distinguished citizens, representatives of foundations, members of the black community, a Mexican American woman, a Puerto Rican, Catholics, physicians, youth (including a 19-year-old student)—and academic demographers headed by Charles Westoff of Princeton University as executive director.[17] The endeavor to have every interest group represented resulted in a final *Report* (1972) with an introduction titled "A Diversity of Views."[18] Of the several research papers commissioned, most were ignored in the final recommendations. After the Commission proposed that the country adopt a number of highly controversial antinatalist policies, the

President rejected the *Report* and Congress took no action concerning it. By 1972, when these recommendations were published, American women aged 18 to 24 reported that they expected to have an average of <2.0 children, or fewer than the 2.1 needed to maintain the population.

Throughout the West, an important factor in reducing fertility has been the fact that persons with fewer family responsibilities have had a greater possibility of rising in the social scale. Ethnic groups that have taken full advantage of the opportunities in America (such as Jews, Japanese, and Chinese) restrict their family responsibilities in order, among other motivations, to move up faster. The association between family size and upward mobility has also been intensified by the expanded ambitions and opportunities of women, many of whom prefer to work outside the home and raise the family income, rather than playing the traditional role of mother-housewife. Those with low incomes, on the other hand, since they sometimes see little chance of bettering themselves no matter what they do, have less incentive to use contraceptives effectively. In short, the operation of the labor market has been stimulating a decline in the reproduction of many Americans, but not always those with the smallest incomes.

Antinatalist Policies in the Third World

When today one reads of a population policy, the likely association with the term is not the pronatalist decrees of long ago or the effort to realize zero population growth in the United States, but rather the more recent, or current, endeavors to reduce the birth rates of less developed countries.

In spite of the wide divergence in these countries' size and population density, their family types, cultural practices affecting reproduction, and the level and rate of growth of their economies, their antinatalist programs have been remarkably similar; for these projects were almost all introduced, sponsored, and largely financed by Western (especially American) or international agencies. Since the administrators arrived with close to a consensus about the nature of the problem, they set a unitary perspective on the means by which it could be solved.[19]

After former colonies had realized their independence and were transformed into "less developed countries," the attendant élan reinforced the myth that earlier social and economic misfortunes had all been the consequence of colonial maladministration and that, therefore, a miraculous renaissance would be effected by the ouster of the imperial ruler. Population pressure, many of the new rulers maintained, had never been a factor in the country's poverty, and now that they controlled their own destiny, therefore, they saw no reason to sponsor family planning.

In 1948 Nehru termed India "an underpopulated country." In the first years after the Communist victory in China, the country's leaders declared its vast population to be its main economic asset; in the words of one official, "Man should be viewed as a producer rather than a consumer." Among an influential sector of Latin American politicians and intellectuals, an increase in numbers was applauded with an almost mystical faith in the benefits that more people would bring. Under Juan Perón, for example, the Argentine state hoped to double its population within a generation. Often these nationalist sentiments merged with the Marxist dogma that, given a just and efficient society, the size of a country's population is an irrelevance. A few decades later feminist doctrine also contributed its bit: as summed up in a recent book, the thesis that population increase is one cause of poverty leads to a pragmatic, even manipulative, approach and thus to a tendency to ignore gender equality and reproductive health.[20] In short, the antinatalist programs carried into the Third World had to cope with not only bureaucratic sloth and corruption but also at least initial doubts about their necessity or urgency.

Long before the euphoria of the new countries' leaders had begun to dissipate, Western demographers, zero populationists, and social workers, happy with their new role, started a massive undertaking to furnish contraceptive means to the peoples of less developed countries. Those who undertook this task assumed not only that the effects of rapid population growth were harmful and ultimately disastrous but also, with little or no evidence, that most of those bringing children into these populations shared this evidently obvious conviction. Thus, once potential parents learned of the existence of effective contraceptives and were helped financially and otherwise to procure them, the average family size and population growth would both decline—or so it was thought. Too often enormously complex dilemmas were presented with a one-dimensional simplicity.

What is Success?

With the frequently general purpose set for family-planning programs, they have often been pronounced "successful" by different, not necessarily complementary, criteria. One large school summarized the purpose of their efforts in the acronym KAP, for knowledge-attitude- practice. The first task, thus, was to spread knowledge about how the available contraceptives worked and where in that locality they could be obtained. The second step, in theory, would be to find out what attitudes among the target population were toward using contraceptives. In fact, however, family-planning administrators generally adopted what they termed "action-research": field workers undertook—simultaneously—to correct what they perceived as mistaken views and to understand their causes. Thus, instead of administrating a questionnaire that would aim at valid responses on how many children the respondents wanted, what their attitude toward contraceptives was, and other key questions about which field workers knew little or nothing, the typical procedure was to get the respondents to become "acceptors." A favorable disposition to the program's goal was first assumed and then confirmed by the mere acceptance of contraceptives that were proffered.

The complexity involved in implementing KAP programs can be portrayed best by concentrating on those in one or two countries, and one obvious choice is India, a prime target for such projects. In an interesting paper, the American demographer Edwin Driver contrasted the premises of American family-planners with those of scholars on Indian culture and society:[21]

- In India, unlike the United States, the basic social units are not the individual and his nuclear family, but rather the extended family, caste, and language community. Villages are not isolated social units, but are tied to outsiders through these structural links.
- Official regional languages are not necessarily understood by everyone in the region. For example, some prospective clients interpreted an announcement in Hindi that "there will be a show of healthy babies up to the age of three" as "there will be a wrestling match of three-year-old children."
- In India traditionalism is not always in conflict with modernism; the two points of view often fit together into patterns that generate neither cultural nor mental conflict.

In the view of the missionaries of our secular age, villagers who resisted their blandishments were ignorant and prejudiced, while those who willingly swallowed them were bathed in approval. In only one family-planning program in India were the results—that "nearly 90 percent were in favor of contraceptives"—checked by an independent scholar on the spot. He was told by one of the "acceptors":

> [The program's field workers] were so nice, you know. And they came from distant lands to be with us....All they wanted was that we accept the [foam] tablets. I lost nothing and probably received their prayers. And they, they must have gotten some promotion.[22]

Most of the "acceptors" said they had thrown the pills away; one of them used the unemptied boxes to build a tiny sculpture, which with calendar prints of movie stars helped to decorate the room.

Those who actually used the contraceptives did not necessarily contribute to a reduction in fertility. Some merely shifted to the means paid for by Western taxpayers, and program directors have pointed out that acceptors were quite happy with this adjustment in their family budgets!

> To argue that people who want contraceptives for their own good reasons do benefit if somebody else--namely, the general taxpayer—pays the bill is, of course, self-evident. But so would the argument that people would benefit from free breakfast, lunch, or dinner, or free shoes, free toothpaste, or free haircuts paid from public funds.[23]

In the best case, those that as a consequence of the crusade did control the number of births in their family were never typical of the target populations; they were the cream skimmed off the top, those most receptive to an antinatalist message.

Birth-control programs have seldom been evaluated by comparing an experimental with a control sector—the test that in other disciplines is routine. In the million-dollar Khanna study, exceptionally, the six Indian villages where the family-planning drive was concentrated were contrasted with six others. There was an overall temporary decline in the birth rate in the targeted area; but it began before the program got under way, for a certain period continued at the same rate among both the test and the control populations, and was the consequence of a rise in the age at marriage rather than an increased use of contraceptives.[24]

During the first decades of India's independence, the country's own family-planning programs were grossly underfunded, and sometimes they were run by principled opponents of their supposed purpose. Successively, various contraceptive means were used, with the effort eventually concentrated on vasectomies, or male sterilizations, which from the state's point of view have the advantage of requiring only a single contact with each person affected.

In the mid-1970s Karan Singh, India's minister for health and family planning, intensified prior antinatalist efforts. He suggested that the country might have to resort to what he termed "compulsuasion," an amalgam of *compul*sion and per*suasion*. Under that heading, civil servants were denied raises or transfers and sometimes even salaries until they had convinced a specified number of eligible parents to undergo sterilization. In some cities officials used the licensing of hotels, theaters, banks, airlines, and other businesses to force firms to induce their employees with three or more children to be sterilized. Opposition to the program was exacerbated by charges that the Hindu government was using it to reduce the proportions of Untouchables and especially of Muslims. Police and family planners were killed; in one antisterilization riot, according to seven opposition Members of Parliament, several dozen protesters were shot dead and 150 wounded.[25] This clash was a significant reason for the fall of the Gandhi government in 1977.

India's family-planning programs, whether those under government auspices or those imported from the West, were perhaps the most extensive, and expensive, in the whole widespread effort to reduce the fertility of the Third World. One of the most interesting comments on India's mission was a book that compared it with the mainly laissez-faire undertaking in Brazil. The decline of fertility in Brazil was both faster and more pervasive than that in India, and the authors analyze why this perhaps unanticipated result came about.[26] The most important point they make is to challenge the assumption underlying most family-planning programs—that if meaningful results are to be attained, the government has to be involved, perhaps even to the extent of using a bit of compulsuation.

China

The most notorious instance of coercion has, of course, been in Communist China. After the census of 1953 recorded an unexpectedly high population of 583 million, China's constitution was revised to include a new canon: "The State advocates and encourages birth control." Laws raised the minimum ages at marriage for the two sexes, and any who married earlier were forcibly separated. Urban families that qualified for a "one-child certificate" received a monthly stipend as well as preferential treatment in housing, jobs, pensions, and the child's schooling.

China's principal means of reducing the population growth, however, soon became a nationwide system of coerced abortions. Steven Mosher, then an American graduate student living in China, wrote an extensive report on the campaign.[27] (When the Chinese government complained to Stanford University about Mosher's all-too-accurate account, its anthropology department ousted him from its doctoral program.) John Aird, the best of American demographers who have specialized on China, wrote a fuller and well-documented record, *Slaughter of the Innocents*.[28] According to one account by a Chinese physician, in that country abortion is now termed "emergency contraception." He and several colleagues conducted a survey on the policy, financed by the World Health Organization.[29] In an interesting attempt to get under official statistics, a researcher compared two sets of records in one county of China, the data of the family-planning surveillance team and those on the vaccination of children. Amazingly, there was no significant difference between the two records—because, she hypothesized, of a consistent omission of above-quota births in *all* statistics: "Omission of births from statistical records is circular: failure to record a birth in the household registration system will be reflected in family-planning and in health records."[30]

There is no doubt, nevertheless, that the program has worked: according to the usual Western estimate, China's one-child policy cut the average family from six to somewhat more than two children. Like the pronatalist policy of Nazi Germany, the antinatalist program of Communist China was the only one that can be designated as unambiguously successful. The two instances suggest that totalitarian controls may be needed to bring about, independently of the couples' desires and whatever social-economic circumstances affect their wishes, either a rise or a fall in average family size.

Taiwan

The sharpest initial declines in the fertility of the Third World took place in small countries with relatively stable governments: Hong Kong,

Taiwan, Thailand, Mauritius, Costa Rica, Trinidad, and so on. The many proclamations of successful programs often based their exaggerated claims by citing these sometimes minuscule instances. Consider, for example, *Population: Dynamics, Ethics and Policy* (published by the American Association for the Advancement of Science), in which a chart is reproduced from an article by R. T. Ravenholt and John Chao, employees respectively of the U.S. Agency for International Development (AID) and the U.S. Bureau of the Census.[31] The chart includes only the 82 countries "with good vital statistics," and in 72 of them the crude birth rate declined over the period from 1960 to 1972--by a full 50 percent in Greenland down to 0.8 percent in St. Lucia. The table also includes Gibraltar, St.Kitts-Nevis, Cook Island, the Isle of Man, and the Faeroe Islands--whose combined population is well under that of the District of Columbia. Omitted are only less developed countries like Communist China, India, Pakistan, Bangladesh, Nigeria—or more than half of the population of the world.

Of 77 microstates (defined as nations with a 1970 population of less than half a million), 79 percent are islands and 15 percent are coastal. In the postcolonial period it was largely their geographic detachment that enabled them to remain independent, rather than being absorbed into larger new nations. For the same reason many had become outposts of Western culture: 85 percent are predominantly Christian, 91 percent have an official language taken over from Europe, and in most the expectation of life has been close to that in Western societies.[32] In short, they are intermediate between Western and non-Western in many of their cultural attributes, and the success of their family-planning programs should not have been taken as a reliable indicator for similar efforts elsewhere.

This category of nations can be more fully analyzed with a detailed exposition on one of them, Taiwan, which was also the site of one of the major efforts to introduce family planning. In 1960, when the Population Council in the United States decided to undertake a major research project in a less developed country, it selected Ronald Freedman of the Population Studies Center, University of Michigan, to head it. He has written a memoir on that experience, an account that reflects both his activities in Taiwan and his modest and thoroughly likable personality.[33]

He began by enlisting a Japanese-speaking native as his on-the-spot assistant, Yuzuru Takeshita. When they began their work in 1962, Taiwan had a small family-planning program in place, euphemistically called the Prepregnancy Health Program. Between 1958 and 1961, the island's total fertility rate (the sum of age-specific maternal fertility rates over the whole of the fecund period) had fallen by 8 percent, with the decline taking place in cities, small towns, and rural districts. As Freedman wrote in 1963:

> The patterns of fertility decline, signs of interest in family planning, and the increasing urbanization, education, and development in Taiwan make a continuing decline likely....[It] may take place while important aspects of the traditional Chinese family are maintained.[34]

As he remarked in retrospect, "This proved to be one of the best forecasts I have ever made, including the idea that the fertility transition would occur while traditional familial values persisted."[35]

In other words, the program lacked the handicaps that typically plagued projects in typical less developed countries. Acceptance of contraception had been developed by the broad social changes under way, as well as the prior three-year Prepregnancy Health Program. Field workers and especially their supervisors had been trained in that earlier effort. Several American physicians cooperated in training local workers in how to insert the IUD that was being used.

Seemingly the effort to reduce the number of children born was successful: from 1956 to 1984, the total fertility rate fell from 6.5 to 2.1. However, about a third of this decline was due to a smaller proportion of women getting married in their 20s.[36] In Freedman's own judgment:

> Taiwan's rapid fertility decline...was undoubtedly in major part a result of the spectacular economic and social development that occurred during that period. However, Taiwan's effective family-planning program probably speeded up the pace of the adoption of contraception.[37]

The contrast between "undoubtedly" and "probably" reflects Freedman's integrity, but it is in sharp opposition to many reports by other family-planning enthusiasts who cited the record in Taiwan as a proof of success in less developed countries generally.

Fertility Trends in the Third World

Positive evaluations of family-planning programs have varied according to the country affected, who judged the program (often the persons in the field who carried out the project—and looked forward to a renewal of their grant), and the criterion of achievement. Properly speaking, there is only one legitimate measure of success for a program that was instituted to reduce a nation's fertility. Statistics on money spent, visitors to clinics, IUDs inserted, and so on are, at best, merely supplementary to the main point: whether the fertility went down as a specific result of the behavior initiated by the program. In fact, thus, such projects cannot be evaluated unambiguously, for to measure their effect one should compare the present fertility not with that of the recent past (for any of a dozen other factors may have been operative) but with the level of fertility there would have been without the program. That can be estimated, but a guess made by the team that carried out the project is obviously suspect.

Until recently, the pattern of fertility in less developed countries was seldom unequivocal enough to settle the long debate between the "technological" and "developmental" schools. The first concentrated on family-planning programs, assuming that KAP marked the road that, irrespective of the social-economic context, most persons in less developed countries would follow. The developmental school focused on what determines the motivation of possible parents to use whatever contraceptives are available to them.

Typically children in the tropics cost very little extra to bring up, and they begin to bring material benefits to their parents at a very early age. A poor peasant, who cannot afford to hire help, depends on his family to furnish labor during the planting and harvesting seasons, and landless agriculturists also earn more if they have sizable families to work with them. For these large social classes, it has been argued, children constitute not only an economic asset but, at the lowest level, a virtual necessity. The Australian demographer John Caldwell summed up the thesis felicitously: fertility begins to fall when the flow of benefits from child to parent is reversed—that is, when any offspring costs the parents more than they contribute.[38]

A recent work that analyzes data collected in sometimes hostile settings gives some details about the conditions under which child labor prevails in India. As portrayed, the lives of working children is horrendous, and laws enacted to protect them are neither well constructed nor adequately enforced.[39] Paradoxically, it is partly because of the country's poverty that a family's numerous progeny are extremely valuable to the parents who exploit their children.

If this generalization is valid at the family level, and if rapid population growth is deleterious at the national level, the contradiction between the two cannot be easily resolved. The dilemma was perceived more clearly after those on both sides of the debate, most of whom had once been certain that their doctrine was inerrant, took account of conflicting evidence. The more reasonable advocates of family-planning programs started to offer more modest claims: *some* potential contraceptors will have fewer children and, because of the programs, fertility will (or may) fall *somewhat*, though possibly more slowly than was once hoped. And on the other side, those who held that family size is essentially a function of broad trends in the society began to admit that rapid population growth is often (or ordinarily) a serious impediment both to economic development generally and to such critical social transformations as a major reduction of illiteracy or a substantial rise in the status of women. Two partisan schools came closer together in a common admission of how ignorant both were of the determinants of fertility and of how to effect a significant change in it.

The United Nations defines the "least" developed countries as those with a combination of low income per capita, low literacy rates, and little manufacturing industry. Of the 36 such countries at a recent date, 26 were in Africa and 8 in Asia, plus Haiti and Samoa. In these populations, the proportion under age 15 ranged from over a third to not quite half, or in most of the countries 43 to 47 percent. In contrast, only 2 to 5 percent were aged 65 and over.[40] (The corresponding proportions of the United States population were, respectively, 22 and 12 percent.)

According to United Nations estimates, the number of children born per woman in "more developed regions" (Northern America, Europe, Japan, and Australia) had fallen to 1.59, or almost 25 percent less than the 2.1 children needed in the long run to maintain a population of the same size. More astoundingly, the trend in less developed countries has been the same, though from a far higher starting point. Over the past three decades the average in less developed countries fell from six children to three, with rates continuing to tumble almost everywhere. By the late 1990s the fertility of 19 less developed countries was below the level of replacement. As estimated for the years 1990-95, the annual rates of population increase in a number of representative less developed and industrial countries were as follows:[41]

Table 10.1

Central African Republic	2.5%	United States	1.0%
Egypt	2.1	Canada	2.2
Nigeria	3.0	Israel	3.5
Mexico	0.9	Japan	0.3
Brazil	1.5	Austria	0.8
China	1.1	Czech Republic	-0.1
India	2.3	France	0.5
Indonesia	1.5	Germany	0.6
Bulgaria	-1.4	Italy	-0.2
Hungary	-0.3	Russia	0.0
Romania	-1.4	Australia	1.1

Even though many of these figures are rough estimates, it is striking how little over-all difference there is between the two categories of nations. There are aberrations in both lists, but even when we include them it is clear that the general trend in population change is a global phenomenon.

According to the best-guess projections of the United Nations, the alternative labeled a "low-medium" future growth of numbers, the population of the world will rise to some 8 billion by the year 2050, and then fall to 6.4 billion over the following century. Indeed, neither the demographers at the United Nations nor any others have established a record for accurate forecasts; but it is at least true that the cries of imminent doom by the antinatalist zealots are somewhat out of date. "The population explosion is over!"[42] It is not likely that the global population of some 5.8 billion in the late 1990s will "double" over the next period, though in screeds of the many doomsayers this has remained the standard forecast.

People and Their Sustenance

The population of the world in 1996 was estimated at almost 5.8 billion, and reportedly it was growing by about 93 million per year, thus (with the same annual increment) reaching something like 7.6 billion by the year 2020. Many in Asia, Africa, Latin America, and elsewhere are hungry, and a frightening percentage of that number are starving. Conventionally these two facts—the growth of the world's population and the persistence of food shortages—are linked. People must eat, and if there are more people, then supplying them with sustenance is more difficult, if not impossible. What could be simpler—or more misleading?

Neither the number of people in the world nor their food supply is known with even modest accuracy. Some population statistics of less developed countries are considered to be of acceptable accuracy, some are not. The basis of most estimates for black Africa, for instance, is made up of more or less equal parts inaccurate local counts, cumbrous mathematical formulas, and wishful thinking. Take as an example the summary appraisal of Nigeria's statistics by the American demographer Etienne van de Walle:

> The very size of its population is uncertain after the last censuses, its mortality is unknown, and its fertility can only be guessed....No sophisticated procedure upon which we would base even a mere guess about what this population would be in 10, 15, or 25 years is justified. Unfortunately this is still true of a large part of Africa.[43]

Since that informed judgment was published, in 1968, social disorder and civil war have rendered Africa's population data even less credible.

The other side of the supposed imbalance, the world's production of food, is yet more elusive. Not only are there areas of total ignorance but the relatively good statistics of a few less developed countries, when used to answer the question of the general availability of sustenance, all contain a fundamental flaw. Data on food production are compiled mainly from commercial transactions, a reasonable enough procedure for the industrial societies that we know best. But in places where hunger is endemic, a large, indeterminate, and sometimes rapidly changing proportion of the food eaten is homegrown. What peasants raise to sustain their families may constitute as much as half, say, of the total consumed without ever appearing in laboriously maintained accounts.

In spite of the deficient record, such facts stand out as that Bangladesh, among the poorest and most densely populated of less developed countries, has been able to cut its grain imports drastically. Chinese corn, until the downturn of all East Asian economies, was flooding the markets of neighboring countries. Saudi Arabia is giving away wheat it no longer wants to store.

In 1987 India, once the usual worst-case example to make the doomsayers' argument, suffered the most destructive drought in 125 years. The two chief grain-producing states, Punjab and Hayana, had almost no rain, and most other states only between 40 and 80 percent of the long-term average. In Uttar Pradesh, the most populous state, half the land was not even sown. Hope that the monsoon would arrive in time to save the rice crop lasted till late July and then was proved futile. Until very recently such a natural disaster would have been the precursor to a major famine. This time the government had in reserve enormous stores out of past surpluses. From 1950 to 1983-84 total domestic production of food grains had tripled, and in mid-1987 the stocks totaled twice the amount probably needed to tide the country over the drought.

Anyone who tries to extrapolate the balance between the world's population and the food to nourish it, a relation impossible to calculate even at any single date, should admit to extreme fallibility. With that hedge, I nevertheless admit to a relative optimism concerning this trend. The so-called green revolution was apparently only the modest start of a new type of vastly improved agriculture. Within a decade or two it may well be possible to create new varieties of grains and other crops that will thrive in hostile climates, far outproduce existent types, and—unlike the present superplants—propagate themselves and establish new species.[44] At the current level of agricultural technology more than enough food could be grown for the present world population plus any likely extrapolation over the next hundred years, and there is every indication that we are on the threshold of a new breakthrough in food production.

This cautious optimism pertains, however, to a worldwide crunch that does not exist and will probably never develop. It does not mean that we should emulate Dr. Pangloss of Voltaire's *Candide* and proclaim this to be the best of all possible worlds. The greatest disservice of the doomsayers is that they have focused our attention on relatively tractable technical or ecological problems, to the neglect of more significant causes. Perhaps the most significant fact about the antinatalist zealots is not that many of them have persisted in their demonstrably wrong-headed propaganda, but that their works have largely obliterated what really warrants our concern.

The Roots of "Overpopulation"

The dramatic photographs of children with swollen bellies indicate not a shortage of food worldwide, either now or in the foreseeable future, but rather institutional blocks that impede or prevent its distribution. In that more relevant context, neither a greater supply of foodstuffs nor more effective family-planning programs, nor both of them together, will solve "the population problem." For in fact the problem is less technological than social-political, with a lack less of expedients than of the will or ability to apply them.

In the typical less developed country the state dominates all the pathways to modernization. Most bureaucracies are incompetent and corrupt, and the middle class—the sector of society that in the West brought about the transformation that the world now fervently desires—is small, weak, and beset by regulations. Partly for convenience but partly also following the antibourgeois ideology of many of their intellectuals, industrial nations have typically funneled much of their aid and investments through the state, thus aggravating its already overlarge power.

In the history of Europe and its overseas daughters, cities were constantly renewed by those in rural areas best suited to take on urban occupations. In less developed countries today, however, people are often pushed out by rural stagnation rather than pulled by urban opportunities, and in that case the innovative minority can be overwhelmed by a flood of unassimilable humanity.

Against that background, rapid population growth must be interpreted not as the sole or prime problem to be faced but as an added burden to societies often just barely managing to hold together, while each year additional thousands reach the age at which they also want to enter the work force. With every institution politicized, those unable to find jobs along what we might term normal routes seek them through family, tribal, or party preferment; and when these do not work, the unemployed may resort to rioting in the streets. Of the scarce jobs, many are improvised to discourage political unrest, fabricated openings more or less irrelevant to the economy. Governments therefore spend much of their scant resources of skill and intelligence merely on staying in power; social and economic bungling are aggravated by the constant growth in the number of persons affected.

The British sociologist Stanislav Andreski has coined the word kleptocracy to denote the rule by thieves that he found in his studies of Latin America and Africa.[45] In these areas (as well as much of Asia), the slumbering traditional economy motivates every ambitious young man to find an alternative to his father's way of life. But since private industry is small and often hampered by governmental restrictions, the best alternatives are limited to government jobs, from cabinet officers through various levels of civil service down to the rural police force. Though the state typically has many more such functionaries than are useful, thousands more clamor for their chance at the posts. Once hired, every new person "on the titty" (as one used to say of corrupt American political machines) knows that he may lose his post next year, or next month; he tries to make the most hay during his probably brief hours in the sun. Bribery is part of doing business; officials differ little in the degree of their rapacity. The rich maneuver successfully to evade taxes by bribing tax collectors. Laws enacted to reform the system create new opportunities to collect new tolls from those who want to evade also the freshly coined regulations.

Western journalists and analysts have often given less attention to such graft and the consequent inefficiency than their prevalence and importance would justify. All too frequently, when thievery is mentioned, we are promptly reminded that our own society is not blameless. The difference is a contrast between aberrations and an all but universal pattern. Businessmen and administrators of relief programs have had to learn, they say, to accommodate to the corruption and help cover up the ubiquitous fraud. For instance, they argue that the assistance projects, in spite of their unequivocal faults, do permit some of the urgently needed help to get through to those in dire need. If sometimes this point may be well based, it also reflects a patent conflict of interest, for the Westerners are also demanding that their programs and their jobs continue to be funded.

The euphoria that greeted the rise of the several remarkably successful economies in East Asia evaporated when that bubble burst. Western observers then began to point out that the role of a few families in running Indonesia, for example, hardly constituted the optimum arrangement for either that country's people or world commerce. Because so much attention had been focused on the relation between people and food, it was only after disaster struck that most analysts and journalists seriously considered the effects of a weak or absent middle class and the correlative dominance of grossly corrupt governments.

11

Conclusions

The most prominent over-all feature of the preceding chapters is technical innovation. New ways of making babies, combined with advances in obstetrics, have extended the boundaries of fecundity and made the study of fertility more complex. One medical breakthrough after another has prolonged life to a span that a generation or two ago would have been called utopian, and a cornucopia of new drugs keeps the aging populations of Western countries in relative comfort. The computer in all its various guises has been a factor in these developments, as well as revolutionizing the collection, compilation, and publication of population statistics.

As with all mammoth changes, these have brought new woes as well as great solace. In vitro fertilization is expensive and cumbersome, and it brings with it legal and ethical dilemmas. The upheaval in medical institutions, ranging from heavy investments in drug research and the implementation of novel techniques to such pioneering procedures as managed care, on balance as great an improvement in disease control as any the world has seen, has nevertheless been a source of complaints and lawsuits, generated in part by an army of lawyers.

Nor has the mechanization of statistical operations been only a benefit. More than ever in the past, the user of the data needs a consumer's guide, which is what I have tried to provide in this book. Every figure is at best an approximation, and all too often a guess. Thousands of Americans are invented in each census; not only their characteristics but their very existence is "imputed" by importing both the being and the attributes of their neighbors into a statistical creature. The neat columns in the tables were well massaged. Nonresponses have disappeared, those who have not answered questions in the schedule have their characteristics supplied for them by an all-knowing computer.

All the data collected are incomplete and in part false. Every consumer should hold to this inescapable fact as he reads the statistics. It is beyond the power of even the most efficient and conscientious staff to compile, without error, a perfect record on several hundred million persons. Even after field-testing every question, the Census Bureau finds time and again that some persons misunderstand its meaning and respond with nonsense. Questions on age, income, education, and other attributes imply a scale from more to less desirable: how many persons answer that they really are younger than their actual age, that they attended college when they did not finish high school, that they really earn as much as they would like to? It hurts no one, a respondent might think, and raises his spirit if he records a few white lies.

In spite of all their flaws and limitations, data on population are in ever greater demand. No businessman, no official of government whether national, state, or local, no person in charge of an educational or other non-profit institution, can function efficiently without detailed knowledge of how many clients or customers he has to serve. The population statistics as collected are valid enough to serve such purposes. The issue is how the users should regard them.

What did President Nixon mean with his remark, "We are all Keynesians now"? Certainly not that everyone had read and understood Keynes's works on economics, nor even that Nixon himself had. When Keynes spoke on policy, Nixon was saying, what he asserted was to be accepted as authoritative. It might be that political leanings dictated some of Keynes's proposals, but that possibility was to be ignored, was not even to be considered.

Today, in that sense, we all used to be demographers, and a major shift in public opinion may have taken place over the past several decades. When the census spoke through its innumerable publications, we used not to ask how the data were compiled, whether a bias or two may have been encapsulated in the questions, how close to reality the statistics were. This was the authoritative word, and anyone who cited the figures won all arguments.

Increasingly, the Bureau of the Census has had to cope with several limitations on its operations. A constant one has been the contrast between expanding tasks and a limited budget. Several decades ago I met Conrad Taeuber, a long-time census official, and he evinced more interest than I could have anticipated in the fact that I was then living in Ohio. What would I recommend, he asked, that the Bureau do about a certain congressman from that state who happened to be on the committee that controlled the Bureau's budget. At a recent hearing, Taeuber told me, he explained to the committee that not only was the decennial enumeration required by the Constitution but the resultant statistics were indispensable for governments at every level and for businesses throughout the country. The man from Ohio said all that was fine, but why did the Bureau have to spend all that money counting the people in every village and town. When he wanted such information, he simply looked up the figure in the *World Almanac*. I was not able to give Taeuber any useful advice.

A second, and incremental, obstacle to efficient operations of the Bureau is that a variety of pressure groups now take a greatly increased interest in what it does. One element of an individual's persona about which feelings often runs very high is race or ethnicity. In a futile attempt to mitigate postcensal criticisms, the Bureau set up special committees of interested persons, who during the past several counts have been consulted on the wording and placement of questions, on how many sectors of America's heterogeneous population were to be specified (in the long or only the short form), and so on. Obviously those who found their way to places on these committees were often the most implacable spokesmen for blacks, Latinos, and other minorities. Their interest was hardly in technical details or even in obtaining the most accurate count, but rather in getting as many of their kind listed as possible. If there are alternative answers, many respondents will choose the first option listed; therefore should not my alleged constituents lead all the others? If some members of a minority want to call themselves "blacks" and others insist on "African Americans," or "Hispanics" versus "Latinos," such disputes do not make the Bureau's task easier.

A more serious restraint on the Bureau's activities has developed as census figures were used to allocate more and more benefits from the federal treasury. Lawyers for large cities, who claimed they lost millions of dollars through undercounts, challenged both the 1980 and the 1990 results. They lost both sets of suits, but the Bureau forfeited some of its earlier automatic authority. As a device to improve the 2000 enumeration, Bureau officials proposed that they count only 90 percent of the population and estimate the remaining residents by sampling, and I have discussed as some length the long and often acrimonious debate over that suggestion. Though sometimes represented as essentially a technical issue, whether to use sampling is basically a political dispute. Is it unreasonable that the Republicans in Congress believe that sampling would be used in 2000 to give Democrats an unlawful advantage in setting the borders of subsequent congressional districts? I think not.

The census has always been in large part a political document, and in recent administrations it has become more so. Paradoxically, it is possible to administer a statistical bureau most objectively when no one cares what the statistical record reveals. But in real life such agencies the world over spend most of their effort gathering data that affect the lives of many powerful people and institutions. The final encumbrance of the Census Bureau is that the likelihood of intrusion by such people and institutions has grown greatly.

One defense against all these limitations is to know about them, and to use the Bureau's statistics keeping that knowledge in mind. It is to give the average citizen some of the background he will need for such a review that I have written this book. It is not a text in demography, though much that would be in such a book has been touched on and students, in my opinion, would benefit from reading it. It is rather an extended commentary on how population data are collected, what flaws they contain, and how a wary consumer should use them.

Notes

Chapter 1: Population: The Fundamentals

1. Cf. Ernst Mayr, *This Is Biology: The Science of the Living World* (Cambridge, Mass.: Belknap Press, 1997), 210-11.
2. Irene B. Taeuber, *The Population of Japan* (Princeton, N.J.: Princeton University Press, 1948), 198-99.
3. G. Pascal Zachary, "Dual Citizenship is a Double-Edged Sword," *Wall Street Journal* (25 March 1998).
4. Frank W. Notestein, "Demography in the United States: A Partial Account of the Development of the Field," *Population and Development Review* 8 (1982): 651-87.
5. United Nations, *The Determinants and Consequences of Population Trends: New Summary of Findings on Interaction of Demographic, Economic, and Social Factors*, 2 vols. (New York, 1973, 1978).
6. Cf. Frank H. Hankins, *Adolphe Quetelet as Statistician* (New York: Columbia University Press, 1908). Marc Lebrun, ed., *Adolphe Quetelet: L'Oeuvre sociologique et démographique, Choix de textes* (Brussels: Office International de Librairie, 1974).
7. Paul Vincent, "Conception d'un dictionnaire démographique," *Population* 8 (1953): 103-20. See also Judith Blake, "Sociological Perspectives on Population Studies," in Robert Schoen and David Landman, eds., *Population Theory and Policy* (Urbana: University of Illinois Press, 1982); "Issues in the Training and Recruitment of Demographers," *Demography* 1 (1964): 258-63.
8. Roland Pressat, "Le vocabulaire de la démographie," *Population* 35 (1980): 849-59; *Dictionnaire de démographie* (Paris: Presses Universitaires de France, 1979).
9. William and Renee Petersen, *Dictionary of Demography*, 5 vols.: *Terms, Concepts and Institutions*; a *Multilingual Dictionary*; and *Biographies* (Westport, Conn.: Greenwood Press, 1985-86).
10. Dennis Hodgson, "Demography as Social Science and Policy Science," *Population and Development Review* 9 (1983): 1-34.
11. Josef Ehrner, "Eine 'deutsche' Bevölkerungsgeschichte? Gunther Ipsens historische-soziologische Bevölkerungstheorie," *Demografische Informationen* (1992-93): 60-70.
12. Philip Kreager, "Histories of Demography: A Review Article," *Population Studies* 47 (1993): 519-39.
13. Nathan Keyfitz, *Resolution of Interdisciplinary Contradictions and the Use of Science in Policy* (Amsterdam: PDOD Paper no. 14, 1993).
14. Walter F. Willcox, "Development of International Statistics," in Milbank

Memorial Fund, *Problems in the Collection and Comparability of International Statistics* (New York, 1949).
15. New York: Columbia University Press, 1948. See also A. J. Jaffe, "Notes on the Population Theory of Eugene M. Kulischer," *Milbank Memorial Fund Quarterly* 40 (1962): 187-206.
16. William Petersen, *Population*, 3rd ed. (New York: Macmillan, 1975).
17. See Fulmer Mood, "The Origin, Evolution, and Application of the Sectional Concept, 1750-1900," in Merrill Jensen, ed., *Regionalism in America* (Madison: University of Wisconsin Press, 1965).
18. These regions were mapped by Management Horizons, Inc., as discussed in Thomas I. Rubel, "Metros, Markets...and More," *American Demographics* 5 (July 1983): 22-25, 40.
19. United Nations, *Demographic Yearbook, 1977* (New York, 1978), Supplement.
20. Walter F. Willcox, "Special Reports, Supplementary Analyses and Derivative Tables," *Twelfth Census of the United States, 1900* (Washington, D.C.: U.S. Bureau of the Census, 1906), 88.
21. *Washington Times* (4-10 March 1996).
22. William Petersen, *Ethnicity Counts* (New Brunswick, N.J.: Transaction, 1997), 121.
23. Romanzo C. Adams, "Japanese Migration Statistics," *Sociology and Social Research* 13 (1929): 436-45.
24. Cf. Barbara S. Mensch, "Quantifying Quality: Examples from Africa," in Laurie Ann Mazur, ed., *Beyond the Numbers: A Reader on Population, Consumption, and the Environment* (Washington, D.C.: Island Press, 1994), 174-76.
25. Judith Banister, "Use and Abuse of Census Editing and Imputation," *Asian and Pacific Census Forum* (6 February 1980): 1-2, 16-20. See also Steven B. Cohen, "An Analysis of Alternative Imputation Strategies for Individuals with Partial Data in the National Medical Care Expenditure Survey," *Review of Public Data Use* 10 (1982): 153-65.
26. Edward Felsenthal, "Supreme Court Expresses Concern over Delay in Census Preparations," *Wall Street Journal* (1 December 1998).
27. Lexington, "The Travails of a Census Man," *Economist* (5 December 1998).
28. Margo Anderson, *The American Census: A Social History* (New Haven, Conn.: Yale University Press, 1988).
29. Petersen, *Ethnicity Counts*, 170.

Chapter 2: Age and Sex

1. Murray Feshbach, "Between the Lines of the 1979 Soviet Census," *Population and Development Review* 8 (1982): 347-61.
2. Larry D. Barnett, "Zero Population Growth, Inc.," *BioScience* 21 (1971): 759-65; "Zero Population Growth, Inc.: A Second Survey," *Journal of Biosocial Sciences* 6 (1974): 1-22.

3. For example, Richard A. Easterlin, *Birth and Fortune: The Impact of Numbers on Personal Welfare* (Chicago: University of Chicago Press, 1987).
4. Cf. Annette Degenhardt, Paul Tholey, and Hedwig Michaelis, "Primary Sex Ratio of 124 Males to 100 Females? Analysis of an Artifact," *Journal of Human Evolution* 9 (1980): 651-54. Jack A. Pritchard, Paul C. MacDonald, and Norman F. Grant, *Williams Obstetrics*, 17th ed. (Norwalk, Conn.: Appleton-Century-Crofts, 1985), 170. James S. Thompson and Margaret W. Thompson, *Genetics in Medicine* (Philadelphia: Saunders, 1986), chap. 7.
5. Michele Marcus et al., "Changing Sex Ratio in the United States, 1969-1995," *Fertility and Sterility* 70 (August 1998): 270-73.
6. David M. Rorvik and Landrum B. Shettles, *Your Baby's Sex: Now You Can Choose* (New York: Dodd, Mead, 1970).
7. Gerald E. Markle, "Sex Ratio at Birth: Values, Variance, and Some Determinants," *Demography* 19 (1982):177-89.
8. Daniel J. Levinson, *The Seasons of a Man's Life* (New York: Alfred A. Knopf, 1978); *The Seasons of a Woman's Life* (New York: Alfred A. Knopf, 1996).
9. Jacob S. Siegel, "Demographic Aspects of Aging and the Older Population in the United States," *Current Population Reports*, Ser. P-23, no. 59 (Washington, D.C.: U.S. Bureau of the Census, 1976).
10. Marcia Mogelonsky, "Road to Adulthood," *American Demographics* (April 1996): 26-35, 56.
11. Charlotte Höhn and Bernd Stötzbach, "Die demographische Alterung in den Ländern der Europäischen Union," *Geographische Zeitschrift* 82 (1994): 198-213. See also Council of Europe, *Recent Demographic Developments in Europe, 1997* (Strasbourg, 1997); Nathan Keyfitz and Wilhelm Flieger, *World Population Growth and Aging: Demographic Trends in the Late 20th Century* (Chicago: Chicago University Press, 1990).
12. Fred Arnold et al., *The Value of Children: A Cross-National Survey*, vol. 1 (Honolulu: East-West Institute, 1975).
13. Michael S. Rendall and Raisa A. Bahchieva, "An Old-age Security Motive for Fertility in the United States?" *Population and Development Review* 14 (1998): 293-307.
14. Basil Hall Chamberlain, *Japanese Things: Being Notes on Various Subjects Connected with Japan* (Rutland, Vermont: Charles E. Tuttle, 1971), 165-66.
15. "Privatising Peace of Mind: A Survey of Social Insurance," *Economist* (24-30 October 1998).
16. Alfred Sauvy, *L'Europe et sa population* (Paris: Éditions Internationales, 1953), 119.
17. Charles R. Morris, *The AARP: America's Most Powerful Lobby and the Clash of Generations* (New York: Random House, 1996).
18. *Wall Street Journal* (13 August 1997).

Chapter 3: Population Composition

1. Cf. William Petersen, "Religious Statistics in the United States," *Journal for the Scientific Study of Religion* 1 (Spring 1962): 165-78.
2. Lisa Miller, "The Age of Divine Diversity," *Wall Street Journal* (10 February 1999).
3. Andrew M. Greeley, *That Most Distressful Nation:The Taming of the American Irish* (Chicago: Quadrangle Books, 1972), chap. 6.
4. Cf. William Petersen, "Jews as a Race," *Midstream* (February-March 1988): 35-37.
5. Ashley Montagu, *Man's Most Dangerous Myth: The Fallacy of Race*, 4th ed. (Cleveland: World Publishing Co., 1964), 25.
6. Pierre L. van den Berghe, *Race and Racism: A Comparative Analysis* (New York: Wiley, 1967), 9; "Class, Race, and Ethnicity in Africa," *Ethnic and Racial Studies* (1983): 221-36.
7. Thomas Sowell, "Three Black Histories," in Sowell, ed., *Essays and Data on American Ethnic Groups* (Washington, D.C.: Urban Institute, 1978).
8. Cf. William Petersen, *Ethnicity Counts* (New Brunswick, N.J.: Transaction Publishers, 1997), chaps. 3-4.
9. U.S. Office of Federal Statistical Policy and Standards, "Race and Ethnic Standards for Federal Statistics and Administrative Reporting," Directive no. 15 (Washington, D.C., May 1978). See also Katherine K. Wallman and John Hodgdon, "Race and Ethnic Standards for Federal Statistics and Administrative Reporting," *Statistical Reporter*, no. 77-10 (July 1977): 450-54.
10. See pp. 8-9.
11. W. Augustus Low and Virgil A. Clift, *Encyclopedia of Black America* (New York: McGraw-Hill, 1981), 656-57.
12. Ralph C. Guzmán, *The Political Socialization of the Mexican American People* (New York: Arno Press, 1970), 187.
13. U.S. Bureau of the Census, *1990 Census of Population and Housing, Summary Population and Housing Characteristics, United States* (Washington, D.C.: 1992), B-11.
14. U.S. Bureau of the Census, "Accuracy of Data for Selected Population Characteristics as Measured by the 1970 CPS-Census Match," PHC (E)-1 (Washington, D.C., 1992).
15. R. A. Hahn, "Inconsistencies in Coding of Race and Ethnicity between Birth and Death in U.S. Infants: A New Look at Infant Mortality, 1983 through 1985," *Journal of the American Medical Association* 267 (8 January 1992): 268-71. 16. U.S. Bureau of Indian Affairs, *Information about the Indian People* (Washington, D.C., 1981).
17. Stephan and Abigail Thernstrom, *America in Black and White: One Nation Indivisible* (New York: Simon & Schuster, 1997), 527.
18. Ibid., 523-27.
19. Ira S. Lowry, *The Science and Politics of Ethnic Enumeration*, Rand Pa-

pers Series, no. P-6435-1 (Santa Monica, Calif., 1980), 19. See also Richard D. Alba, "Assimilation's Quiet Tide," *Public Interest*, no. 19 (Spring 1995): 3-18.

Chapter 4: From Fecundity to Fertility

1. Raphael Jewelowicz and Sharon B. Jaffe, "Amenorrhea," in John J. Sciarra, ed., *Gynecology and Obstetrics* (Philadelphia: Lippincott, 1994), vol. 5, chap. 21.
2. James S. Thompson and Margaret W. Thompson, *Genetics in Medicine* (Philadelphia: Saunders, 1986), chap. 2.
3. Sergio C. Stone and Gregory F. Rosen, "Physiology of Puberty," in Sciarra, *Gynecology and Obstetrics*, vol. 5, chap. 9. Robert W. Rebar, "Puberty," in Jonathan S. Berek, ed., *Novak's Gynecology*, 12th ed. (Baltimore: Williams & Wilkins, 1996), 771-807.
4. Joginder Kumar, "The Recent Level of Age at Menarche and the Effect of Nutrition Level and Socio-economic Status on Menarche: A Comparative Study," *Eastern Anthropologist* 28 (1975): 99-131. Grace Wyshak and Rose E. Frisch, "Evidence for a Secular Trend in Age at Menarche," *New England Journal of Medicine* 306 (1982): 1033-35.
5. Phillips Cutright, "The Teenage Sexual Revolution and the Myth of an Abstinent Past," *Family Planning Perspectives* 4 (1972): 24-38.
6. Raymond Pearl, *The Natural History of Population* (New York: Oxford University Press, 1939), 57-58. Robert R. Kuczynski, *The Measurement of Population Growth: Methods and Results* (London: Sidgwick & Jackson, 1935), 106-10.
7. Ansley J. Coale, *The Growth and Structure of Human Populations: A Mathematical Investigation* (Princeton, N.J.: Princeton University Press, 1972), 5-6.
8. Leon Speroff et al., *Clinical Gynecologic Endocrinology and Infertility* (Baltimore: Williams & Wilkins, 1973), chap. 12. 9. F. J. Schoeneck, "The 'Normal' Menstrual Cycle," *Obstetrics and Gynecology*
9. (1957): 739; cited in S. Leon Israel, *Diagnosis and Treatment of Menstrual Disorders and Sterility*, 5th ed. (New York: Hoeber Medical Division, Harper & Row, 1967), 99.
10. Steven F. Palter and David L. Olive, "Reproductive Physiology" in Berek, *Novak's Gynecology*, 149-72.
11. Israel, *Diagnosis and Treatment*, 72, 101.
12. Cf. Jeffrey A. Kurland, "Paternity, Mother's Brother, and Human Sociality," in Napoleon A. Chagnon and William Irons, eds., *Evolutionary Biology and Human Social Behavior: An Anthropological Perspective* (North Scituate, Mass.: Duxbury Press, 1979). See also Richard D. Alexander and Katharine M. Noonan, "Concealment of Ovulation, Parental Care and Human Social Evolution," in Chagnon and Irons, *Evolutionary Biology*

and Human Social Behavior; Ronald D. Lee, "Population Dynamics of Humans and Other Mammals," *Demography* 24 (1987): 443-65.
13. Katharine Bement Davis, *Factors in the Sex Life of Twenty-two Hundred Women* (New York: Harper, 1929). See also Cynthia Hedricks et al., "Peak Coital Rate Coincides with Onset of Luteinizing Hormone Surge," *Fertility and Sterility* 48 (1987): 234-38.
14. Bronislaw Malinowski, *Sex, Culture, and Myth* (New York: Harcourt, Brace and World, 1962).
15. Peter Laslett et al., eds., *Bastardy and Its Comparative History* (Cambridge, Mass.: Harvard University Press, 1980), Introduction.
16. Beth Berkov and June Sklar, "Does Illegitimacy Make a Difference? A Study of the Life Chances of Illegitimate Children in California," *Population and Development Review* 2 (1976): 356-71.
17. Robert Darnton, *The Kiss of Lamourette: Reflections in Cultural History* (New York: Norton, 1990), 10.
18. La Leche League International, *The Womanly Art of Breastfeeding*, 4th ed. (Franklin Park, Ill., 1987).
19. Roger Short, "Nature's Contraceptive," *Journal of Biosocial Science*, Supplement 9 (1985): 1-3.
20. Ron Lesthaeghe and Hilary J. Page, "The Postpartum Nonsusceptible Period: Development and Application of Model Schedules," *Population Studies* 34 (1980): 143-70. Kathleen Ford and Young Kim, "Distribution of Postpartum Amenorrhea: Some New Evidence," *Demography* 24 (1987): 413-30. World Health Organization, "Multinational Study of Breast-feeding and Lactational Amenorrhea. I," *Fertility and Sterility* 70 (September 1998): 448-60.
21. Miriam H. Lubbock and Virginia H. Laukaran, "Breastfeeding and Family Planning," in Sciarra, *Gynecology and Obstetrics*, vol. 6, chap. 36. Marjorie P. Elias et al., "Nursing Practices and Lactation Amenorrhea," *Journal of Biosocial Science* 18 (1986): 1-10. Gigi Santow, "Reassessing the Contraceptive Effect of Breastfeeding," *Population Studies* 41 (1987): 147-60. Robert Buchanan et al., "Breast-feeding: Aid to Infant Health and Fertility Control," *Population Reports: Family Planning Programs*, Series J, no. 4 (Washington, D.C.: George Washington University Medical Center, 1975). Jeroen K. van Ginneken, "Prolonged Breastfeeding as a Birth-spacing Method," *Studies in Family Planning* 5 (1974): 201-6; "The Impact of Prolonged Breastfeeding on Birth Intervals and on Postpartum Amenorrhea," in William H. Mosley, ed., *Nutrition and Human Reproduction* (New York: Plenum, 1978). James B. Brown et al., "A Study of Returning Fertility after Childbirth and during Lactation by Measurement of Urinary Oestrogen and Pregnanediol Excretion and Cervical Mucus Production," *Journal of Biosocial Science* 9 (1985): 5-23.
22. For example, Ron Lesthaeghe, "The Breast-feeding Hypothesis and Regional Differences in Marital Fertility and Infant Mortality in the Low Countries During the 19th Century: Comments on a Debate," Interuniversity Programme in Demography, *Working Papers 1987-3* (Brussels: Vrije

Universiteit, 1987). Sølvi Sogner, "Allaitement au sein et abstinence sexuelle au Moyen Age," *Annales de Démographie Historique* (1986): 353-59.
23. Nancy Howell, "The Population of the Dobe Area !Kung," in Richard B. Lee and Irven DeVore, eds., *Man the Hunter* (Chicago: Aldine, 1968).
24. Ibid.
25. Lorna Marshall, *The !Kung of Nyae Nyae* (Cambridge, Mass.: Harvard University Press, 1976), chaps. 3-4.
26. Chung-li Chang, *The Chinese Gentry: Studies on Their Role in the Nineteenth-Century Chinese Society* (Seattle: University of Washington Press, 1955), 112-13.
27. Wolfram and Alide Eberhard, "Family Planning in a Taiwanese Town," in Wolfram Eberhard, *Settlement and Social Change in Asia* (Hong Kong: Hong Kong University Press, 1967).
28. John Hajnal, "European Marriage Patterns in Perspective," in D. V. Glass and D. E. C. Eversley, eds., *Population in History* (Chicago: Aldine, 1965).
29. Jack Goody, *The Development of Family and Marriage in Europe* (Cambridge, England: Cambridge University Press, 1983).
30. George Homans, *English Villagers of the Thirteenth Century* (Cambridge, Mass.: Harvard University Press, 1941), 136-37.
31. J. A. Banks, *Prosperity and Parenthood: A Study of Family Planning among the Victorian Middle Classes* (London: Routledge & Kegan Paul, 1954), 48 and passim.
32. David Sven Reher, "Family Ties in Western Europe: Persistent Contrasts," *Population and Development Review* 24 (1998): 203-34.
33. Malcolm Potts, "History of Contraception," in Sciarra, *Gynecology and Obstetrics*, vol. 6. chap. 8.
34. Robert V. Wells, "Fertility Control in Nineteenth-Century America: A Study of Diffusion, Technique, and Motive," in American Academy of Arts and Sciences, "Historical Perspectives on the Scientific Study of Fertility in the United States" (Boston: mimeographed, 1978).
35. Louise B. Tyrer and Jacqueline Darroch Forrest, "Fertility Regulation in the United States," in Sciarra, *Gynecology and Obstetrics*, vol. 6, chap. 11.
36. Alex M. Freedman, "Why Teenage Girls Love 'the Shot,'" *Wall Street Journal* (14 October 1998).
37. Ian H. Thorneycroft et al., "Multi-dose Depo Provera 400mg/ml Is an Effective Contraceptive," Sixteenth World Congress on Fertility and Sterility, San Francisco, October 4-9, 1998, *Abstracts*, S164.
38. Leon Speroff, Robert H. Glass, and Nathan G. Kase, *Clinical Gynecologic Endocrinology and Infertility* (Baltimore: Williams & Wilkins, 1973).
39. M. G. Bulmer, *The Biology of Twinning in Man* (Oxford: Clarendon, 1970).
40. William D. Mosher, "Reproductive Impairments in the United States, 1965-1982," *Demography* 22 (1985): 415-30; "Infertility Trends among U.S. Couples: 1965—1976," *Family Planning Perspectives* 14:1 (1982): 22-27. Stanley K. Henshaw and Margaret Terry Orr, "The Need and Unmet

Need for Infertility Services in the United States," *Family Planning Perspectives* 19:4 (1987): 180-87.
41. Elizabeth Hervey Stephen and Anjani Chandra, "Updated Projections of Infertility in the United States: 1995-2025," *Fertility and Sterility* 70 (July 1998): 30-34.
42. Elwyn M. Grimes and Marilyn R. Richardson, "Management of the Infertile Couple," in Sciarra, *Gynecology and Obstetrics*, vol. 5, chap. 50.
43. Mark D. Hornstein and Daniel Schust, "Infertility," in Berek, *Novak's Gynecology*, 915-62.
44. Anne Retel-Laurentin, *Infécondité en Afrique Noire: Maladies et conséquences sociales* (Paris: Masson, 1974); *Infécondité et maladies chez les Nzakara, République Centrafricaine* (Paris: Institut de la Statistique et des Études Économiques, 1974); "Évaluation du rôle de certaines maladies dans l'infécondité: Un exemple africain," *Population* 33 (1978): 101-18; "Causes de l'infécondité dans la Volta Noire," *Population* 35 (1980): 1151-62.
45. Odile Frank, *Infertility in Sub-Saharan Africa*, Center for Policy Studies, Working Paper no. 97 (New York: Population Council, 1983); "Infertility in Sub-Saharan Africa: Estimates and Implications, *Population and Development Review* 9 (1983): 137-44.
46. Abate Mammo and S. Philip Morgan, "Childlessness in Rural Ethiopia," *Population and Development Review* 12 (1986): 533-46.
47. *Lancet*, 351 (24 January 1998): 232-34. *New York Times* News Service (28 October 1998).
48. Rose E. Frisch, "Population, Food Intake, and Fertility," *Science*, 199 (6 January 1978): 22-30; "Population, Nutrition, and Fecundity: Significance for Interpretation of Changes in Fertility," in Nick Eberstadt, ed., *Fertility Decline in Less Developed Countries* (New York: Praeger, 1981). John Bongaarts, "Malnutrition and Fecundity: A Summary of the Evidence," Center for Policy Studies, *Working Papers*, no. 51 (New York: Population Council, 1979).
49. Phelim P. Boyle and Cormac Ó Gráda, "Fertility Trends, Excess Mortality, and the Great Irish Famine," *Demography* 23 (1986): 543-62, as well as other studies cited there.
50. L. H. Lumey and Aryeh D. Stein, "In Utero Exposure to Famine and Subsequent Fertility: The Dutch Famine Birth Cohort Study," *American Journal of Public Health* 87 (1997): 1962-70.
51. Thomas G. Stovall and Marian L. McCord, "Early Pregnancy Loss and Ectopic Pregnancy," in Berek, *Novak's Gynecology*, 497-523. See also Speroff et al., *Clinical Gynecologic Endocrinology and Infertility*, chap. 15.
52. Deborah Yaeger, "Doctors Make Progress in Treating Infertility, But Costs Are High," *Wall Street Journal* (12 October 1984).
53. Margaret A. Jacobs, "Women Seek Infertility Benefits in Suits," *Wall Street Journal* (12 June 1996). For an informative book on the same theme, see Judith Steinberg Turiel, *Beyond Second Opinions: Choices about Fertil-*

ity Treatments (Berkeley: University of California Press, 1998). See also K. M. Hill et al., "Women's Described Experiences of an In Vitro Fertilization (IVF) Cycle," Sixteenth World Congress on Fertility and Sterility, San Francisco, October 4-9, 1998, *Abstracts*, S38.

54. Peter Singer and Deane Wells, *Making Babies: The New Science and Ethics of Conception* (New York: Charles Scribner's Sons, 1985), chaps. 1-3.
55. David R. Meldrum, "In Vitro Fertilization and Embryo Transfer," in Sciarra, *Gynecology and Obstetrics*, vol. 5, chap. 97.
56. William S. Andereck et al., "The Ethics of Guaranteeing Patient Outcomes" and Richard T. Scott, Jr. and Kaylen Silverberg, "Ethics of Guaranteeing Patient Outcome: A Complex Issue Whose Time Has Not Come," *Fertility and Sterility* 70 (September 1998): 416-24.
57. M. R. Maifeld et al., "Decision-making regarding Multifetal Reduction," Sixteenth World Congress on Fertility and Sterility, San Francisco, October 4-9, 1998, *Abstracts*, S36.
58. George L. Annas, "The Shadowlands—Secrets, Lies, and Assisted Reproduction," *New England Journal of Medicine* 339 (1998): 935-39.
59. David Rorvik, *In His Image: The Cloning of a Man* (New York: Lippincott, 1978). Cf. Singer and Wells, *Making Babies*, chap. 6.
60. John A. Calhoun, "The 1980 Child Welfare Act," *Children Today* 9 (September-October 1980), 2-4, 36.
61. Virgil L. Klunder, *Lifeline: The Action Guide to Adoption Search* (Cape Coral, Fla.: Caradium Publishing, 1991). O. Robin Sweet and Patty Bryan, *Adopt International: Everything You Need to Know to Adopt a Child from Abroad* (New York: Farrar, Straus and Giroux, 1996).
62. Carl L. Harter, "The Fertility of Sterile and Subfecund Women in New Orleans," *Social Biology* 17 (1970): 195-206.
63. Joseph W. Eaton and A. J. Mayer, *Man's Capacity to Reproduce: The Demography of a Unique Population* (Glencoe, Ill.: Free Press, 1954).
64. Ansley J. Coale, "The Decline of Fertility in Europe from the French Revolution to World War II," in S. J. Behrman et al., eds., *Fertility and Family Planning* (Ann Arbor: University of Michigan Press, 1970).
65. Louis Henry, *Population: Analysis and Models* (New York: Academic Press, 1976).
66. William H. James, "The Fecundibility of U.S. Women," *Population Studies* 17 (1973): 493-500.
67. Louis Henry, "Fondements des mesures de la fécondité naturelle," *Revue de l'Institut International de Statistique* 21 (1953): 135-51.
68. John E. Knodel, "From Natural Fertility to Family Limitation: The Onset of Fertility Transition in a Sample of German Villages," *Demography* 16 (1979): 493-521.
69. Deborah Maine and Allan Rosenfield, "Maternal and Child Health Benefits of Family Planning," in Sciarra, *Gynecology and Obstetrics*, vol. 6, chap. 5.
70. Arlene T. Geronimus, "On Teenage Childbearing and Neonatal Mortality

in the United States," *Population and Development Review* 13 (1987): 245-79.
71. Nancy E. Reichman and Deanna L. Pagnini, "The Complicated Relation between Maternal Age and Birth Outcomes," OPR Working Paper no. 96-4 (Princeton, N.J.: Office of Population Studies, 1996).
72. Dorothy Nortman, "Parental Age as a Factor in Pregnancy Outcome and Child Development," *Reports on Population/Family Planning*, no. 16 (New York: Population Council, 1974): 6-7. See also George Acsadi and Gwendolyn Johnson-Acsadi, *Optimum Conditions for Childbearing* (London: International Planned Parenthood Federation, 1986), chaps. 3-5.
73. Fédération des Centres d'Études et de Conservation du Sperme Humain et al., "Female Fecundity as a Function of Age," *New England Journal of Medicine* 306 (1982): 404-6. Cf. A. H. DeCherney and G. S. Berkowitz, "Female Fecundity and Age," *New England Journal of Medicine* 306 (1982): 424-26.
74. John Bongaarts, "Infertility after Age 30: A False Alarm," *Family Planning Perspectives* 14:2 (1982): 75-78. Jane Menken, "Age and Fertility: How Late Can You Wait?" *Demography* 22 (1985): 469-83.
75. Gerry E. Hendershot et al., "Infertility and Age: An Unresolved Case," *Family Planning Perspectives* 14:5 (1982): 287-89.
76. David E. Soper, "Genito-urinary Infections and Sexually Transmitted Diseases," in Berek, *Novak's Gynecology*, 429-45.
77. Valerie K. Oppenheimer, "Women's Employment and the Gain of Marriage: The Specialization and Training Model," *Annual Review of Sociology* 23 (1997): 431-53.
78. Hendershot et al., "Infertility and Age."
79. Nortman, "Parental Age."

Chapter 5: Mortality

1. UNICEF, *The State of the World's Children* (New York, 1990), 8.
2. Nicholas Eberstadt, *The Tyranny of Numbers: Mismeasurement and Misrule* (Washington, D.C.: AEI Press, 1995), 221.
3. Jean Fourastié, "De la vie traditionnelle à la vie 'tertiaire,'" *Population* 14 (1959): 417-32; translated by William Petersen as "From the Traditional to the 'Tertiary' Life," in William Petersen, ed., *Readings in Population* (New York: Macmillan, 1972).
4. Peter Newman, *Malaria Eradication and Population Growth, with Special Reference to Ceylon and British Guiana* (Ann Arbor: University of Michigan School of Public Health, 1965); R. H. Gray, "The Decline in Mortality in Ceylon and the Demographic Effects of Malaria Control," *Population Studies* 28 (1974): 205-29.
5. *Economist* (1 August 1998).
6. Ad Hoc Committee, "A Definition of Irreversible Coma," *Journal of the American Medical Association* 205 (1968): 85-88.

7. H. Tristram Engelhardt, Jr., "Definitions of Death: Where to Draw the Line and Why," in Ernan McMullin, ed., *Death and Decision* (Boulder, Colo.: Westview Press, 1978).
8. Robert S. Morison, "Death: Process or Event?" *Science* 173 (20 August 1971): 694-98.
9. Leon R. Kass, "Death as an Event: A Commentary on Robert Morison," *Science* 173 (20 August 1971): 698-702.
10. Ivan V. Polunin, "Health and Disease in Contemporary Primitive Societies," in Don Brothwell and A. T. Sandison, eds., *Disease in Antiquity: A Survey of Diseases, Injuries and Surgery of Early Populations* (Springfield, Mass.: Thomas, 1967).
11. Joel E. Cohen, "Childhood Mortality, Family Size and Birth Order in Preindustrial Europe," *Demography* 12 (1975): 35-55. Jean-Noël Biraben, "Les Aspects médico-écologiques de la mortalité différentielle des enfants aux 18ème et 19ème siècles," in IUSSP International Population Conference, *Proceedings* (Manila, 1981).
12. Jacques Vallin, "La Mortalité infantile dans le monde: Évolution depuis 1950," *Population* 31 (1976): 801-38. Cf. Abdul-Aziz Farah and Samuel H. Preston, "Child Mortality Differentials in Sudan," *Population and Development Review* 8 (1982): 365-83.
13. Mary Ellen Avery and H. William Taeusch, Jr., eds., *Schaffer's Diseases of the Newborn*, 5th ed. (Philadelphia: Saunders, 1984), chap. 4.
14. James F. Fries and Lawrence M. Crapo, *Vitality and Aging: Implications of the Rectangular Curve* (San Francisco: W. H. Freeman, 1981).
15. Helen C. Chase, "Registration Completeness and International Comparisons of Infant Mortality," *Demography* 6 (1969): 425-33; "The Position of the United States in International Comparisons of Health Status," *American Journal of Public Health* 62 (1972): 581-89.
16. Avery and Taeusch, *Schaffers Diseases of the Newborn*.
17. Fries and Crapo, *Vitality and Aging*.
18. Kenneth W. Wachter and Caleb E. Finch, eds., *Between Zeus and the Salmon: The Biodemography of Longevity* (Washington, D.C.: National Academy Press, 1997). See also the review of the book by S. Jay Olshansky in *Population and Development Review* 24 (June 1998): 381-93.
19. David W. E. Smith, *Human Longevity* (New York: Oxford University Press, 1993).
20. Sherwin B. Nuland, *How We Die: Reflections on Life's Final Chapter* (New York: Vintage Books, 1995), 43.
21. Francis C. Madigan, "Are Sex Mortality Differentials Biologically Caused?" *Milbank Memorial Fund Quarterly* 35 (1957): 202-23.
22. Frank Trovato and N. M. Lalu, "Causes of Death Responsible for the Changing Sex Differential in Life Expectancy between 1970 and 1990 in Thirty Industrialized Nations," *Canadian Studies in Population* 23 (1996): 99-126.
23. Herbert Goldhamer and Andrew W. Marshall, *Psychosis and Civilization: Two Studies of the Frequency of Mental Disease* (Glencoe, Ill.: Free Press, 1953), 92.

24. See also above, pp. 23-24.
25. John Snow, *On Cholera: Being a Reprint of Two Papers* (Oxford: Commonwealth Fund, 1936), ix-x.
26. Ibid., 39.
27. Ibid.
28. Ibid., 45-46.
29. Brian MacMahon and Thomas F. Pugh, *Epidemiology: Principles and Methods* (Boston: Little, Brown, 1970), 21.
30. The sources of numerical data that are not identified in this section, usually collected by one or another federal agency, were compiled in *The Wall Street Journal Almanac, 1998* (New York: Ballantine, 1997). Since the statistics are no more than illustrative of general points, no specific references are given here.
31. Annette Flanagin and Thomas B. Cole, "Violence, a Neglected Epidemic: Call for Papers," *Journal of the American Medical Association* 280 (23/30 December 1998): 2121.
32. Allard E. Tempe, *Occupation and Disease: How Social Factors Affect the Conception of Work-related Disorders* (New Haven: Yale University Press, 1996).
33. Saad Z. Nagi, *Disability and Rehabilitation: Legal, Clinical, and Self-Concepts and Measurement* (Columbus: Ohio State University Press, 1969).
34. Émile Durkheim, *Suicide* (New York: Free Press, 1951).
35. George Howe Colt, *The Enigma of Suicide* (New York: Summit Books, 1991), 245. See also Herbert Hendin, *Suicide and Scandinavia* (New York: Anchor Books, 1965).
36. Colt, *Enigma of Suicide*, 222.
37. B. M. Barraclough, "Are the Scottish and English Suicide Rates Really Different?" *British Journal of Psychiatry* 120 (1972): 267-73. Norman Kreitman, "Suicide in Scotland in Comparison with England and Wales," *British Journal of Psychiatry* 121 (1972): 83-87.
38. William E. Datel, "The Reliability of Mortality Count and Suicide Count in the United States Army," *Military Medicine* 144 (1979): 509-12.
39. Derek Humphry and Mary Clement, *Freedom to Die: People, Politics, and the Right-to-Die Movement* (New York: St. Martin's Press, 1998), chaps. 16-18.
40. Ibid., 337.
41. Robert O'Brien et al., *The Encyclopedia of Drug Abuse*, 2nd ed. (New York: Facts on File, 1992), 7.
42. Ibid., 48.
43. Monroe Lerner and David N. Nurco, "Drug Abuse Deaths in Baltimore, 1951-1966," *International Journal of the Addictions* 5 (1970): 693-715.
44. Karin L. Swisher and Katie de Koster, eds., *Drug Abuse: Opposing Views* (San Diego: Greenhaven Press, 1994).
45. For example, Elvin M. Jellinek, "Recent Trends in Alcoholism and in

Alcohol Consumption," *Quarterly Journal of Studies on Alcohol* 8 (1947): 1-42.
46. Paul Johnson, *A History of the American People* (New York: HarperCollins, 1997), 680.
47. Robert A. Hummer et al., "Sociodemographic Differentials in Adult Mortality: A Review of Analytic Approaches," *Population and Development Review* 24 (1998): 553-78.
48. Cf. Alfred I. Tauber, *The Immune Self: Theory or Metaphor?* (New York: Cambridge University Press, 1996).
49. William B. Schwartz, *Life Without Disease: The Pursuit of Medical Utopia* (New York: Columbia University Press, 1998).
50. Roy Porter, *The Greatest Benefit to Mankind: A Medical History of Humanity* (New York: Norton, 1997), 715. See also the review essay by S. Ryan Johansson, *Population and Development Review* 24 (1998): 624-32.
51. "The Urgent Need to Improve Health Care Quality," *Journal of the American Medical Association* 280 (16 September 1998): 1000-05.
52. Porter, *The Greatest Benefit to Mankind*, 60.
53. Nuland, *How We Die*, 60.

Chapter 6: Health

1. Eric Partridge, *Origins: A Short Etymological Dictionary of Modern English* (New York: Macmillan, 1959), 804-05.
2. A. H. Pollard, "The Interaction between Morbidity and Mortality," *Journal of the Institute of Actuaries* 107, Part 3 (1980): 233-313.
3. *The American Heritage Dictionary of the English Language*, 3rd ed. (Boston: Houghton Mifflin, 1992), 833.
4. Horacio Fábrega, Jr., *Evolution of Sickness and Healing* (Berkeley: University of California Press, 1997), chap. 3. Ivan V. Polunin, "Health and Disease in Contemporary Primitive Societies," in Don Brothwell and A. T. Sandison, eds., *Diseases in Antiquity: A Survey of the Diseases, Injuries, and Surgery of Early Populations* (Springfield, Mass.: Thomas, 1967).
5. Philip Singer and Elizabeth A. Titus, *Resources for Third World Health Planners: A Selected Subject Bibliography* (New York: Trado-Medic Books, 1980).
6. World Health Organization, *Traditional Medicine and Its Role in the Development of Health Services in Africa* (Geneva, 1976).
7. Adele Baleta, "South Africa to Bring Traditional Healers into Mainstream Medicine," *Lancet* 352 (15 August 1998), 554-56.
8. P. K. Sanyal, *A Story of Medicine and Pharmacy in India* (Calcutta: Sanyal, 1964). Ralph C. Croizier, "Medicine, Modernization, and Cultural Crisis in China and India," *Comparative Studies in Society and History* 12 (1970): 275-91.
9. William R. Morse, *Chinese Medicine* (New York: Hoeber, 1934).
10. See a summary and commentary in *Science* 178 (1972): 9ff.

11. Diane Umansky, "A Chinese Herbal Primer," *Vegetarian Times* 248 (April 1998), 24ff.
12. Penelope Ody, *The Complete Medicinal Herbal* (New York: Dorling Kindersley, 1993).
13. Ibid., 90-91.
14. Marcia Angell and Jerome P. Kassirer, "Alternative Medicine—The Risks of Untested and Unregulated Remedies," *New England Journal of Medicine* 339 (17 September 1998): 839-41.
15. NIH Consensus Development Panel on Acupuncture, "Acupuncture," *Journal of the American Medical Association* 280 (4 November 1998): 1518-24.
16. "Fact and Fiction about Chiropractic," *Harvard Health Letter* 24:3 (January 1999): 1-3.
17. Arthur J. Rubel, "Concepts of Disease in Mexican- American Culture," *American Anthropologist* 62 (1960): 795-814.
18. Cf. David Boadella, ed., *In the Wake of Reich* (Boston: Sigo Press, 1991).
19. Cf. James I. Cleeman and Claude Lenfant, "The National Cholesterol Education Program: Progress and Prospects," *Journal of the American Medical Association* 280 (23/30 December 1998): 2099-2104.
20. Jean Anderson and Barbara Deskins, *The Nutrition Bible* (New York: Morrow, 1995). Editors of the University of California, Berkeley, Wellness Letter, *The Wellness Encyclopedia* (Boston: Houghton Mifflin, 1991).
21. Ronald Klatz, *Grow Young with HGH* (New York: HarperCollins, 1997).
22. Consumer Reports, "How to Digest Nutrition News,"*On Health* (February 1999): 5-9.
23. Michael Fumento, *Science under Siege: Balancing Technology and the Environment* (New York: Morrow, 1993), 13.
24. Cf. Lee Coleman, *The Reign of Error: Psychiatry, Authority, and Law* (Boston: Beacon Press, 1984), chap. 7.
25. Cf. Elizabeth Haiken, *Venus Envy: A History of Cosmetic Surgery* (Baltimore: Johns Hopkins University Press, 1998).
26. Daniel Callahan, *What Kind of Life: The Limits of Medical Progress* (New York: Simon and Schuster, 1990), 33.
27. James A. Nolan, Jr., *The Therapeutic State: Justifying Government at Century's End* (New York: New York University Press, 1998).
28. *American Heritage Dictionary*, 2026.
29. S. Jay Olshansky, "On the Biodemography of Aging: A Review Essay," *Population and Development Review* 24 (1998): 381-93.
30. William H. Harris and Judith S. Levey. eds., *The New Columbia Encyclopedia* (New York: Columbia University Press, 1975), 2044.
31. David B. Morris, *The Culture of Pain* (Berkeley: University of California Press, 1991), 30, 74-76.
32. Quoted in ibid., 172.
33. Stanley Kranczer, "Record High U.S. Life Expectancy," *Statistical Bulletin* 78:4 (1997): 2-8.
34. Cf. Frank Ryan, *The Forgotten Plague: How the Battle against Tuberculosis Was Won—and Lost* (Boston: Little, Brown, 1992).

35. Cf. Laurie Garrett, *The Coming Plague: Newly Emerging Diseases in a World out of Balance* (New York: Farrar, Straus and Giroux, 1994).
36. Gerard Piel, "AIDS and Population 'Control,'" *Scientific American* 270 (February 1994), 124.
37. Bryan Appleyard, *Brave New Worlds: Staying Human in the Genetic Future* (Harmondsworth, England: Viking Penguin, 1998).
38. Michael J. Reiss and Roger Straughan, *Improving Nature? The Science and Ethics of Genetic Engineering* (New York: Cambridge University Press, 1996), 222-23.

Chapter 7: Prehistoric and Primitive Populations

1. Ellen Bielawcki, "Dual Perceptions of the Past: Archaeology and Inuit Culture," in Robert Layton, ed., *Conflict in the Archaeology of Living Traditions* (London: Routledge, 1989).
2. Lewis R. Binford, *In Pursuit of the Past: Decoding the Archaeological Record* (New York: Thames and Hudson, 1983), 14-15.
3. Richard Fortey, *Life: A Natural History of the First Four Billion Years of Life on Earth* (New York: Alfred A. Knopf, 1998), chap. 1.
4. Binford, *In Pursuit of the Past*, 15.
5. Robert C. Schmitt, "Garbled Population Estimates of Central Polynesia," *Journal of the Polynesian Society* 74 (1965): 57-62; reprinted in William Petersen, ed., *Readings in Population* (New York: Macmillan, 1972).
6. Margaret Mead, *Coming of Age in Samoa* (New York: Morrow, 1973; first ed. 1928).
7. Derek Freeman, *Margaret Mead and Samoa: The Making and Unmaking of an Anthropological Myth* (Cambridge, Mass.: Harvard University Press, 1983); *The Fateful Hoaxing of Margaret Mead: A Historical Analysis of Her Samoan Research* (Boulder, Colo.: Westview Press, 1999).
8. Freeman, *The Fateful Hoaxing*, 139.
9. Mead, *Coming of Age*, 197.
10. A. L. Kroeber, *Anthropology*, rev. ed. (New York: Harcourt, Brace, 1948). Ángel Rosenblatt, *La población indígena de América desde 1492 hasta la actualidad* (Buenos Aires: Institución Cultural Española, 1945). Henry F. Dobyns, "Estimating Aboriginal American Population: An Appraisal of Techniques with a New Hemispheric Estimate," *Current Anthropology* 7 (1966): 395-416.
11. Russell Thornton, *American Indian Holocaust and Survival: A Population History Since 1492* (Norman: University of Oklahoma Press, 1987), chap. 2. See also C. Matthew Snipp, *American Indians: The First of This Land* (New York: Russell Sage Foundation, 1991), chap. 1.
12. Kim A. McDonald, "New Evidence Challenges Traditional Model of How the New World Was Settled," *Chronicle of Higher Education* (13 March 1998).
13. Thornton, *American Indian*, 44.
14. Ibid., 47-53.
15. Snipp, *American Indians*, chap. 2.

16. See above, 45-46.
17. Thornton, *American Indian*, 189.
18. James A. Clifton, ed., *The Invented Indian: Cultural Fictions and Government Policies* (New Brunswick, N.J.: Transaction Publishers, 1990).
19. Thornton, *American Indian*, 212-31. Snipp, *American Indians*, chap. 3.
20. See William Petersen, *Ethnicity Counts* (New Brunswick, N.J.: Transaction Publishers, 1997), chap. 6.
21. Ibid.
22. Willard Libby, *Radiocarbon Dating* (Chicago: University of Chicago Press, 1955). See also Brian M. Fagan, *Time Detectives: How Archaeologists Use Technology to Recapture the Past* (New York: Simon & Schuster, 1995).
23. Paul G. Bahn, ed., *The Cambridge Illustrated History of Archaeology* (New York: Cambridge University Press, 1996), 284.
24. Thomas H. Charlton, "Population Trends in the Teotihuacán Valley, A.D. 1400-1969," *World Anthropology* 4 (1972): 106-23.
25. David Hurst Thomas, cited in Bahn, *Cambridge Illustrated History*, 287.
26. Sherburne F. Cook, *Prehistoric Demography* (Reading, Mass.: Addison-Wesley, Module 16, 1972), Table 1.
27. See W. W. Taylor, *A Study of Archaeology* (Menasha, Wisc.: Memoirs of the American Anthropological Association, no. 69, 1948), 193.
28. Ann Gibbons, "Pleistocene Population Explosions," *Science* 262 (10 January 1993), 27-28.
29. David E. Reich and David B. Goldstein, "Genetic Evidence for a Paleolithic Human Population Expansion in Africa," *Proceedings of the National Academy of Sciences* 95 (1998): 8119-23.
30. Cf. Michael A. Glassow, "The Concept of Carrying Capacity in the Study of Culture Process," in Michael B. Schiffer, ed., *Advances in Archaeological Method and Theory* (New York: Academic Press, 1978).
31. Noel D. Broadbent et al., "Why Only Some Became Farmers," in Göran Burenhult, ed., *The People of the Stone Age: Hunter-gatherers and Early Farmers* (New York: American Museum of Natural History, 1993).
32. Ibid., 190.
33. James A. Brander and M. Scott Taylor, "The Simple Economics of Easter Island: A Ricardo-Malthus Model of Renewable Resource Use," *American Economic Review* 88 (1998): 119-38.
34. Asen Balikci, "The Netsilik Eskimos: Adaptive Processes," in Richard B. Lee and Irven DeVore, eds., *Man the Hunter* (Hawthorne, N.Y.: Aldine de Gruyter, 1968).
35. Robert L. Carneiro and Daisy F. Hilse, "On Determining the Probable Rate of Population Growth during the Neolithic," *American Anthropologist* 68 (1966): 177-80.
36. A. M. Carr-Saunders, *The Population Problem: A Study in Human Evolution* (Oxford: Clarendon Press, 1922), 214-16.
37. Norman E. Himes, *Medical History of Contraception* (Baltimore: Williams & Wilkins, 1936), 3.

38. John M. Riddle, *Contraception and Abortion from the Ancient World to the Renaissance* (Cambridge, Mass.: Harvard University Press, 1992).
39. Frederick L. Dunn, "Epidemiological Factors: Health and Disease in Hunter-gatherers," in Lee and DeVore, *Man the Hunter*.
40. Stephen J. Kunitz, *Disease and Social Diversity: The European Impact on the Health of Non-Europeans* (New York: Oxford University Press, 1994).
41. John C. Caldwell et al., with comments and a reply, "Anthropology and Demography: The Mutual Reinforcement of Speculation and Research," *Current Anthropology* 28 (1987): 25-43.
42. George Acsádi and János Nemeskéri, *History of Human Life Span and Mortality* (Budapest: Akadémiai Kiadó, 1970). Don Brothwell and A. T. Sandison, eds., *Diseases in Antiquity: A Survey of Diseases, Injuries, and Surgery of Early Populations* (Springfield, Mass.: Thomas, 1967).
43. Audrey I. Richards and Priscilla Reining, "Report on Fertility Surveys in Buganda and Buhaya, 1952," in Frank Lorimer, ed., *Culture and Human Fertility* (Paris: UNESCO, 1954).
44. Wolf Bleek, "Lying Informants: A Fieldwork Experience from Ghana," *Population and Development Review* 13 (1987): 316-22.
45. Norma McArthur, "Essays in Multiplication: European Seafarers in Polynesia," *Journal of Pacific History* 1 (1966): 91-105.

Chapter 8: Population Theories

1. Charles Emil Stangeland, *Pre-Malthusian Doctrines of Population: A Study in the History of Economic Theory* (New York: Columbia University Press, 1904), chap. 1. Edward Prince Hutchinson, *The Population Debate: The Development of Conflicting Theories up to 1900* (New York: Houghton Mifflin, 1967), chap. 1.
2. Stangeland, *Pre-Malthusian Doctrines*, 30-38.
3. John Thomas Noonan, Jr., *Contraception: A History of Its Treatment by the Catholic Theologians and Canonists* (Cambridge, Mass.: Belknap Press, 1965).
4. Cf. Vernon J. Bourke, "Thomas Aquinas, St.," *Encyclopedia of Philosophy*, vol. 8, 105-16.
5. Eli F. Heckscher, *Mercantilism* (London: Allen & Unwin, 1935), vol. 2, 158, 300.
6. David V. Glass, *Numbering the People: The Eighteenth-Century Population Controversy and the Development of Census and Vital Statistics in Britain* (Farnborough, Hants: Saxon House, 1973).
7. Anita Fage, "La Révolution française et la population," *Population* 8 (1953): 311-38.
8. William Petersen, *Malthus: Founder of Modern Demography* (New Brunswick, N.J.: Transaction Publishers, 1998), chap. 4.
9. Thomas Robert Malthus, *An Essay on the Principle of Population: Or, A*

View of Its Past and Present Effects on Human Happiness, 7th ed. (London: Reeves & Turner, 1872), 436-41.
10. Petersen, *Malthus*, Introduction.
11. Karl Marx, *Capital* (Chicago: Kerr, 1906), vol. l, 652.
12. Ibid., 692.
13. Ibid., 697.
14. Ibid., 672.
15. Ibid., 693.
16. Quoted in Franz Mehring, *Karl Marx: The Story of His Life* (New York: Covici-Friede, 1935), 632-45.
17. Quoted in Alfred Sauvy, *Théorie générale de la population* (Paris: Presses Universitaires de France, 1952), vol. 1, 174.
18. John F. Besemeres, *Socialist Population Politics: The Political Implications of Demographic Trends in the USSR and Eastern Europe* (White Plains, N.Y.: M. E. Sharpe, 1980).
19. Raul Hilberg, *The Destruction of the European Jews* (Chicago: Quadrangle Paperbacks, 1967). Robert Conquest, *The Great Terror: Stalin's Purge of the Thirties* (Harmondsworth, England: Penguin Books, 1971).
20. Adolphe Landry, *La Révolution démographique: Études et essais sur les problèmes de la population* (Paris: Librairie du Recueil Sirey, 1934). Warren S. Thompson, "Population," *American Journal of Sociology* 34 (1929): 959-75. Frank W. Notestein, "Population—The Long View," in Theodore W. Schultz, ed., *Food for the World* (Chicago: University of Chicago Press, 1945).
21. William Petersen, "A Demographer's View of Prehistoric Demography," *Current Anthropology* 16 (1975): 227-45. See also above, 120-21.
22. See above, pp. 58-59.
23. David M. Heer, "Economic Development and Fertility," *Demography* 3 (1966): 423-44.
24. Cf. Ansley J. Coale, "The Demographic Transition Reconsidered," in IUSSP, International Population Conference, Liège, 1973, *Contributed Papers* (1973-74).
25. Kingsley Davis, "The Sociology of Demographic Behavior," in Robert K. Merton et al., eds., *Sociology Today* (New York: Basic Books, 1959).
26. Frank W. Notestein, "Comment" on "Population Theory," in B. F. Haley, ed., *Survey of Contemporary Economics* (Homewood, Ill.: Irwin, 1952).
27. David Coleman and Roger Schofield, eds., *The State of Population Theory: Forward from Malthus* (Oxford: Basil Blackwell, 1986), Introduction.
28. Ibid.
29. See above, 4-6.

Chapter 9: Forecasts and Projections

1. Jaegwon Kim, "Explanation in Science," in Paul Edwards, ed., *The Encyclopedia of Philosophy* (New York: Macmillan, 1967), vol. 32, 160-63.
2. Karl R. Popper, *The Poverty of Historicism* (London: Routledge, 1988).

3. Winslow C. Watson, ed., *Men and Times of the Revolution; or Memoirs of Elkanah Watson* (New York: Dana, 1856), 257-58.
4. Raymond Pearl, *The Biology of Population Growth* (New York: Alfred A. Knopf, 1925). See also Pearl and Lowell J. Reed, "On the Rate of Growth of the Population of the United States since 1790 and Its Mathematical Representation," *Proceedings of the National Academy of Sciences* 6 (1920): 275-88.
5. R. R. Kuczynski, *The Measurement of Population Growth: Methods and Results* (London: Sidgwick & Jackson, 1935).
6. Wilson H. Grabill, Clyde V. Kiser, and Pascal K. Whelpton, *The Fertility of American Women* (New York: John Wiley, 1958), 73.
7. Nathan Keyfitz, "The Social and Political Context of Population Forecasting," in William Alonso and Paul Starr, eds., *The Politics of Numbers* (New York: Russell Sage Foundation, 1987).
8. National Resources Committee, Committee on Population Problems, *The Problems of a Changing Population* (Washington, D.C.: U.S. Government Printing Office, 1938).
9. See Harold F. Dorn, "Pitfalls in Population Forecasts and Projections," *Journal of the American Statistical Association* 45 (1950): 311-44.
10. Nathan Keyfitz, "The Limits of Population Forecasting," *Population and Development Review* 7 (1981): 579-93.
11. Nathan Keyfitz, "Can Knowledge Improve Forecasts?" *Population and Development Review* 8 (1982): 729-51.
12. Nicholas Eberstadt, "Asia Tomorrow, Gray and Male," *National Interest* no. 53 (Fall 1998): 56-65.
13. Soumitra R. Eachempati et al., "'The Demographics of Trauma in 1995': An Assessment of the Accuracy and Utility of Trauma Predictions," *Journal of Trauma: Injury, Infection, and Critical Care* 45 (1998): 208-14.
14. E. P. Hutchinson, *The Population Debate: The Development of Conflicting Theories up to 1900* (Boston: Houghton Mifflin, 1967).
15. Johann Peter Süssmilch, *Die Göttliche Ordnung in der Veränderung des menschlichen Geschlechts, aus der Geburt, dem Tode und der Fortpflanzung desselben erwiesen*, 4th ed. (Berlin, 1775), 175ff.
16. David Hume, "Of the Populousness of Ancient Nations" (1752) in *Essays, Moral, Political and Literary* (New York: Longmans, Green, 1898), 384.
17. Donella H. Meadows et al., *The Limits to Growth: A Report for the Club of Rome's Project on the Predicament of Mankind* (New York: American Library, 1972).
18. *Economist* (11 March 1972). See also H. S. D. Cole et al., *Thinking about the Future: A Critique of* The Limits to Growth (London: Chatto Windus, 1973).
19. U.S. Council on Environmental Quality and U.S. Department of State, *The Global 2000 Report to the President: Entering the Twenty-First Century* (Washington, D.C.: U.S. Government Printing Office, 1980).
20. Julian L. Simon and Herman Kahn, eds., *The Resourceful Earth: A Re-*

sponse to Global 2000 (Oxford: Basil Blackwell, 1984). See also Simon, *Population Matters: People, Resources, and Immigration* (New Brunswick, N.J.: Transaction Publishers, 1990).
21. Philip Ball, *Made to Measure: New Materials for the 21st Century* (Princeton, N.J.: Princeton University Press, 1997).
22. James Gleick, *Chaos: Making a New Science* (New York: Viking, 1987), 11-58.
23. See above, p. 135.
24. Gleick, *Chaos*, 59-80.
25. See, for example, Jeff Berkowitz, *Fractal Cosmos: The Art of Mathematical Design* (San Francisco: Amber Lotus, 1998).
26. Gleick, *Chaos*, 304.

Chapter 10: State Control of Population

1. See above, pp. 123-24.
2. See William Petersen, *Malthus: Founder of Modern Demography* (New Brunswick, N.J.: Transaction Publishers, 1998), chap. 7.
3. Joseph J. Spengler, "Optimum Population Theory," *International Encyclopedia of the Social Sciences*, vol. 12, 358-62.
4. Edwin Cannan, *Wealth: A Brief Explanation of the Causes of Economic Welfare*, 3rd ed. (London: King, 1928). See also Lionel Robbins, "The Optimum Theory of Population," in T. E. Gregory and Hugh Dalton, eds., *London Essays in Economics in Honour of Edwin Cannan* (London: Routledge, 1927).
5. E. F. Penrose, *Population Theories and Their Application with Special Reference to Japan* (Stanford, Calif.: Food Research Institute, 1934), 90.
6. Gunnar Myrdal, *Population: A Problem for Democracy* (Cambridge, Mass.: Harvard University Press, 1940), 26-27.
7. S. Fred Singer, *Is There an Optimum Level of Population?* (New York: McGraw-Hill, 1971).
8. Joseph J. Spengler, "Adam Smith on Population," *Population Studies* 24 (1970): 377-88; "Adam Smith on Population Growth and Economic Development," *Population and Development Review* 2 (1976): 167-80. See also Samuel Hollander, *The Economics of Adam Smith* (Toronto: University of Toronto Press, 1973).
9. John Knodel and Etienne van de Walle, "Lessons from the Past: Policy Implications of Historical Fertility Studies," *Population and Development Review* 5 (1979): 217-45.
10. Joseph J. Spengler, *France Faces Depopulation* (Durham, N.C.: Duke University Press, 1938). Hans Harmsen, *Bevölkerungsprobleme Frankreichs unter besonderer Berücksichtigung des Geburtenrückgangs* (Berlin-Grunewald: Vowinckel, 1927).
11. James C. Vadakin, *Family Allowances: An Analysis of Their Development and Implications* (Miami: University of Miami Press, 1958), 304.
12. Hervé LeBras and Georges Tapinos, "Perspectives à longe terme de la

population française et leurs implications économiques," *Population* 34 (1979): 139-45.
13. Brian E. Pendleton, "An Historical Description and Analysis of Pronatalist Policies in Italy, Germany, and Sweden," *Policy Sciences* 9 (1978): 45-70. See also Carl Ipsen, "Population Policy in the Age of Fascism: Observations on Recent Literature," *Population and Development Review* 24 (1998): 579-92.
14. D. V. Glass, *Population Policies and Movements in Europe* (Oxford: Clarendon, 1940).
15. William Petersen, "Parents vs. State," *American Scholar* (Winter 1997): 121-27. See also Jacqueline Kasun, "Too Many People? The Myth of Excess Population," *Economic Affairs* 9 (June-July 1989): 15-23.
16. Dirk J. van de Kaa, "Recent Trends in Fertility in Western Europe," in Robert W. Hiorns, ed., *Demographic Patterns in Developed Societies* (London: Taylor & Francis, 1980).
17. Charles F. Westoff, "The Commission on Population Growth and the American Future: Its Origins, Operations, and Aftermath," *Population Index* 39 (1973): 491-507.
18. Commission on Population Growth and the American Future, *Population Growth and the American Future* (Washington, D.C.: U.S. Government Printing Office, 1972).
19. William Petersen, "American Efforts to Reduce the Fertility of Less Developed Countries," in Nick Eberstadt, ed., *Fertility Decline in the Less Developed Countries* (New York: Praeger, 1981).
20. Frank Furadi, *Population and Development: A Critical Introduction* (New York: St. Martin's Press, 1997).
21. Edwin D. Driver, *Essays on Population Policy* (Lexington, Mass.: D.C. Heath, 1972), 101-25.
22. Mahmood Mamdani, *The Myth of Population Control: Family, Caste, and Class in an Indian Village* (New York: Monthly Review Press, 1972), 33.
23. Paul Demeny, "Population on the World Agenda, 1984: A View from Bucharest," *Population and Development Review* 10 (1984): 353-59.
24. John B. Wion and John E. Gordon, *The Khanna Study: Population Problems in the Rural Punjab* (Cambridge. Mass.: Harvard University Press, 1971).
25. Veena Soni, "Thirty Years of the Indian Family Planning Program: Past Performance, Future Prospects," *International Family Planning Perspectives* 9 (1983): 35-45.
26. George Martine et al., eds., *Reproductive Change in India and Brazil* (New York: Oxford University Press, 1998).
27. Steven W. Mosher, *Broken Earth: The Rural Chinese* (New York: Free Press, 1983).
28. John S. Aird, *Slaughter of the Innocents: Coercive Birth Control in China* (Washington, D.C.: AEI Press, 1990). See also Aird, "Fertility Decline in China," in Eberstadt, *Fertility Decline*.
29. Cheng Yimin et al., "Emergency Contraception: Knowledge and Desire

among Unmarried Women," Sixteenth World Congress on Fertility and Sterility, San Francisco, October 4-9, 1998, *Abstracts* (Birmingham, Ala.: American Society of Reproductive Medicine, 1998), S162.
30. M. Giovanna Merli, "Underreporting of Births and Infant Deaths in Rural China: Evidence from Field Research in One County in Northern China," *China Quarterly* no. 155 (September 1998), 637-55.
31. R. T. Ravenholt and John Cho, "World Fertility Trends, 1974," *Population Report*, Series J, no. 2 (Washington, D.C.: Medical Center, George Washington University, 1974).
32. John C. Caldwell et al., "The Demography of Microstates," *World Development* 8 (1980): 953-67.
33. Ronald Freedman, *Observing Taiwan's Demographic Transition: A Memoir* (Taichung: Taiwan Provincial Institute of Family Planning, 1998).
34. Ronald Freedman, Y. Takeshita, and T. H. Sun, "Fertility Trends in Taiwan: Tradition and Change," *Population Studies* 10 (1963): 219-36.
35. Freedman, *Observing Taiwan*, 10.
36. Griffith Feeney, "Fertility Decline in Taiwan: A Study Using Parity Ratios," *Demography*, 28 (1991): 467-79.
37. Freedman, *Observing Taiwan*, 44-45.
38. James C. Caldwell, "Towards a Restatement of the Demographic Transition Theory," in Caldwell, ed., *The Persistence of High Fertility: Population Pressure in the Third World*, 2 vols. (Canberra: Department of Demography, Australian National University, 1977). See also Hillard Kaplan, "Evolutionary and Wealth-flow Theories of Fertility Decline: Empirical Tests and New Models," *Population and Development Review* 20 (1994): 753-91.
39. Neera Burra, *Born to Work: Child Labour in India* (New York: Oxford University Press, 1998).
40. United Nations, *Statistical Yearbook*, 42nd ed. (New York, 1977).
41. Ibid., Table 8.
42. Ben J. Wattenberg, "The Population Explosion Is Over," *New York Times Magazine* (23 November 1997).
43. In William Brass et al., eds., *The Demography of Tropical Africa* (Princeton, N.J.: Princeton University Press, 1968).
44. Julian L. Simon and Herman Kahn, eds., *The Resourceful Earth: A Response to Global 2000* (New York: Basil Blackwell, 1984). Simon, *Population Matters: People, Resources, and Immigration* (New Brunswick, N.J.: Transaction, 1990).
45. Stanislav Andreski, *The African Predicament: A Study in the Pathology of Modernisation* (London: Michael Joseph, 1968).

Index

Abortion, 63, 64, 78; partial-birth, 73
Abstinence, 56-57
"Acceptors," 152-53
Accidents, 83, 89, 152-53
Acupuncture, 101
Adamkus, Valdas, 3
Addiction, 88, 91-93
Adolescence, 51-52
Adoption, 65
Affirmative action, 41
Africa, Africans, 7, 55-56, 62, 74, 99, 114, 116, 121, 161, 163. See also particular countries
Age, chap. 2, 90; at marriage, 51, 70, 84-85, 130; statistics on, 12-13; structure, 23-29, 35, 136-37. See also population
Aggregation, 8-9, 42-43, 113
Aging, 35-36, 82, 140
Agriculture, 118, 162. See also Nutrition
Aid to Families with Dependent Children, 30
AIDS, 62, 108
Aird, John, 155
Alaskan natives. See Eskimos.
Alcohol, alcoholism, 93
Algeria, 77, 85
Aliens, 2
Amenorrhea, 50, 55
American Academy of Pediatrics, 80
American Association for the Advancement of Science (AAAS), 147, 156
American Association of Retired Persons (AARP), 34
American Civil Liberties Union (ACLU), 40
Americans for Generational Equity (AGE), 30
American Heritage Dictionary, 106
American Indians, 24, 40, 42, 45-46, 113-16
American Medical Association, 86, 89, 101
Anderson, Margo, 18

Andreski, Stanislav, 163
Anilepiman, 57
Anstie, Francis, 93
Anthropology, 41, 55-56, 110-13. See also Archaeology
Aquinas, Thomas, 124
Arable land, 142. See also agriculture
Archaeology, 109-10, 116-18. See also Anthropology
Argentina, 151
Aristotle, 123
Asia, 140, 164. See also particular countries
Asians and Pacific Islanders (API), 9, 42, 43-44, 46
Asian Indians. See Indians
Astrology, 57, 99
Athens, 123
Augustus, 124
Australia, 77, 160
Austria, 21-22, 149, 160
Ayurveda, 99-100

Baby boom, 27-28, 32, 35, 138
Baby food, 54
Ball, Philip, 142-43
Bangladesh, 13, 77, 156, 161
Barbour, Haley, 11
Basbaum, Allan I., 107
BEA economic areas, 107
Besant, Annie, 58
Binford, Lewis, 110, 117
Biodemography, 106
Biology, 1, 128
Birth, 51
Birth control, 9, 52, 56, 58-59, 73, 119, 151-57
Bismarck, Otto von, 33
Blacks, 9, 20, 24, 29, 42-43, 46-47
Boas, Franz, 111-13
body mass index (BMI), 1-4
Bongaarts, John, 69-71
Boserup, Ester, 132
Botswana, 62

Bradlaugh, Charles, 50
Brazil, 13, 154, 160
breastfeeding, 53, 54-56
Brown, Louise, 64
Bruton, Ogden C., 90
Budin, Pierre-Constant, 80
Bulgaria, 160
Bureau of Economic Analysis, 8-9, 107
Bureau of Indian Affairs, 46
Bureau of the Census, 12, 31, 38, 47, 115, 138-39, 166-68
Butterfly effect, 143

Caldwell, John, 158
California, 13-14, 64-65, 90
Cancers, 83, 88, 108
Cannan, Edwin, 146
Cantillon, Richard, 125
Capitalism, 127
Cardiovascular diseases, 88, 104, 108
Carinthia, 21
Carmel, 13-14
Carr-Saunders, A. M., 119-20
Carrying capacity, 117-18, 142
Castro, Josué de, 63
Catholic, Catholicism, 38, 89-91, 124, 148
CECOS, 69-71
Census, 1-2, 166-67; Act of 1976, 18; Bureau of the, 12, 31, 38, 47, 115, 138-39, 166-68; definition of, 9-10; editing of, 13-15; errors in, 11-15; ethnicity in, 12; funding of, 16, 20-21; future of, 15-21; imputation in, 14-15, 19, 165; languages in, 19, 21, 43; of 1990, 13-15, 15-21; race in, 21; sampling in, 15-21, 167-68; self-identification in, 2, 44-45, 46; validation check, 14
Central African Republic, 160
Ceylon, 75
Chamberlain, Basil Hall, 33
Chang, Chung-li, 56-57
Chao, John, 156
Chaos, 143-44
Chapel Hill, 12
Child, children, 51, 158; labor, 127, 158; value of, 32
China, 7, 13, 56-57, 77, 151, 154-55, 156, 160, 161
Chinese in U.S., 30, 43, 150
Chinese medicine, 99-100
Chiropractic, 101-02

Cholera, 85-87
Cholesterol, 103
Christianity, 124. See also Catholic, Protestant
Cirrhosis, 88, 93
Citizen, citizenship, 2-3, 40
Clifton, James, 115
Clinton, William J., 16, 20, 73, 106
Cloning, 65
Club of Rome, 142
Coale, Ansley, 51, 66
Cohen, Misha, 110
Cohorts, 26-27
Coitus interruptus, 67
Colonies, 150-51
Commission on Narcotic Drugs, 92-93
Commission on Population Growth and the American Future, 149-50
"compulsuation," 154
Condorcet, Marquis de, 125
Confucius, 140
Constantine, 124
Constitution, U.S., 16, 17-18
Consumer Reports, 104
Contraception. See Birth control
Cook Island, 156
Cook, James, 111
Coresidence, 37
Correlation, 87
Costa Rica, 156
Cubans in U.S., 12, 44
Cultural relativism, 41
Culture, 112-13
Current Population Surveys, 12
Czech Republic, 160

Darwinian fitness, 98, 119
Dating, radiocarbon, 116
Davis, Kingsley, 131
DDT, 75-76
Death, 46, 77-78, 82, 87. See also Mortality
Declaration of Independence, 1
Demographers, 4
Demographic dictionaries, 5-6, 74
Demograpahic transition, 129-31
Demographics, 6
Demography, 4-5, 22, 24, 55, 69-70, 132
Denmark, 77, 90, 147, 149
Dependency ratio, 32
Depo-Provera, 59
Depression, economic, 138

Diabetes, 88
Diseases, cancers, 83, 88, 108; cardiovascular, 88, 104, 108; cholera, 85-87; cirrhosis, 103; diabetes, 88; malaria, 75-76, 84; occupational, 89; pneumonia, 83, 95; sexually transmitted, 56, 62, 63, 70, 88, 95; sickle-cell anemia, 98; tuberculosis, 108
Divorce, 90
Dobyns, Henry F., 113
Driver, Edwin, 152
Drugs, 92
Dual citizenship, 2-3
Durkheim, Émile, 89-90

Easter Island, 108
Easterlin, Richard, 28
Eberstadt, Nicholas, 140
Economic Commission for Europe, 10
Education, 13
Egypt, 77, 160
Ehrlich, Paul, 27
Eisenhower, Dwight, 149
Engels, Friedrich, 127-28
England. See Great Britain
Epidemiology, 84-87
Errors in population data, 11-15
Eskimos, 33, 42, 109, 118
Estrous cycle, 53
Ethiopia, 60
Ethnicity, 22, 24, 37, 39, 41-47
Ethnoarchaeology, 109
Ethnographic analogy, 109
European marriage pattern, 57, 130
European Union, 3, 32
Evolution, 39
Expectation of life, 74-75, 83, 94, 97, 107-08

Faeroe Islands, 156
Family, 74-75, 128-29; cycle, 28, 31; definition of, 30; human, 53-54; nuclear, 30-31; planning programs, 130, chap. 10; size, 30-31, 135-36; work, 157, 158
Fecundability, 66-67
Fecunditiy, chap. 4, 165; by age, 68-71; definition of, 49; genetic effect on, 60-61; nutrition and, 63
Feminism, 151
Fertility, chap. 4, 165; by age, 23, 25, 50-52, 66, 67-71; definition of, 49; 73; maximum, 66-67; measures, 133-36; natural, 67; optimum age for, 67-71; by social class, 57-58; transition, 67, 147
Fertilization, 49-50; in vitro, 64, 165
Feshbach, Murray, 24
Fetus, 80-81
Filipinos, 23, 43
Folk medicine, 98-99
Food and Drug Administration, 100, 102, 103
Food, 160-62. See also Nutrition
Fordham Institute for Social Policy, 91
Foreign-born, 40
Fourastié, Jean, 74-75
fractal, 144
France, 13, 22, 34, 54, 69-71, 74-75, 124, 125, 147-48, 160
Frank, Odile, 62
Freedman, Ronald, 156-57
Freeman, Derek, 112-13
Frontier areas, 5, 30
Frost, Wade Hampton, 85
Fumento, Michael, 105

Galen, 100
Gabon, 62
Gannet, Henry, 8
Gene therapy, 108
Generations, conflict of, 34
Genetics, 50, 117
Genocide, 39
George III, 1
Germans, Germany, 6, 7, 21, 24, 39, 67, 77, 128, 148, 149, 155, 160
Gerontocide, 33
Gerontology, 36
Ghana, 121
Gibraltar, 156
Gini, Corrado, 66-67
Glass, David, 148-49
Glavin, Matthew, 18-19
Godwin, William, 125
Gonorrhea, 62
Goodman, Paul, 102
Graunt, John, 124
Great Britain, 21, 22, 57-58, 81, 90, 147, 148
Greece, ancient, 123
Greeley, Andrew, 38
Green revolution, 162
Greenland, 156

Guillard, Achille, 4
Guzmán, Ralph, 44

Hajnal, John, 57, 139
Harpending, Henry, 117
Harmsen, Hans, 148
Harvard Medical School, 78, 102
Hawaii, 12, 111
Health, chap. 6, 165
Hemlock Society, 90-91
Herbs, 100
Henry, Louis, 67
Himes, Norman, 119
Hippocrates, 100
Hispanics in U.S., 12, 20, 42, 44
Hmong, 43-44
Hollick, Frederick, 58-59
Homeopathy, 99
Homicide, 88, 91
Hong Kong, 155
Honseki, 3
House of Representatives, U.S., 19
Household, 30
Human Genome Project, 108
Human statistics, 4
Humanae Vitae, 54
Hume, David, 141
Hungary, 22, 51, 149, 160
Hunter-gatherers, 118-120, 129
Husband, 57
Hutchinson, E. P., 141
Hutterites, 66
Huxley, Aldous, 108

Immigration, U.S., 2, 23-24, 40
Immigration and Naturalization Service, 2
Immune system, 94, 108
Impotence, 60
Imputation, 14-15, 19, 165
Income, 9, 14, 24, 43-44
India, Indians, 43-45, 58, 77, 99, 130, 151, 152-54, 156, 158, 160, 161-62. See also American Indians
Indian medicine, 99
INED, 148
Infant mortality, 67-68, 74-77, 79-82
Infanticide, 55-56, 73, 119-20, 140
Infertility, 59-66
Institute of Society, Ethics, and the Life Sciences, 78
International statistics, 68
Interracial marriage, U.S., 47

Intrinsic rates, 136
Ipsen, Gunther, 6
Ireland, Irish, 3, 24, 38, 63
Isle of Man, 156
Israel, 3, 160
Italy, Italians, 22, 24, 38, 148, 160
Ithaca, 34

Japan, Japanese, 3, 12, 33, 44, 65, 77, 130, 150, 160
Jefferson, Thomas, 18
Jews, 24, 37-38, 39, 89-90, 129, 150
Johns Hopkins University, 76

Kahane, Meir, 3
Kansas, 78
KAP (knowledge-attitude-practice), 152, 158
Kass, Leon R., 79
Keyfitz, Nathan, 6, 139
Keynes, John Maynard, 166
Khanna study, 152
King, Gregory, 124
Klatz, Ronald, 103-04
Kleptocracy, 163-64
Knodel, John, 67
Korea, 26
Kroeber, A. L., 113
Kuczynski, R. R., 135-36
Kulischer, Eugene M., 7-8
!Kung, 55-56

Lactation, 53, 54-56
La Leche League, 54
Latin America, 12, 65, 74, 151, 163
Legitimacy, 25, 53
Less developed countries, 7-8, 11, 13, 22, 32, 54, 62, 74, 76-77, 130-31, 136-37, 141, 150-51, 163-64. See also particular countries
Levinson, Daniel, 31
Libby, Willard F., 116
Libido, 53
Life, expectation, 74-75, 83, 94, 97, 107-08; span, 82, 93, 108, 165; table, 124
Limits of Growth, 132, 142
Lithuania, 3
Logistic curve, 135
London, 142

Madigan, Francis, 83
Mailer, Norman, 102

Malaria, 75-76, 84
Malinowski, Bronislaw, 53-54
Malthus, Thomas Robert, 4, 118, 125-26, 141, 146; principle of population of, 49, 126, 134-35
Mammals, 52-54
Mandelbrot, Benoit, 144
Marcuse, Herbert, 102
Marriage, 124, 140; age at, 51, 70, 84-85, 130; interracial, U.S., 47; pattern, European, 57, 130
Marx, Karl, 127-28
Marxism, 133, 151
Maryland, 90
Massachusetts, 23, 85
Maturity, 31
Mauritius, 156
May, Robert, 144
McArthur, Norma, 121
Mead, Margaret, 111-113
Medicare, 32
Medicine, advances in, 76, 93-95; alternative, 100-01; Chinese, 99-100; folk, 98-99; future of, 107-08; holistic, 100-01; Indian, 99
Mefloquine, 76
Menarche, 51
Menken, Jane, 69-71
Menominee Reservation, 16
Menopause, 52, 106
Menstrual cycle, 50, 52-53, 57
Mental illness, 85
Mercantilism, 124-25, 147
Meteorology, 143
Mexican Americans, 3, 12, 24, 44, 45, 102
Mexico, 3, 77, 117, 160
Microstates, 156
Migration, illegal, 10, 11; international, 10, 131, 134
Military personnel, 90
Mill, John Stuart, 146
Milton, John, 30
Mississippi, 11
Mixed race, 45, 46-47
Montesquieu, 125
Morison, Robert S., 78-79
Mortality, chap. 5; by age, 77, 79-82, 106; causes of, 84-93, 94; child, 75, 76, 80-82; decline in, 74-78, 93-95, 97, 131; fetal, 73-74; infant, 67-68, 74-77, 79-82; neonatal, 67-68, 79, 81; political, 129; postneonatal, 67-68, 79; prehistoric, 121; by race, 90; by sex, 83-84, 94
Mortara, Giorgio, 13
Mosher, Steven, 155
Myrdal, Gunnar, 146-47

National Academy of Sciences, 95, 103
National Association for the Advancement of Colored People (NAACP), 42-43
National Center for Health Statistics, 59, 68-69, 74, 82, 87, 136
National Institute of Demographic Studies (INED), 148
National Opinion Research Center (NORC), 38
Nationality, 2, 40-41
Negroes See blacks
Nehru, Jawaharial, 151
Neo-Malthusianism, 58
Netherlands, 21, 38, 63, 81-82
New England Journal of Medicine, 104
New Mexico, 78
New Orleans, 66
Nigeria, 156, 160
Nixon, Richard, 149, 166
Nomads, 11
Norway, 90
Notestein, Frank, 4, 21
Nuclear family, 30-31
Nutrition, 6, 51, 63, 88, 103-05, 142

Obesity, 104
O'Connor, Sandra Day, 18
Oppenheimer, Valerie, 70
Oregon, 90-91
Orgone box, 102
Osler, William, 95
Overpopulation, 162-64
Overweight, 104
Ovulation cycle, 52-53

Pain, 106-07
Pakistan, 56, 107
Paleontology, 110
Palmer, D. D., 101
Passing, 42
Pearl, Raymond, 9
Pebble Beach, 13
Pellagra, 86
Pelvic inflamatory disease (PID), 70
Perón, Juan, 151
Petersen, Renee, 5

Petersen, William, 5, 8, 13-14, 27, 107
Petty, William, 4, 124
Pfizer Inc., 60
Pharmacology, 101
Philippines, 23, 43
Pittsburgh, 34
Plato, 123
Pneumonia, 83, 95
Political arithmetic, 4, 124
Polynesia, 111, 112, 121
Population, by age, 31-36; aged, 31-36; composition, chap. 3; definition of, 1-2; errors in data, 11-15; forecasts, chap. 9; future, 160; growth, 27-29, 127, 132, 149, chap. 10; optimum, 128, 145-47; policy, 6, 123-24, 128, chap. 10; pre-Columbian, 112-14; prehistoric, chap. 7; primitive, chap. 7, 80; principle of, 49, 126, 134-35; projections, chap. 9; pyramid, 25-26; stable, 29; state control of, chap. 10; stationary, 26, 29; statistics, 7, 165-68; structure, chap. 2; theories, chap. 8; world, 141-43, 160
Population Association of America, 49, 69
Population Council, 156
Porter, Roy, 94-95
Post Census Local Review, 21
Post-enumeration survey, 21
Predators, 118, 143-44
Pregnancy, 63, 80-81
Prematurity, 80-81
Pressat, Roland, 5
Prewitt, Kenneth, 20-21
Primitive societies, 33, 55-56, 80, 98. See also Hunter-gatherers, Less developed countries
Princeton University, 131, 149-50
"Problem minorities," 19-20
Prohibition, 93
Projections, chap. 9
Pronatalism, 124, 128, 147-49
Protestantism, 89-90
Prussia, 125, 147
Puberty, 50-51
Puerto Ricans, U.S., 12, 24, 44

Quesnay, Francois, 125
Quetelet, Adolphe, 5

Race, 38-40, 45, 90, 92
Rates, 24-25

Ravenholt, R. T., 156
Reagan, Ronald, 16
Refugees, 41
Regions, 8
Registration areas, U.S., 10
Rehnquist, William, 16, 19
Reich, Wilhelm, 102
Religion, 37-38
Rentenberg, 34
Reproduction rates, 135-36
Residence, 12, 32, 117
Retel-Laurentin, Anne, 62
Retirement, 32, 34
Romania, 160
Rome, ancient, 10, 26, 123-24
Rosenblatt, Ángel, 113
Roses, 100
Rousseau, Jean Jacques, 125
Russia, 160

Sacramento, 16
Samoa, 111-13
Sampling, 15-21, 117, 167-68
San Francisco, 100
Saudi Arabia, 161
Sauvy, Alfred, 34
Scalia, Antonin, 16
Schmitt, Robert, 111
Scotland, 90
Scots-Irish, 38
Self-identification, 2, 44-45, 46
Sex, 29-31, 53, 90; ratio, 29-30, 140
Sexual permissiveness, 51, 112-13
Sexually transmitted diseases, 56, 62, 63, 70, 88, 95
Shoshone, 117
Sickle-cell anemia, 98
Siegel, Jacob, 31
Simon, Julian, 142-43
Simpson, Alan, 34
Singh, Karan, 154
Slaves, 40
Slovenes, 21
Smith, Adam, 147
Snow, John, 85-87
Social, classes, 9; security, 32, 34, 36
Socialism, utopian, 128, 146
South America, 11
Southwestern Legal Foundation, 18-19
Soviet Union, 7, 22, 24, 128-29, 148
Sowell, Thomas, 40
Spanish-American War, 23

Index   197

Sparta, 123
Spengler, Joseph, 148
St.-Juste, Louis de, 125
St. Kitts-Nevis, 156
St. Lucia, 156
Stanford University, 155
Statistics, 4; human, 4; international, 6-8; moral, 5; population, 7, 165-68; vital, 10
Steig, William, 102
Sterilization, 58-59
Sterility, 59-65
Stillbirths, 73-74
Stufenlehre, 129
Subfecundity, 60-61, 63-65
Subfertility, 59-66
Suicide, 88, 89-90; physician-assisted, 90-91
Süssmilch, Johann Peter, 124-25, 141
Sweden, 26, 51, 77, 81-82, 90, 147, 148
Switzerland, 21, 26

Tahiti, 111
Taiwan, 57, 155-57
Takeshita, Yuzuro, 156-57
Technology, 142-43
Teenagers, 68
Term (of pregnancy), 80
Texas, 102
Thailand, 156
Therapeutic State, 105-06
Thompson, Warren, 137-38
Thornton, Russell, 113-14
Totalitarianism, 128-29, 155
Trauma centers, 140
Trinidad, 156
Tuberculosis, 108

UNICEF, 74
United Nations, 5, 7, 62, 159
United Nations Population Commission, 128
University of California, 107
University of Michigan, 156
University of North Carolina, 12
University of Washington, 101
Upward mobility, 57-58, 126, 150

Van de Kaa, Dirk, 149
Van de Walle, Etienne, 161
Vasectomy, 154
Venereal diseases, 56, 62, 63, 70, 88, 95
Viagra, 60
Vincent, Paul, 5-6
Vital statistics, 10
Vitamins, 103
Voltaire, 125, 162

War, 75, 114
Washington, D.C., 23
Washington State, 90
Watson, Elkanah, 134
Welfare, state, 33-36
Wellness, 106
Westoff, Charles, 149-50
Whelpton, P. K., 137-38
White, Walter, 42
Widows, widowers, 84
Wilkins, Roy, 43
Willcox, Walter F. 11
Wilson, Edmund, 93
Woods, Tiger, 46
World Archaeological Congress, 109
World Bank, 88
World Health Organization (WHO), 73-74, 76, 80, 89, 91-92, 97-99, 155
World population, 141-43, 160

X-rays, 102-03

Zero Population Growth, 27-28
Zimbabwe, 61